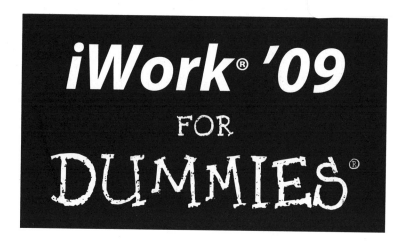

iWork® '09

FOR

DUMMIES®

by Jesse Feiler

WILEY

Wiley Publishing, Inc.

iWork® '09 For Dummies®

Published by
Wiley Publishing, Inc.
111 River Street
Hoboken, NJ 07030-5774
www.wiley.com

Copyright © 2009 by Wiley Publishing, Inc., Indianapolis, Indiana

Published by Wiley Publishing, Inc., Indianapolis, Indiana

Published simultaneously in Canada

No part of this publication may be reproduced, stored in a retrieval system or transmitted in any form or by any means, electronic, mechanical, photocopying, recording, scanning or otherwise, except as permitted under Sections 107 or 108 of the 1976 United States Copyright Act, without either the prior written permission of the Publisher, or authorization through payment of the appropriate per-copy fee to the Copyright Clearance Center, 222 Rosewood Drive, Danvers, MA 01923, (978) 750-8400, fax (978) 646-8600. Requests to the Publisher for permission should be addressed to the Permissions Department, John Wiley & Sons, Inc., 111 River Street, Hoboken, NJ 07030, (201) 748-6011, fax (201) 748-6008, or online at http://www.wiley.com/go/permissions.

Trademarks: Wiley, the Wiley Publishing logo, For Dummies, the Dummies Man logo, A Reference for the Rest of Us!, The Dummies Way, Dummies Daily, The Fun and Easy Way, Dummies.com, Making Everything Easier, and related trade dress are trademarks or registered trademarks of John Wiley & Sons, Inc. and/or its affiliates in the United States and other countries, and may not be used without written permission. iWork is a registered trademark of Apple, Inc. All other trademarks are the property of their respective owners. Wiley Publishing, Inc., is not associated with any product or vendor mentioned in this book.

LIMIT OF LIABILITY/DISCLAIMER OF WARRANTY: THE PUBLISHER AND THE AUTHOR MAKE NO REPRESENTATIONS OR WARRANTIES WITH RESPECT TO THE ACCURACY OR COMPLETENESS OF THE CONTENTS OF THIS WORK AND SPECIFICALLY DISCLAIM ALL WARRANTIES, INCLUDING WITHOUT LIMITATION WARRANTIES OF FITNESS FOR A PARTICULAR PURPOSE. NO WARRANTY MAY BE CREATED OR EXTENDED BY SALES OR PROMOTIONAL MATERIALS. THE ADVICE AND STRATEGIES CONTAINED HEREIN MAY NOT BE SUITABLE FOR EVERY SITUATION. THIS WORK IS SOLD WITH THE UNDERSTANDING THAT THE PUBLISHER IS NOT ENGAGED IN RENDERING LEGAL, ACCOUNTING, OR OTHER PROFESSIONAL SERVICES. IF PROFESSIONAL ASSISTANCE IS REQUIRED, THE SERVICES OF A COMPETENT PROFESSIONAL PERSON SHOULD BE SOUGHT. NEITHER THE PUBLISHER NOR THE AUTHOR SHALL BE LIABLE FOR DAMAGES ARISING HEREFROM. THE FACT THAT AN ORGANIZATION OR WEBSITE IS REFERRED TO IN THIS WORK AS A CITATION AND/OR A POTENTIAL SOURCE OF FURTHER INFORMATION DOES NOT MEAN THAT THE AUTHOR OR THE PUBLISHER ENDORSES THE INFORMATION THE ORGANIZATION OR WEBSITE MAY PROVIDE OR RECOMMENDATIONS IT MAY MAKE. FURTHER, READERS SHOULD BE AWARE THAT INTERNET WEBSITES LISTED IN THIS WORK MAY HAVE CHANGED OR DISAPPEARED BETWEEN WHEN THIS WORK WAS WRITTEN AND WHEN IT IS READ.

For general information on our other products and services, please contact our Customer Care Department within the U.S. at 877-762-2974, outside the U.S. at 317-572-3993, or fax 317-572-4002.

For technical support, please visit www.wiley.com/techsupport.

Wiley also publishes its books in a variety of electronic formats. Some content that appears in print may not be available in electronic books.

Library of Congress Control Number: 2009925035

ISBN: 978-0-470-43372-0

Manufactured in the United States of America

10 9 8 7 6 5 4 3

WILEY

About the Author

Jesse Feiler has been a user of Macs and Mac software since the beginning in 1984. Through his consulting company, North Country Consulting (www.northcountryconsulting.com), he provides services to small businesses and nonprofits, with an emphasis on FileMaker and Mac OS X.

Active in the community, he has served on a variety of nonprofit boards and projects primarily in community development, the arts, and public libraries. The New York State Association of Library Boards honored him with an award for "exemplary service and dedication to libraries" in part for his role in bringing public access Internet to small rural libraries in upstate New York.

Jesse has written extensively on Mac OS X (and its precursor, Rhapsody), FileMaker, and contemporary technologies such as Facebook applications and Mashups. He lives in Plattsburgh, New York with a rescued greyhound, Trainwreck Toby, who has been absolutely no help on this (or any other) book.

Dedication

For Joseph Arguelles

Author's Acknowledgments

Many people have helped bring this book together. First of all, my agent, Carole McClendon, at Waterside Productions, provided her usual valuable insight and suggestions. Colleagues and clients at North Country Consulting put in their comments and suggestions about the book and the features they use most in the iWork applications.

Susan Pink, copy editor and project editor, has been an enormous help as we've struggled through the complexities of capitalization of technical terms (a constantly moving target). Dennis Cohen has provided invaluable technical assistance. Thanks also to Laura L. Bowman, the proofreader.

In addition to the names of those listed on the Publisher's Acknowledgments page, my thanks to the Apple technical documentation staff, who have maintained their usual high standard of documentation for developers, making it easy to see how the software is put together.

Publisher's Acknowledgments

We're proud of this book; please send us your comments through our online registration form located at http://dummies.custhelp.com. For other comments, please contact our Customer Care Department within the U.S. at 877-762-2974, outside the U.S. at 317-572-3993, or fax 317-572-4002.

Some of the people who helped bring this book to market include the following:

Acquisitions and Editorial

Project Editor: Susan Pink

Acquisitions Editor: Kyle Looper

Copy Editor: Susan Pink

Technical Editor: Dennis Cohen

Editorial Manager: Jodi Jensen

Editorial Assistant: Amanda Foxworth

Sr. Editorial Assistant: Cherie Case

Cartoons: Rich Tennant
    (www.the5thwave.com)

Composition Services

Project Coordinator: Patrick Redmond

Layout and Graphics: Claudia Bell, Reuben W. Davis, Melissa K. Jester, Christin Swinford, Christine Williams

Proofreader: Laura L. Bowman

Indexer: Rebecca Salerno

Special Help: Laura L. Bowman

Publishing and Editorial for Technology Dummies

Richard Swadley, Vice President and Executive Group Publisher

Andy Cummings, Vice President and Publisher

Mary Bednarek, Executive Acquisitions Director

Mary C. Corder, Editorial Director

Publishing for Consumer Dummies

Diane Graves Steele, Vice President and Publisher

Composition Services

Debbie Stailey, Director of Composition Services

Contents at a Glance

Table of Contents

Introduction

iWork '09 For Dummies addresses the basics of all three iWork applications — Pages, Keynote, and Presentations — and then delves into the specifics of each. Tools such as page layouts, charts and tables, and slide presentations can show up in any iWork application. This reflects the way people work, although it doesn't often reflect the way in which other office products have been built. If you're used to another office suite, some of this may be disorienting. Everyone knows that tables and charts are part of spreadsheets, page layout tools are part of word processing, and slideshows are for presentations.

As is often the case with things that "everyone knows," this approach is often wrong. You can easily find an office suite in which a word processor can be used to build charts and tables while spreadsheets can also be used to build charts and tables. The commands and the results can be quite different.

In iWork, the basic commands for page layout, charts and tables, and graphic objects are the same for all iWork applications. Some expanded options and features are added for specific applications. For example, you use the same basic tools to create and edit charts and tables in all three applications, but Numbers, which is the spreadsheet application, has added features for charts and tables beyond those available in Pages and Keynote.

How This Book Is Organized

iWork '09 For Dummies has five parts and two appendixes. In Part I, I provide an overview of iWork as well as the commands and techniques you can use for any of the iWork applications. Here's where you find how to create charts and tables and how to use the menus, toolbar, and inspectors that are available in each iWork application. Finally, you see how to format text, shapes, and images.

If you come away from this part of the book thinking that there's really only one iWork application with a variety of options, you won't be far wrong. A major feature of iWork and its applications is that there's only one program to understand.

In Part II you find out about Pages, the word processing component of iWork. Pages is actually two applications in one: a standard word processing application (much like Microsoft Word) and a page layout application (think Quark XPress or InDesign).

Part III describes Numbers, the spreadsheet application, and the newest component of iWork. For a long time, spreadsheets were the domain of people who worked only with numbers, but studies showed that many users didn't use all (or even many) of the features built into their spreadsheets. The folks at Apple have thought long and hard about spreadsheets, charts, and tables, and Numbers is the result.

In Part IV, I describe Keynote, the tool for presentations. As Apple has focused more and more on media (everything from iTunes and iPods to iMovie and iPhoto), the components of successful presentations have been available to all users on all Macs. Keynote has been a matter of pulling all those tools and features together into a simple-to-use presentation tool. In so doing, Keynote has redefined people's expectations for presentation software. In Part IV, you see how to create slides, work with transitions, and integrate your own media with your presentations. The tools that let you see the next slide and your notes on one display while a large projection screen displays your slides for your audience are among the most powerful available on any platform.

Part V is an overview of tips and techniques that apply to all three iWork applications.

The two appendices can help you explore iWork further. Appendix A introduces iWork.com, a beta product that comes with iWork '09 that lets you share iWork documents over the Web. You and people you choose can annotate the documents. In addition, anyone to whom you give permission can download the documents in various formats.

The process of adding an image to a shape is the same whether you do it in a word processing document, a spreadsheet, or a presentation. In Appendix B, you find a list of all the techniques in the book along with the specific chapter where the technique is described.

Icons Used in This Book

This icon identifies things to remember. If you want to highlight the text with a colored marker, feel free to do so.

This is not a developer book, but sometimes if you know how parts of the applications have evolved, it can help you understand how to use those applications better. This information is separated from the main text so you can decide for yourself whether or not to use it.

This icon provides shortcuts and hints for improving your iWork documents and streamlining your work process.

It's really hard to make a major mistake on the Mac: Almost every command is undoable, and Mac developers use the built-in undo mechanism to encourage people to experiment with new commands and features. Still, this icon warns you of the few times when you have to be careful.

Where to Download the Example Files

I use two lengthy documents as examples (one is a Pages document and the other is a Numbers document). If you want to download them and experiment for yourself, go to my Web site at www.northcountryconsulting.com and look for Downloads.

Part I

Introducing iWork '09

"The odd thing is he always insists on using the latest version of iWork."

In this part . . .

*i*Work's three applications — Pages for word processing and page layout, Numbers for spreadsheets, and Keynote for presentations — let you create very different kinds of documents. But the iWork infrastructure means that each one of those documents can use common features. You add shapes, tables, or charts to Pages in basically the same way you add them to Keynote. iWork has broken down artificial barriers so that you do the same things in the same way in all iWork applications.

This part provides an introduction to iWork and to these common interface element and to working in iWork — manipulating fonts, colors, and shapes; using the toolbar at the top of every iWork window; and taking advantage of the powerful inspectors.

Chapter 1

Starting Out with iWork '09

* *

In This Chapter

▶ Leaving the past behind

▶ The iWork timesavers: Do it once, do it right, and reuse it

* *

Word processing and spreadsheet applications are among the most widely used software products on personal computers; presentation software is a close runner-up. Having started from scratch on the hardware side and then the operating system side, people at Apple started dreaming about what they could do if they were to start from scratch to write modern versions of word processing, spreadsheet, and presentation programs. They knew they'd have to follow their recent advertising campaign theme: *Think Different.*

Freed from supporting older operating systems or from foregoing features that couldn't be implemented on Windows, they began to dream about how good those programs could be if they could start over.

So they did.

Welcome to iWork.

I assume you already have a Mac with iWork '09 installed. If you need more assistance with installations, go to www.apple.com/support/software.

Living the Suite Life

A suite of applications provides a collection of applications that can work together. For example:

✔ Adobe Creative Suite combines graphics-oriented applications.

✔ Apple iLife combines iPhoto, iTunes, iMovie, iWeb, iDVD, and GarageBand.

✔ Microsoft Office is a suite of applications that comes in a variety of flavors: on Mac OS X, it normally includes Microsoft Office, Microsoft Excel, and Microsoft PowerPoint. On Windows, there are further variations, some of which include Microsoft Access (a database).

Here's how iWork fits into the picture.

Official business

iWork is an *office suite,* like Microsoft Office. Office suites provide applications that are, well, office oriented. An office suite usually includes at least

✔ A *word processing* application such as Microsoft Word or iWork's Pages

✔ A *spreadsheet* application such as Microsoft Excel or iWork's Numbers

✔ A *presentation* application such as Microsoft PowerPoint or iWork's Keynote

One of the coolest advantages of iWork is that major features, not just small operations such as changing a font or selecting a color, are available in the same way in all its applications. You really have only one program to learn when you're using iWork.

One piece at a time

A lot of technical trickery is in the background, but you *use* iWork through three applications that are similar to Microsoft Office applications (but way cooler, I think).

Pages

For many people, word processing is the core of an office suite. In fact, many people don't get beyond it. You can create two types of word processing documents with iWork:

✔ **Standard word processing documents,** in which the text flows from page to page as needed (for example, add a paragraph on page three, and the bottom of page three flows onto the top of page four automatically). In general, the automatic flowing of word processing documents is used for documents that will be read in the way in which letters and memos are read.

✔ **Page layout documents,** which have the type of structure you see in newspapers and magazines — articles don't just flow one after the other. Instead, an article on page one may be continued on page four while another article on page one may be continued on page eight. Also, objects such as photos are often placed in a specific position on a page, and they don't move as text is added or deleted.

iWork provides you with a variety of sophisticated tools to create your Pages documents. These include advanced font handling, color, tables, and charts, as well as the ability to place QuickTime movies and hypertext links in your Pages documents. Of course, printed versions of those documents won't support QuickTime movies or hypertext links, but they will be active when you look at the document on a computer screen. Or on your iPhone.

Apple starts you off with a variety of templates for various documents. Figure 1-1 shows you the templates available for newsletters in the Page Layout set of templates.

Figure 1-1: Choose a Pages template as a starting point.

If you choose one of the templates, it opens in Pages. You see in later chapters how to explore that document, but here's a sneak preview. A Pages pop-up menu in the interface shows you the template's pages, as shown in Figure 1-2.

Figure 1-2:
Explore
the pages
within the
template.

You can customize the templates and the pages as you see fit. But before you do so, take the time to look at what you have in front of you. It isn't just a matter of nicely formatted pages. In addition, the specific pages in each template (they're different in each template) should give you ideas not just for laying out and constructing your document but also for the types of information you should consider for different types of documents.

For example, the Program template from the Brochures set of templates has a page laid out already for mailing information. Had you thought of putting mailing information on your brochure? Maybe you did and maybe you didn't — but Pages did.

Numbers

Spreadsheet programs let you enter data in rows and columns. One of their main features is that you can also enter formulas. That way, if you have a column listing your grocery expenditures for a week, for example, the addition of another bill will cause the column's total to be recalculated. Spreadsheets are about data (usually numbers) and fast calculation updates.

You probably think you know what a spreadsheet looks like, but take a look at the Numbers document in Figure 1-3. This is a Numbers document based on the Numbers Home Improvement template. A single document can have a number of *sheets* (like sheets in a Microsoft Excel workbook). But there the similarity ends. A Numbers sheet can contain a variety of objects: zero or more tables (traditional spreadsheets), zero or more charts, as well as other iWork objects, such as graphics, text boxes, movies, and audio. In Figure 1-3, the sheet is shown with a table, a chart, and a picture.

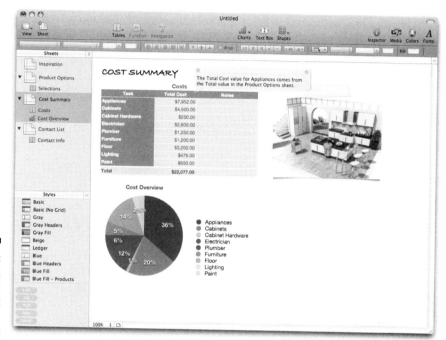

Figure 1-3: Numbers is more than a spreadsheet application.

A *comment* is attached to the table. All iWork applications support comments, although each has its own method of displaying them. Sometimes they look like those colored notes you stick on memos and refrigerator doors.

Keynote

It's only been a few thousand years since people starting giving presentations. Call them lectures, classes, sermons, or sales pitches, they're all pretty much the same: Someone stands in front of a large or small group of people and explains, teaches, or informs them. Sometimes, the presentation has multimedia elements: slides in an architecture class, music in a history lecture about a composer, and movies in a talk about "My Summer Vacation."

The Keynote authoring and presentation tools are unsurpassed, but it doesn't stop there. Take a look at Figure 1-4 to see the variety of export formats available in Keynote. When you're preparing a Keynote presentation, you're simultaneously authoring a QuickTime movie, a Flash animation, HTML, or even a DVD. All you have to do is click one extra button to start the export process.

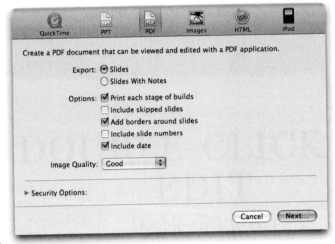

Figure 1-4:
Keynote
exports pre-
sentations
in a variety
of formats.

Keynote was the original iWork application. Built by Apple engineers for MacWorld keynote speeches delivered by Steve Jobs, Keynote has been refined over the years to the powerful tool it is today.

The Big Difference

You can do similar things with various office suites, but the big difference with iWork comes from two aspects of iWork that are hallmarks of Apple's approach to software development:

- ✔ **It's all about communication:** From the beginning of the Mac, the people at Apple have focused not merely on raw computing power but also on how that power and technology can be used to help people communicate.

- ✔ **Do it once, do it right, and reuse it:** Apple's pioneering use of scripting languages (AppleScript primarily) helped people turn the Macs into devices that could learn, as in "watch what I do and then do it automatically."

Perhaps the clearest indication of where Apple's values lie came in its recent corporate name change: It's now Apple, not Apple Computer. Computers are a means to an end.

It's all about communication

For decades, people have been hailing the advent of the paperless office, but the flood of paper has only increased. When you think about what people are trying to do with all that paper, you realize that it's not about automating the production of documents — it's about communicating. That's what iWork is about — helping you communicate as effectively and easily as possible. Apple has provided elegant interfaces and sophisticated designs for your communications, but this isn't done for decoration. The focus is communication.

If you don't think it's all about communication, take a look back at Figure 1-3, which shows Numbers in action. In the upper left you can see a recognizable table (or part of a spreadsheet). There's a pie chart and an image showing how the items in the spreadsheet could look if used together. If you think spreadsheets aren't about communication, think about how many spread-sheets you've seen that look like this. (If the number is zero, don't be alarmed: Not everyone in the world uses iWork . . . yet.)

As you explore iWork, don't be dazzled by the wide variety of communication tools. The most effective communication is the clearest. If you want someone to understand how to change the toner cartridge in a photocopy machine, a movie might be the best tool. If you want to explain the structure of an organization, a static diagram might be the clearest representation. And remember the many documents that have changed the world through their words alone.

Look at the iWork communication tools not as a challenge in which you must use them all; instead, look at them as a wonderful array of tools from which you can select the most appropriate ones for any task. Too much of anything — graphics, movies, or even words — is counterproductive.

For every iWork document, ask yourself these questions:

- ✔ What am I trying to say?
- ✔ Who am I trying to say it to?

After you can answer those two questions, you're ready to go.

Do it once, do it right, and reuse it

iWork has a variety of tools that save you time by letting you easily reuse work you've done already. Not only can you reuse your own work, but you can also reuse the work of other people.

Customizing with themes and templates

The iWork applications have a variety of tools for reuse; the chief ones are themes and templates:

- ✔ **Themes (Keynote):** A *theme* allows only certain types of modifications. The limits on what you can change means that an application that supports themes knows the basics about what to expect. You can switch from one theme to another without compromising your data. This happens with Keynote and with other applications, such as Bento.

- ✔ **Templates (Pages and Numbers):** A *template* is a document that's ready for you to modify with your own data and formatting. It has formatting set for you that you can then customize. It may have placeholders for text and images that you later insert; it may have text and images that will be used without change in your documents. After you change a margin in a template, for example, your new margin is used in documents you create from that modified template.

All iWork applications support themes or templates and allow you to save a document as a theme or a template. If you choose to modify a theme or a template, you can then resave it as a theme or a template of your own. Figure 1-5 shows how easy it is to create your own theme in Keynote with a simple command. Design the presentation you want to reuse, and then choose Save Theme. When you want to reuse it, use the Choose Theme command.

New	⌘N
New from Theme Chooser...	
Open...	⌘O
Open Recent	▶
Close	⌘W
Save	⌘S
Save As...	⇧⌘S
Revert to Saved...	
Reduce File Size	
Record Slideshow	
Clear Recording...	
Choose Theme...	
Save Theme...	
Print...	⌘P

Figure 1-5: Create your own theme in Keynote.

The iWork applications ship with themes and templates ready for you to use (see Figure 1-6). These are worth exploring even if you plan to start from scratch because you can find ideas in all the themes and templates that you can use in your own ways. Apple has built on the real-life experiences of iWork users. The themes and templates may remind you of features or issues that you haven't thought of.

Figure 1-6:
Use the
iWork
themes and
templates.

Reusing parts of documents

All iWork applications let you create parts of your documents that you can reuse. These reusable parts can be

- **Sections** in Pages word processing documents
- **Pages** in Pages page layout documents
- **Master slides** in Keynote
- **Sheets or tables** in Numbers

To break down a project to a manageable size, look for the intermediate size parts that you can work on. For example, if you're part of a committee of ten people working on a 200-page planning document for a company, a community, or an event, where do you begin? If you just start writing, you're likely to be at the task a long time. Very long. Try to break down the task. What are the logical components? These will probably become chapters.

If you're working on a budget for your school, you may soon be looking at hundreds of rows and hundreds of columns. Use Numbers tables to divide and conquer. Instead of budgeting expenses for the Language Arts department in five columns; make Language Arts into its own small table. Numbers makes it easy to integrate many small tables into a large whole.

Whether a Pages document, a Numbers project, or a Keynote presentation, if you make the components about one page in length, you almost always have an easier-to-understand document.

Sharing styles

A *style* is a collection of attributes, such as fonts, typefaces, colors, and number formatting. You set up a style and give it a name, and then you can reuse it throughout your document. Common styles have names, such as Header, Subheader, Address, or Footnote. Using styles means you can set one attribute — the *style* — rather than individually setting the various parts of the style.

If you use styles, you can change an attribute of the style so that it's changed in every occurrence of the style.

iWork supports styles in all its applications.

Letting your Mac do the work

Mac OS X and iWork support scripting of applications. The two primary tools for scripting are AppleScript and Automator. With a script, your work is automated. You start the script, and it runs. You can either write scripts or use the Record feature in ScriptEditor so that your actions are captured automatically into a script.

Scripts are particularly useful for the following:

- ✔ **Repeated tasks:** If you have a task that needs to be carried out several times with only slight variations, AppleScript is your savior. For example, you can write a script that retrieves text and images from a FileMaker database and places them in a Pages document to automatically produce a catalog.

- ✔ **Complex tasks:** One of the challenges of complex tasks is remembering all the steps and sequences. AppleScript can remember them for you. You may not save time, but a script does the task the same way every time.

- ✔ **Integration tasks:** AppleScript excels at integrating applications and their data. For example, a FileMaker/Pages script would communicate with FileMaker to retrieve some data, switch to Pages to place it, switch back to FileMaker to get some more data, and so forth.

Chapter 2

Working Effectively

The iWork applications share much of the basic interface. This means that once you know how to do something in Pages, you generally know how to do the same thing in Numbers. This chapter helps you use the common tools that apply across all iWork applications.

These tools fall into two broad categories: user interface tools, such as buttons, and traditional menu commands. In many cases, you can do the same thing using either buttons or menu commands. In other cases (font and text management, for example), you can do the basics with menu commands and much more extensive customization with buttons. In all cases, you can switch back and forth between buttons and menu commands depending on your needs and your mood.

Common commands such as Quit work the same way in all Mac OS X applications, including iWork applications. Sometimes there are slight variations from program to program, even within the iWork suite. In general, I mention those variations in the specific chapters for each iWork application.

The Menu System

The menu system for iWork provides a great deal of standardization so that each iWork app functions in very much the same way. This section provides an introduction to the menus, highlighting some of the features you'll find in each one.

The Application menu in Pages, Numbers, and Keynote

Common Mac OS X menu commands, such as Save, Quit, Cut/Copy/Paste, and Undo/Redo aren't covered in this chapter.

The Application menu is where you set preferences (which can be different for each application). This menu is also where you find the About command, shown in Figure 2-1, which shows the version information and your license key.

Figure 2-1: Set preferences in the Application menu.

Take a moment now to write down the license key for your iWork applications. Keep it on a piece of paper or in your Bento database in case you need to reinstall the software. There is only one license key for all three applications.

You can show or hide all application windows (this applies to all Mac applications, including iWork). You can also show all application windows.

The Application menu is also where you can register your software or try it out before you buy it. And, at the end of the menu, you find the Quit command.

The File menu

The File menu, shown in Figure 2-2, has the basic commands to create and open documents (including reopening recent documents) as well as print them. All of these are standard commands for most File menus. In iWork, two sets of special menu commands relate to themes and templates. You can use built-in templates for Numbers and Pages documents; when you create a new document from one of these, formatting, colors, and fonts are predetermined to give your document the best appearance. When it comes to colors in charts or tables, iWork coordinates those with the palette of colors in the template you have chosen.

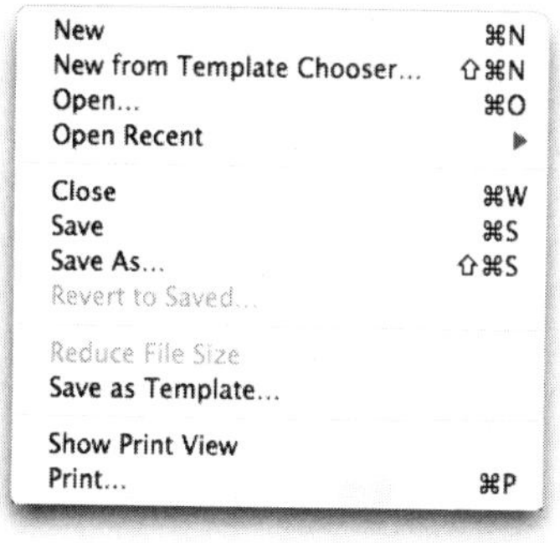

```
New                              ⌘N
New from Template Chooser...    ⇧⌘N
Open...                          ⌘O
Open Recent                       ▶

Close                            ⌘W
Save                             ⌘S
Save As...                      ⇧⌘S
Revert to Saved...

Reduce File Size
Save as Template...

Show Print View
Print...                         ⌘P
```

Figure 2-2:
The File
menu.

Towards the bottom of the File menu for Numbers and Pages is a command to save the current document as a template. All the settings are saved in this template so that you can easily create a document based on it.

A *template* is a collection of settings that can be applied to a new iWork document when you create it. You can modify those settings as you see fit, and you can save the modified template.

In the case of Keynote, instead of templates, you have *themes.* The difference between themes and templates is that a theme can be reapplied to a document as you are editing it. This is possible with a highly structured document such as a Keynote presentation (it's also possible with a Bento library). Because the document's structure is strict, Keynote knows where all the elements are, and it can always reformat slides and bullet items when you apply a new theme.

The Edit menu

Like all Edit menus in Mac OS X, the iWork Edit menu combines the standard Undo and Redo commands as well as commands for Select, Copy, and Paste, as shown in Figure 2-3. Writing tools such as Find and Spelling are available to enhance your text; there's more on the Find and Spelling tools in Chapter 23.

One of the important commands in the Edit menu is the Paste and Match Style command. This command pastes selected text in the document, but it picks up the current style of the location where the text is pasted. As a result, the pasted text fits right in.

Undo Typing	⌘Z
Redo	⇧⌘Z
Cut	⌘X
Copy	⌘C
Paste	⌘V
Paste and Match Style	⌥⇧⌘V
Delete	
Clear All	
Duplicate	⌘D
Select All	⌘A
Deselect All	⇧⌘A
Find	▶
Spelling	▶
Special Characters...	

Figure 2-3:
The Edit menu lets you use the standard cut-and-paste commands.

The Insert menu

The Insert menu lets you insert files and objects into your iWork document. The following types of objects can be inserted into any iWork document:

✔ Comments

✔ Text boxes

✔ Shapes

✔ Charts

✔ Tables

✔ Functions (such as sums)

The fact that these items are all available in menu commands and on the toolbar is a great feature of iWork. I discuss them in Chapter 3.

You use the Insert⇨Choose command to open a standard Open File dialog so you can select a document to insert into your iWork document at the current insertion point or inside a selected object. The types of files that are available depend on the iWork application and the selected object. In general, when you want to insert a file into an iWork document, the Choose command is the command you want.

You can insert a file into an iWork document also by dragging it from a Finder window to the appropriate location in the document. Each iWork application has additional objects to insert.

The Slide menu (Keynote)

The Slide menu lets you manage slides in a presentation. You often do this by using the buttons in the Keynote window and dragging slides in the Slides pane, as shown in Figure 2-4.

Figure 2-4:
Rearrange
Keynote
slides.

You can reorder slides and move them into a hierarchical structure. You can also use commands in the Slide menu to manage them.

The Table menu (Numbers)

You use the Table menu to manage Numbers tables. As you can see from Figure 2-5, there are many commands you can use to add or change rows and columns.

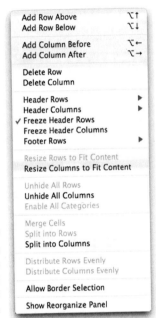

You can also use triangles in the frame of rows and columns to invoke relevant row and column commands, as shown in Figure 2-6. Whether you use the Table menu or the commands in the table frame, the basic procedure is the same: Select a row or column, and then use the appropriate command to modify it.

The Format menu

The Format menu gives you commands for working with fonts and text. In fact, you find a variety of ways to accomplish the same goal in the Format menu.

Formatting fonts with menu commands

The Format➪Font submenu and its submenus give you a lot of control, but not as much as the Fonts window. Figure 2-7 shows the Format➪Font submenu structure and its Kerning submenu.

Figure 2-6:
Use triangle
pop-up
menus in
the table
frame to
modify a
single row
or column.

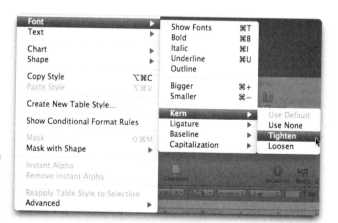

Figure 2-7:
Adjust
kerning

You can switch back and forth between the menu commands and the Fonts
window.

The first part of the Font menu covers the basics, such as italics (and covers them with less precision than the Fonts window). But then you start to see the differences:

✔ Instead of setting a font size, you can select some text and make it bigger or smaller until it looks right to you (use the keyboard shortcuts to do this quickly).

✔ Kerning (the horizontal spacing between characters) can be tightened or loosened; you don't have to set specific values.

Formatting text with menu commands

You can use the Format➪Font submenu to set alignment or justification. *Alignment* refers to the way the text in a paragraph is set: It can be aligned left (with a flush left margin, like in this book), aligned right (with a flush right margin), or centered. Fully justified text is aligned flush at both margins.

The Arrange menu

All the iWork apps allow you to place objects on a page (or sheet, in the case of Numbers). You can organize and arrange these so that they make sense and look good. One of the keys to this is the Arrange menu, which is shown in Figure 2-8.

Figure 2-8:
Use the
Arrange
menu.

You can create long sections of text and large tables of numbers, but most of the time you're better off focusing on smaller units: a paragraph or two, a table of a few rows and columns, or a short sequence of slides that presents a concept.

You may find that the simplest way to start to arrange a page (or sheet or slide) is to place the components you want to use on the page. Figure 2-9 shows a page where I've started an arrangement.

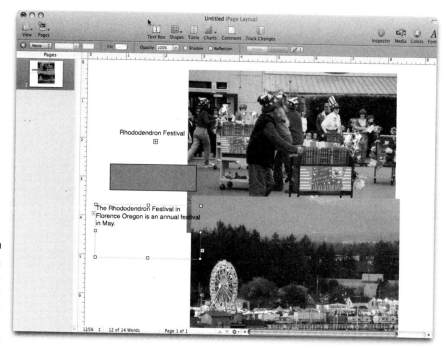

Figure 2-9:
Begin to
arrange
your
content.

You can arrange content in many ways. Most of the time, it's a matter of trial and error as you experiment to see what works best. Here's a sequence of steps you can try:

1. **Resize the objects.**

   If you are using images and objects from various sources, they're likely to be different sizes. Resize them so that they're basically the same size, with the more important ones (the title, for example) a bit larger.

2. **Bring objects forward or backward.**

   The Ferris wheel photo in Figure 2-9 has plenty of sky. It covers up part of the book cart. If you select the book cart image, you can choose Arrange➪Bring Forward to place the book cart in front of the sky so that the details of the cart are more visible, as shown in Figure 2-10.

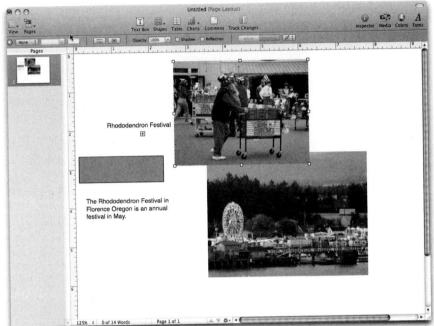

Figure 2-10:
Move the
book cart
forward.

3. Create a title.

Figure 2-9 also contains a text box ("Rhododendron Festival") and a colored shape designed as its background. Together, they'll make a good title. (This combination of shape and text box is a common iWork technique.) Select the text box and the shape, and then choose Arrange⇨Align Objects⇨Middle. The result is shown in Figure 2-11. (Note that at this point, all you see of the title is the plus icon at the bottom of the text. You'll fix that shortly.)

Aligning two objects in the middle aligns them in the vertical middle. To totally align two objects, follow up the middle alignment with center alignment, which aligns them horizontally. You usually need both commands (middle and center) to properly align objects on top of one another.

4. Create a text box.

Another text box is shown in Figure 2-11. Unlike the Rhododendron Festival text box that will become a title with a colored background, this second text box will stand on its own without a special background. You can see the beginning of this second text box with the text, "The Rhododendron Festival in Florence Oregon is a special event in May."

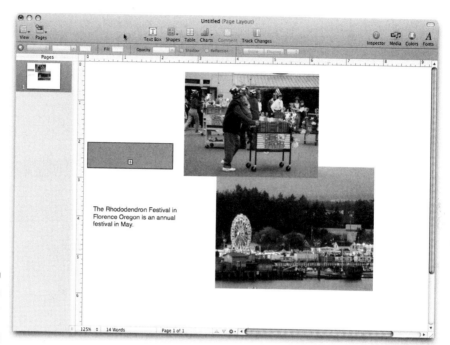

Figure 2-11:
Start to cre-
ate a title.

5. Move the shape backward.

As you can see in Figure 2-11, the Rhododendron Festival text box is visible only with its handles. That's because it's behind the colored shape.
Select the shape and choose Arrange⇨Send to Back. The shape moves
back and the text is now visible, as shown in Figure 2-12.

6. Correct the alignment.

Something is a bit wrong with the spacing in Figure 2-12. This is common
as you move objects around and resize them. Sometimes the correction
is a matter of trial and error; other times you can see what the problem
is immediately.

A simple way of correcting alignment issues like this is to click in the
text and display the format bar. Figure 2-13 shows the problem: The title
text is aligned left; it will look better if it's aligned in the center. This is a
common (and easily solved) issue: Just click the Align Center button,
which is immediately to the right of the Align Left button.

These are the little tweaks that make the difference between an elegant document and one that doesn't quite cut the mustard.

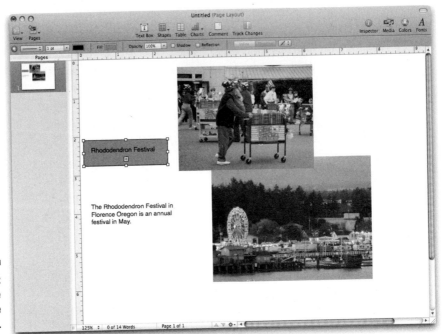

Figure 2-12:
Move the
shape
backward.

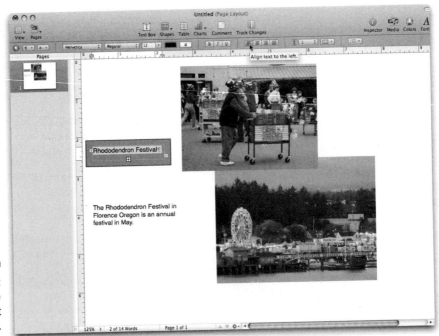

Figure 2-13:
Change the
text
alignment.

The View menu

The View menu lets you show or hide parts of the iWork window. The View pop-up menu on the toolbar provides the same functionality. Each app has its own features; they're described in the relevant chapters.

The Play menu (Keynote)

You use the Play menu, shown in Figure 2-14, to control how a Keynote slideshow is played. There's more information on this in Chapter 19.

Figure 2-14:
Use the
Play menu
for Keynote
presenta-
tions.

The Windows menu

The Windows menu is a standard part of Mac OS X. You use it to minimize the current window (which you can also do with the yellow minimize button in the upper-left corner of the window). You can also maximize the window, just as you do with the green button at the upper left of the window.

The Windows menu lists all of the application's windows. You can choose Windows⇨Bring All to Front to bring all of an application's windows forward. You can also choose Pages/Keynote/Numbers⇨Hide Others so that no other windows are visible on the screen.

The Share menu

Finally, the Share menu lets you share documents on the Web and with users in other formats. There's more on the Share menu in Chapter 21.

Shortcuts

The iWork menus group commands by their basic functions, such as editing, inserting, and formatting. The menu commands are generally static. Some are disabled if they don't make sense for the selected objects, but generally their names and their order remain static. (The exceptions are toggle commands such as Show Inspector/Hide Inspector; depending on whether an inspector is shown, one command or the other is shown in the menu.)

Sometimes you aren't certain exactly what you want to do, but you know what you want to do it to. Shortcut menus come to the rescue.

Select one or more objects in an iWork window, and then hold down the Control key while you press the mouse button. A *shortcut menu* (sometimes called a *contextual menu*) pops up next to the object. This shortcut menu assembles all menu commands from the various iWork menus that are relevant to the object. Most of the disabled commands in the menu bar are excluded from the shortcut menu, so you wind up with just the commands you can actually use on the selected object. Occasionally, some of the commands in the shortcut menu are disabled, but they're the exception rather than the rule.

Figure 2-15 shows a shortcut menu in Numbers when a spreadsheet cell is selected. Commands relevant to the cell and to its column or row, as well as the standard editing commands, are all in one place.

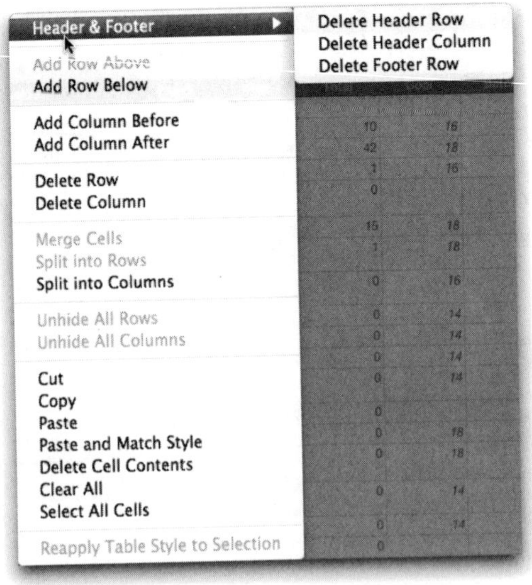

Figure 2-15: Use shortcut menus to save time.

Standard Elements

A brief tour of the common interface elements will not only get you ready to use all of the iWork applications but will also show you the richness of features available for you to use.

Many of the commands in the command interface let you manipulate objects: text, graphics, shapes, table cells, and the like. The way that you manipulate similar objects is the same across the iWork applications. What is different is often how you create the objects. There is a great deal of similarity in creating a text box in Pages, Numbers, and Keynote, but there is almost total similarity in manipulating the text box once it has been created. If you're primarily interested in creating objects, you might want to explore the later chapters of this book first. However, if you're interested in manipulating them, this chapter is your key. Depending on your specific needs, you may want to switch back and forth between chapters.

The format bar, located just below the toolbar, is a common interface element. However, its components are sufficiently different for each of the iWork applications that it is described in the context of each specific application rather than in this chapter.

The iWork window

Figure 2-16 shows you the bare bones of an iWork window, with a Business Card template in Pages. What stays the same for all iWork applications is the outer frame: the title bar at the top with the close, minimize, and zoom buttons at the upper left; the bottom frame with (from left) a pop-up menu to set the zoom factor for the window, the page information, and up- and down-arrows to move to the next or previous page (if there is no next or previous page, the appropriate arrow appears dimmed). At the right, the scrolling tools common to many Mac windows are provided. Finally, in the lower right the resize corner lets you resize (and reshape) the window.

The iWork Toolbar

But what is that oblong button at the right of the title bar? Click it and you'll find out, as shown in Figure 2-17. The oblong button is the toolbar button: It shows and hides the toolbar. Each iWork application has its own toolbar, but some basics apply to all of them. (Chapter 3 goes into toolbars in depth.)

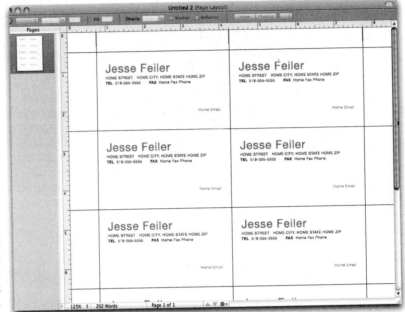

Figure 2-16:
A bare-
bones iWork
window.

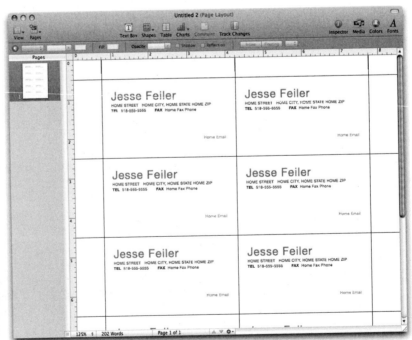

Figure 2-17:
Show the
toolbar.

The gray background of the toolbar behaves just like the background of the window's title bar. You can drag the window by clicking anywhere in that gray background.

If the window isn't wide enough to show the toolbar, the icons at the right are shown (text only) just beyond the right side of the toolbar when you click the double arrow shown at the right in Figure 2-18.

Figure 2-18:
Click the double arrow at the right to see icons that don't fit on the toolbar.

Some toolbar icons have small downward-pointing arrows that bring up a menu of choices. Usually, the choices are visual, as shown in Figure 2-19, but sometimes the choice is a traditional menu with text commands.

Some toolbar icons have a plus symbol at the upper left, as shown in Figure 2-20. These icons add something to the document: another page, another table, or whatever the icon indicates. In the case of Pages, these icons can represent a specific type of page to add based on the chosen template. As you see in Figure 2-20, you can choose to add a blank page or a page with eight or ten new labels.

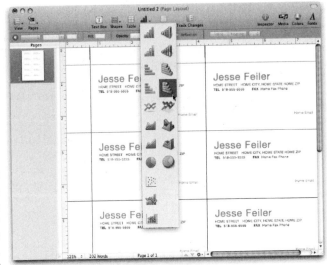

Figure 2-19:
Some
toolbar
icons have
submenus.

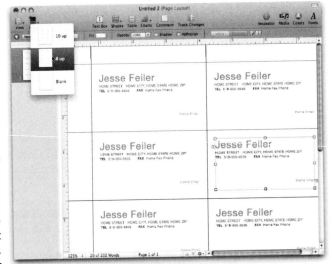

Figure 2-20:
Some icons
let you add
objects to
the current
document.

Colors window

Color has become an essential part of today's documents both on paper and on the screen. The days of black-and-white printing for most documents is long gone. You can use color to create the most garish and distracting documents that confuse and annoy people, but you can use color also to enhance your communication and make your work more attractive. One of the Mac's most useful features is a consistent and integrated approach to color management. While not all applications on the Mac use the common interface, all iWork applications use it. So do many applications from Apple and third parties. You will find yourself wanting to set colors for text, graphics, and graphics in iWork. You set color in one place: the Colors window. This section provides you with a fast way to set a color. Then, you find out how to use the advanced features of the Colors window.

The Colors window is a floating window that appears only when the application is active. That means if you switch to another application by clicking one of its windows (or by launching it), the Pages window will remain visible behind the other application's windows, but the Colors window and any other floating windows will disappear. When Pages once again becomes active (most commonly when you click one of its windows in the background of another application), its floating windows come forward and become active. In addition, the Colors window reappears, in its last location. Other floating windows discussed in this chapter, such as the Fonts panel and the Inspector window, have the same behavior.

The Colors window is part of Mac OS X; it is used in many applications, not just iWork.

The process for applying a color depends on how you're using the color. You can

- ✔ Color a selected object.
- ✔ Color a nonselected object.
- ✔ Add a color to your palette in the Colors window.
- ✔ Copy a color from an object in the window.

Coloring a selected object using the Colors window

To color a selected object, such as text or a graphic element, follow these steps:

1. **Select the object you want to color.**

2. **Click the Colors button on the toolbar or choose View⇨Show Colors to open the Colors window, which is shown in Figure 2-21.**

   If the color wheel isn't shown as you see it in Figure 2-21, click the color wheel button at the top left of the Colors window. If you don't see the set of five buttons across the top of the Colors window, click the oblong button at the top right of the window and then click the color wheel button at the left.

To brighten or darken the colors in the color wheel, use the slider at the right.

3. **Click a color from the color wheel.**

   The center of the wheel is white. It shades into other colors:

   • Yellows in the upper right

   • Reds in the lower right

   • Blues in the lower left

   • Greens in the upper left

   The selected color is applied to the selected object automatically.

Coloring a nonselected object using the Colors window

Follow this process if you want to select a color and then apply it to one or more elements that aren't selected:

1. **Click the Colors button on the toolbar or choose View⇨Show Colors to open the Colors window, which is shown in Figure 2-21.**

   If the color wheel isn't shown as you see it in Figure 2-21, click the color wheel button at the top left of the Colors window.

   If you don't see the set of five buttons across the top of the Colors window, click the oblong button at the top right of the window and then click the color wheel button at the left.

2. **Use the slider at the right to brighten or darken the colors in the color wheel.**

3. **Click a color from the color wheel.**

   The center of the wheel is white; it shades into specific colors: yellows in the upper right, reds in the lower right, blues in the lower left, and greens in the upper left.

   The color appears in the rectangular box at the top of the Colors window. This box is called the *color well*.

4. **Drag the color from the color well to the object you want to color.**

5. **Repeat with any other object you want to color with the same color.**

Saving a color in your color palette

The Colors window lets you save swatches of color in a *palette* at the bottom of the window. This palette shows up in all Colors windows. It consists of ten rows of swatches; its width is determined by the width of the Colors window. Figure 2-22 shows the palette with all ten rows shown in a widened window.

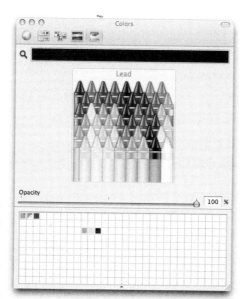

Figure 2-22:
Use the
Colors
window
palette.

Using the preceding steps, select the color you want. But instead of dragging the color to the object to color (in Step 4), drag it to a swatch in the color palette.

Organize the colors in your palette so that you know what they will be used for. You can leave spaces, as shown in Figure 2-22, so that colors for your Web site are separated from colors for your brochures, for example. If you put the green for your Web site next to the green for your Keynote presentation backgrounds, you may have trouble telling them apart. Millions of colors are available on modern computers such as the Mac; using a selected subset makes your work elegant and consistent. It also makes it much easier to set colors in your iWork documents, as you will see in the next step.

Coloring a selected object using the palette

Once you have set up colors in the palette, the process of coloring a selected object is much simpler.

1. **Select the object.**
2. **Open the Colors window as described in the preceding steps.**
3. **Double-click the color from the palette.**

Coloring a nonselected object using the palette

Likewise, the process for coloring nonselected objects is simpler with the palette:

1. **Open the Colors window as described in the preceding steps.**
2. **Single-click the color you want.**

   The color appears in the color well.
3. **Drag the color from the color well to any object you want to color.**

Copying a color from the screen

Any color you see on the screen can be copied to the color well. This can be a color from a Web site, from a photo, or from an interface element of an application. (Colors themselves aren't copyrighted, but combinations of them may be copyrighted logos and images.) To copy a color from the screen:

1. **Open the Colors window.**
2. **Click the magnifying glass to the left of the color well.**
3. **Move it over the color on the screen you want to copy.**

   The pixels under the magnifying glass are enlarged, and you can position the center of the magnifying glass directly over the color you want.

4. Click and the color is placed in the color well. From there, you can apply the color to objects in your document or place it in your palette.

Graphics often have a row of pixels along their edges to make them appear better on the screen. You may think that you have a red circle on a background of a blue square, but when you look at the individual pixels, you may find one or two rows of pixels in intermediate colors that make the image more attractive and remove fuzziness. For that reason, make certain that you center the magnifying glass on the color you want and not on the special pixels at its edge.

Setting opacity

Opacity refers to the degree of transparency of the color — the extent to which objects behind it can be seen. Now that you've selected a color, you may want to set its opacity with the slider at the bottom of the window. Lower numbers (dragging the slider to the left) make the color more transparent so that objects behind it are visible.

Advanced color management

The Colors window gives you as much control as you want over color. If you want red, you can just click a red crayon. If you want exactly the shade of red that you remember from your first grown-up prom gown, you can have that. But before you go too far, you should know that color is one of the most subjective perceptions we have. Artists and philosophers as diverse as Wolfgang Goethe in the eighteenth century and Josef Albers in the twentieth century wrote and thought perceptively about color (and they didn't agree).

Colors look different in different lighting conditions; even more important, reflected color (that is, color that is reflected from a wall, painting, or physical object) looks different from color that is transmitted (such as on a computer screen or a projection screen). You can use whatever color model you want. If you're trying to match colors on other documents, they may be specified in one of the slider models and values, so it is easiest to use them. You can use different color models for different objects in the same document. The only way to accurately match colors is to use the actual method that will be used to display them. Don't even try to match a color in a newspaper with a color on a flat-panel TV screen.

The Colors window (shown in Figure 2-23) gives you as much or as little complexity as you want. At the top of the Colors window, five buttons let you choose between five *color pickers* — ways of comparing and identifying colors:

Figure 2-23:
Use RGB
sliders to
set a color.

✔ **Color wheel:** Maybe you learned about the color wheel in school. The center point of the color wheel is always white. Individual colors move out from there, with greens in the upper left, blues in the lower left, reds in the lower right, and yellows in the upper right. The colors merge into one another. When you click a color in the color wheel, it fills the box just above the color wheel. Set the brightness for the entire color wheel with the slider at the right.

✔ **Color sliders:** The second button lets you select from among color sliders, which allow you to specify a color using numbers. These may seem to have more precision than the color wheel, but they actually have less because the numbers are integers: one value for gray scale, three for RGB and HSB, and four for CMYK. If you want a color that is just between grayscale 65 and 66, for example, you can't compromise on 65.6. In the color wheel, are least theorctically, every gradation is possible (the hardware limits the actual gradations). Four separate models are supported for sliders:

 • **Gray scale slider:** This slider shows shades of gray. You can move it until the color in the box at the top of the Colors window is the shade of gray you want. You also can type a percent from 0 percent (black) to 100 percent (white).

 • **RGB sliders:** This color model uses three numbers to define the colors red, green, and blue (hence RGB). Each can have a value from 0 to 255 as shown in Figure 2-23. As you move the slider or type a number, the color at the top changes. If you want a basic red, set red to 255 and set the blue and green values to 0. RGB colors are often used to set colors for the Web and other screen-display devices.

- **CMYK sliders:** These behave just like RGB sliders, but they use a different model based on four values: cyan (C), magenta (M), yellow (Y), and black (K). CMYK is often used to specify colors that will be used in printing.

- **HSB sliders:** This is yet another color model based on three values: hue, saturation, and brightness. This model is often used in television.

✔ **Palettes:** Here you will find palettes of color. You can also create your own. Perhaps the most commonly used palette is Web Safe colors, as shown in Figure 2-24. These are the colors that are safe to use on the Web for all displays on all operating systems and all browsers. If you're designing documents to be published on the Web, you should use these colors. To select a color, use the Palette pop-up menu at the top of the Palettes tab of the Colors window to select Web Safe and then click whatever color you want. The color will appear in the color well at the top of the Colors window.

Create and name a palette if it will be used for a specific project. The palette at the bottom of the Colors window applies to all of your iWork projects and documents.

✔ **Spectrum:** The fourth button from the left is another attempt to represent all colors, but in a different layout from the color wheel. Give it a try and click the color you want to use.

✔ **Crayons:** If you don't have to precisely match colors, maybe you're longing for a simple box of crayons. That's exactly what the last icon provides, as shown in Figure 2-25.

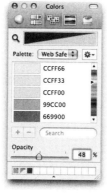

Figure 2-24:
Use Web
Safe colors
for docu-
ments to be
published
on the Web.

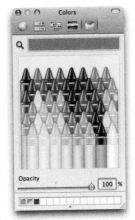

Figure 2-25:
Get out the
crayons!

The Fonts window

All iWork applications use the Fonts window to provide the greatest amount of control over text fonts. The menus have font commands, as you will see later in this chapter, but for the greatest control, the Fonts window is what you'll want to use.

Your basic font settings can be overridden for individual paragraphs, sentences, or even individual characters. Use the Fonts window to set the font for the whole document, and then modify sections as needed by selecting them and returning to the Fonts window.

The Fonts window is part of Mac OS X; it is used in many applications, not just iWork.

Selecting fonts

Setting a font and its size is the most basic thing you do with fonts:

1. **Select the text you want to change.**

   If you want to set fonts for text before you type, click the insertion point where you want to begin typing. If this is a new document, the pointer is automatically positioned at the beginning of the document.

   If you have selected text in your iWork document, you will see it change as you work in the Fonts window.

2. **Open the Fonts window by clicking the Font button on the toolbar (at the right in Figure 2-17) or by choosing Format⇨Font⇨Show Fonts.**

   The Fonts window is shown in Figure 2-26.

Figure 2-26:
Set fonts
with the
Fonts
window.

3. Select the font you want to use from the second column, Family.

The first column, Collections, lets you group font families. Mac OS X
has already built several collections into the Fonts window. You see
how to add new collections and how to add font families to collections
later in this section. Font families can be in more than one collection.
Collections are just an organizing mechanism for font families.

4. Select the typeface from the Typeface column.

Typefaces are somewhat intuitive. Font families are developed by different vendors, and they may use different naming conventions. For
example, one vendor's italic might look like another vendor's oblique in
different font families.

Figure 2-26 illustrates an issue with font families that you should be
aware of. Not only do vendors use different typeface names (such as
oblique versus italic), but one vendor's typeface variation is another
vendor's font family. Notice that the Gill Sans font family in Figure 2-26
has a Bold typeface. Just below it is another font family called Gill Sans
Ultra Bold, which is exactly what its name suggests. But it isn't another
typeface for Gill Sans; it is its own font family.

5. Select the size you want to use.

You can type a font size in the size box at the upper right of the Fonts
window, you can click to select a font from the scrolling list of font sizes,
or you can use the slider at the far right of the Fonts window to quickly
move to the size you want.

You can close the Fonts window, if you want, by clicking its close button. If you do more formatting, however, just click in your iWork document window and keep working; the Fonts window remains open behind the document window

Previewing fonts

If you select text in your document (rather than using the insertion point to set the font for new text that hasn't been typed), you can see the selected text change as you work with the Fonts window. But what do you do if you want to experiment directly in the Fonts window?

Use the small dot in the top center of the Fonts window, shown in Figure 2-26, to pull down an area that provides a live preview of your selection, as shown in Figure 2-27.

Figure 2-27:
See your font choices in action.

Setting basic effects

At the top of the Fonts window is a set of controls for font effects. You can show or hide this area using the Fonts panel actions, which you display using the gear icon in the lower left of the Fonts window.

If you're using the preview feature of the Fonts window, be aware that it reflects the choices for font family, typeface, and font size. The settings for font effects, such as underlining and color, are shown just below the preview pane in the Effects pane, but they aren't shown in the preview pane.

Actions are menus that pop up from a window. They're always shown with the gear icon. Figure 2-28 shows the Fonts window actions.

Figure 2-28:
Fonts
window
actions.

The first four buttons for font effects provide common controls:

- ✔ **Underlining:** The icon with an underlined T sets underlining. Use the pop-up menu to choose from None, Single, Double, and Color. The Color option is a single underline with the color you choose. You already know how to choose the color. Select this choice and the Colors window opens.

- ✔ **Strikethrough:** The icon with a T and a strikethrough bar sets the options for strikethrough settings. They're the same as for underlining.

- ✔ **Text color:** The third icon opens the Colors window to let you set the text color.

- ✔ **Paragraph color:** The fourth icon opens the Colors window to let you set the paragraph's background color.

Applying text shadows

The five controls at the right of the Effects pane all control text shadows.

Shadowed text isn't as easy to read as unshadowed text. Use it for headlines and labels — short sections of big letters.

Here is how to set up text shadows:

1. **Select the text you want to shadow.**

2. **Open the Fonts window by clicking the Font button on the toolbar or by choosing Format⇨Font⇨Show Fonts.**

3. **Click the text shadow button (fifth from the left in the Fonts window).**

   This toggles text shadowing on and off. The text shadow button should be highlighted. If it isn't, click it again.

4. **The slider to the right of the text shadow button changes the opacity of the shadow.**

   Move the slider to the right to make the shadow more opaque. You may want to experiment with the sliders in their most extreme positions to see their effects. Keep watching the selected text in the iWork document window to see what happens.

   Click elsewhere in the document to deselect the text: It's hard to distinguish between the highlighting of the selection and the text shadowing.

5. **The next slider blurs the far edge of the shadow more (to the right) or less (to the left).**

6. **The final slider moves the shadow farther away from the text it shadows. (This is called the *offset*.)**

   If you're experimenting, try moving this slider all the way to the right. That lets you see the shadow clearly. If you're having trouble, choose View⇨Zoom⇨Zoom In to zoom the window. You can also use the zoom control at the left of the bottom window frame of your iWork document.

7. **Drag the wheel to set the angle for the shadow.**

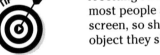

   A setting such as 320 degrees usually looks good. On a computer screen, most people are used to an assumed light source at the upper left of the screen, so shadows normally are drawn below and to the right of the object they shadow.

Customizing typography

You can gain even more control over your fonts by using typography options that are supported for some fonts. Here is how to gain access to the typography options:

1. **In your iWork document, select the text to which you want to apply the typography options.**

2. **In the Fonts window, select the font.**

3. **Choose Typography from the Fonts window actions (the gear icon at the bottom of the window).**

   The Typography dialog shown in Figure 2-29 opens.

   The typography options vary for each font. Some fonts support none of them; others such as Helvetica Neue and Hoefler Text support many of them.

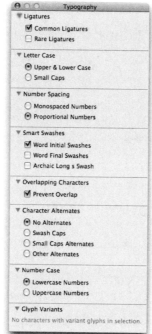

Figure 2-29:
Use
typography
options.

Managing collections

Collections are sets of fonts that you want to be able to find quickly. You can add any fonts to your collections. By default, the following collections are provided for you: All Fonts, English, Favorites, and Recently Used.

If you want to add a new collection, click the add button (the + symbol) below the Collections column in the Fonts window. You can name your collection; it will be alphabetized automatically.

To remove a collection (but not the fonts within it), select it and then click the delete (– symbol) button below the Collections column.

To add a font family to a collection, just drag it in. To remove it, drag it out. This affects only the collection: Nothing happens to the font itself.

The Fonts window Actions menu lets you add a selected font family to the Favorites collection.

Chapter 3

Tooling around the Toolbar

In This Chapter

▶ Customizing the toolbar

▶ Drawing and modifying shapes

▶ Working with tables and charts

*T*oolbars are an integral part of the Mac OS X user interface. Although each application's toolbar is different (and not all applications have toolbars), the basics of the toolbar are managed by Mac OS X.

This chapter introduces you to the iWork toolbar. Each application has its own toolbar, but many of the commands on the toolbar are similar (often the same) for all iWork applications.

Looking at the Toolbar

Figure 3-1 shows an iWork toolbar for Keynote. Every toolbar button causes an immediate action that is visible in the document. The buttons on the toolbar perform commands; sometimes these commands are also available on the menu.

In the default view, the buttons have both text and an icon. When you customize the toolbar, you can change the default view so that only the text or only the icon is shown. For example, Figure 3-2 shows a Pages toolbar with only text on the toolbar buttons.

Many toolbar buttons add an object to the document. In Figure 3-1, the New button adds a slide (because this is the Keynote toolbar), and the Text Box, Table, and Comment buttons add a text box, table, and comment, respectively.

The icons for toolbar buttons often have small variants in their images. Most common is the downward-pointing arrow, which brings up a pop-up menu for that toolbar. In Figure 3-1, menus are available for View, Themes, Masters, Shapes, Charts, and Smart Builds.

Often the menu for a toolbar button lets you add a particular type of object to the document (a specific type of shape, for example). Other times, the menu lets you choose various options. Figure 3-3 is the menu for the View button in Keynote; you can use the menu to choose which parts of the window to show or hide. The View button contains the same commands as the View menu.

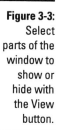

Figure 3-3:
Select
parts of the
window to
show or
hide with
the View
button.

You can customize the toolbar, but the default toolbar has a consistency across the iWork applications.

The toolbar buttons on the left side

For example, the left side of each app's toolbar provides application-specific toolbar buttons:

- ✔ **Numbers:** The first toolbar buttons at the left display the Numbers View menu and add a sheet to your Numbers document.

- ✔ **Keynote:** The first toolbar buttons in Keynote create a new slide and play your presentation. Next, pop-up toolbar buttons let you choose views, themes, and slide masters.

- ✔ **Pages:** The first toolbar buttons in Pages are the View menu and the Sections menu, which lets you insert a new section in your Pages word processing document. For page layout documents, the Pages View menu is accompanied by a Pages menu that lets you add page layout pages.

The toolbar buttons in the center

All buttons in the center of the toolbar add objects to the current document. For Pages and Keynote, these toolbar buttons let you add text boxes, shapes, tables, charts, and comments; you can also turn track changes on and off. In Numbers, you can add tables, insert functions, and reorganize (sort) your data.

The toolbar buttons on the right side

The buttons to the right of the toolbar open other windows or dialogs. In Figure 3-1, they open the Inspector window, Colors window, and Fonts window. This chapter focuses on the default set of toolbar buttons. Because you can customize the toolbar, you may have other buttons in your toolbar.

Using the Toolbar View Button to Customize the Window

Towards the left of each iWork toolbar is a View button that displays a pop-up menu. (The Keynote View pop-up menu was shown in Figure 3-3.) You can use the menu to show or hide parts of your iWork window, such as rulers, the format bar, or comments. Each window can have its own settings, which are preserved with the document.

Three areas of the window can be shown or hidden for any iWork app:

- ✓ **Rulers:** Rulers appear around the main part of the window to help you position objects precisely. You can adjust the settings for rulers in each application's Preferences window.

- ✓ **Format bar:** Located just below the toolbar, the format bar lets you format text and other objects.

- ✓ **Left pane:** Located on the side of an iWork window, the left pane contains program-specific information. You can click any image in the left pane to select it or to navigate to it in the main part of the window. In Keynote, the pane can contain images of master slides as well as slides. In Pages, the pane can contain page thumbnails or a search box. In Numbers, the pane can contain sheets and tables. The View menu identifies the individual items in the left pane (such as master slides); the left pane itself is not shown in the View menu.

- ✓ **Main window:** Other options in the View menu control what is shown in the main part of the window, such as presenter notes (Keynote), invisible characters (Pages), and a formula list (Numbers).

If you aren't certain what a certain interface element is called, experiment with showing and hiding the various items in the View menu. As soon as you find the command that hides or shows the element you're interested in, you will find its name.

Creating Shapes

You can create shapes in any iWork application. Shapes can have colors, borders, and other attributes that you set with inspectors. You also can click in a shape and type text within it. All shapes except lines can contain text.

Shapes work the same way in all iWork applications. Usually, the toolbar is the easiest way to create shapes. iWork has two kinds of shapes:

- ✔ **Predrawn shapes:** iWork can create predrawn shapes such as circles and arrows. You can *modify* predrawn shapes.

- ✔ **Custom shapes:** Draw any shape that you want. You can constrain the shape to horizontal or vertical as well as to a regular shape (that is, a circle instead of an oval, or a square instead of a rectangle).

 Inspectors are the interface elements that let you change settings such as colors, line widths, arrowheads, and the distance created around a shape as you move it through other objects. You can also use an inspector to place an image in an object. This chapter shows you how to use inspectors.

Inserting a predrawn shape from the toolbar

Follow these steps to insert a predrawn shape from the toolbar in any iWork document:

1. **Click Shapes on the toolbar.**

   Hold down the mouse button to bring up the menu of shapes shown in Figure 3-4.

    The bottom shape is the *custom* shape. You use custom shape later in the chapter.

2. **Select the shape you want.**

   The shape is inserted in the center of the document. Later, you find out how to move it, resize it, and modify it.

Figure 3-4:
Select a
shape to
insert.

Inserting a predrawn shape with the mouse

You can use the mouse to add a predrawn shape in the size and location that you want. Here's how:

1. **Create or open your iWork document.**

2. **Hold down the Option key while you click the Shape button on the toolbar.**

3. **Using the mouse, draw the shape.**

   As you move the mouse, the size of the shape grows or shrinks. Also, instead of automatically being placed in the center of the document as is the case when you use the Insert command in the menu bar, the shape is placed where you started drawing it.

Inserting a shape from the menu bar

Finally, you can use the Insert menu command to insert a shape rather than using the toolbar:

1. **Open or create your iWork document.**

2. **Choose Insert➪Shape➪<the kind of shape you want>.**

   The shape is created. If you want to edit it, continue with the next section.

Editing a shape

Once you've created a shape in any of the ways I just described, you can change it. Click the shape to select it, and you see a *bounding box* and eight *handles,* small boxes along the bounding box, as shown in Figure 3-5.

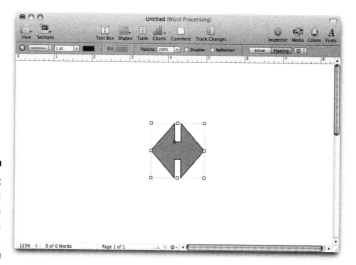

Figure 3-5:
Select a
shape to
show its
handles.

Four handles are in the corners of the shape; the other four are located at the midpoints of the bounding box. The bounding box is the smallest rectangle that can contain the shape. Even if the shape is not rectangular, it will fit inside a rectangle. Shapes such as triangles have a different number of sides, but the functionality is the same.

Here are the types of edits you can perform on a shape:

- ✓ **Resize the shape:** Drag one of the four corner handles to enlarge or reduce a shape's size.

- ✓ **Reshape the shape:** Drag one of the four midpoint handles to change the shape's proportions. The midpoint handle in the top line moves the top line up and down; the midpoint handle in the bottom line moves that line up and down. Similarly, the midpoint handles on the left and right lines move them in and out.

✔ **Move the shape:** Drag inside the bounding box to move the entire shape. Don't use one of the handles because that will resize or reshape the shape.

✔ **Change special sizes:** Some shapes have additional handles:

    • **Arrow depth:** A small handle lets you vary the length of the arrow shaft.

    • **Double-arrow width:** The double-headed arrow has a tiny handle in the center of the shape that you can drag back and forth to change the distance between the two arrowheads.

    • **Star and polygon points:** When you select a star or polygon, a slider below the shape lets you change the number of points, as shown in Figure 3-6. Note the small round handle between two of the points. Drag it in or out to make the valley deeper or shallower.

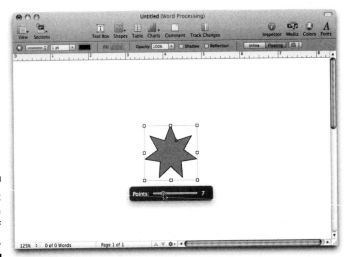

Figure 3-6:
Change the
number of
points.

Editing a shape's geometry

The changes to a shape described in the preceding section don't change the basic geometry of a shape. The formula that describes a circle, a rectangle, or another shape is the same regardless of its values. For example, a circle is always round; a rectangle is always rectangular, with four sides. A special case of a rectangle is a square with four sides of identical length.

There are many reasons for changing a shape's geometry. Perhaps the most common is after you've created a shape and carefully set its size and color only to realize that it would look better as another shape. Editing the shape will preserve is color and other attributes. This section describes how you can change a shape's geometry:

1. **Select the shape you want to edit.**

2. **Choose Format⇨Shape⇨Make Editable.**

   In addition to the handles, red circular controls appear in the middle of each arc of the shape, as shown in Figure 3-7.

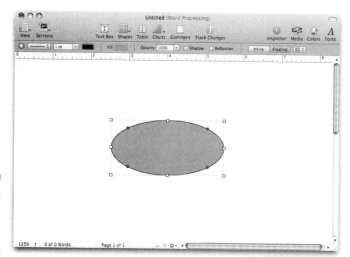

Figure 3-7:
Make a
shape
editable.

3. **If you want to change an arc, drag the circular control to the new position, as shown in Figure 3-8.**

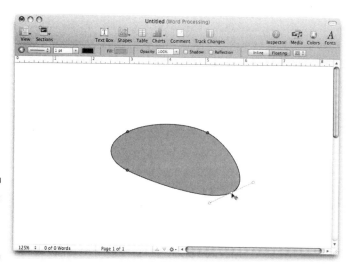

Figure 3-8:
Change a
rounded
shape.

4. **The clicked control has a control handle. Pull either end of the handle to change the arc.**

   Compare Figure 3-8 with Figure 3-9 to see how these control handles modify the shape.

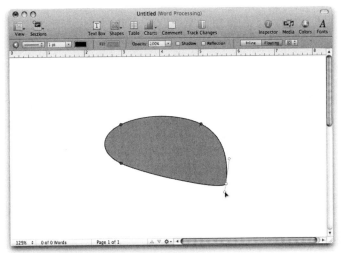

Figure 3-9:
Change
an arc.

Creating Tables and Charts

Charts and tables present data in a highly structured way, which can help to make your documents clearer. Numbers has its own very sophisticated tables, but Keynote and Pages also provide powerful tables.

Creating a table

In any iWork app, click Table on the toolbar to create a table, as you can see in Figure 3-10. Just as with shapes, if you hold down the Option key while you click Table, you can then draw the table where you want it.

As you can see, tables, like shapes, have handles in their corners and the midpoints of each side. You can drag the handles and resize just as you drag and resize shapes. The default table for Pages documents has three columns, a header, and three rows beneath the header. In Keynote, the default table is a simple three by three table. (In Numbers, much more specific tables are provided; they are described in Chapter 12.)

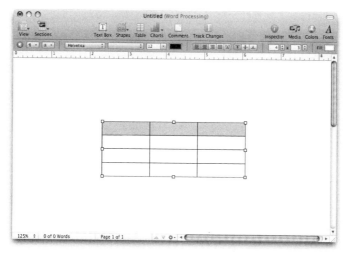

Figure 3-10:
Create
tables in
Keynote
and Pages
documents.

When you create a table, Table inspector opens immediately so that you can further customize the table. The next chapter shows you how to use Table inspector.)

Creating charts

Pages charts are among the most sophisticated and simple features of the Pages program. Click Charts on the toolbar to open the chart menu shown in Figure 3-11.

Two-dimensional charts are shown in the first column; three-dimensional charts are shown in the second. To create a chart type, simply click it, just like you click a shape or a table. If you hold down the Option key while you click a chart type, you can draw the chart in the location and size you want.

If you choose to create a two-dimensional chart such as the combined bar/ line chart, the chart itself behaves just like a shape or a table, with eight handles, as you can see in Figure 3-12. A legend is also created (in Figure 3-12 it is above the chart) and is in its own draggable and resizable shape.

But there's more. A floating window containing data for the chart is also opened. (The window is below the chart in Figure 3-12.) And still more! Chart inspector also opens. You'll see how to use Chart inspector in the next chapter.

Figure 3-11:
Choose a
chart type.

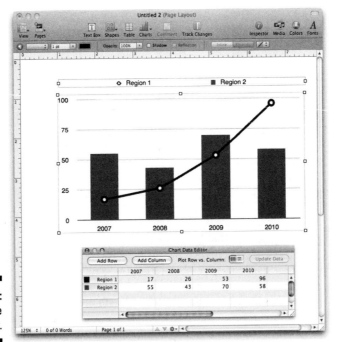

Figure 3-12:
Create the
chart.

You can edit the chart data in Chart Data Editor. You add rows or columns and switch how the chart is drawn. Pages takes care of everything for you. For example, suppose you want to change the value in Region 1 for 2007 from 17 (the default value created by Pages) to 170. You type the new value in the Region 1/2007 field, and leave the field by clicking out of it or by pressing the tab key. (Until you leave the field to finish editing the data, Pages will not redraw the chart.)

As shown in Figure 3-13, Pages not only moves the point but also rescales the chart so that the value of 170, which is significantly larger than any value in Figure 3-12, is shown properly. There's more on Chart Data Editor in Chapter 15.

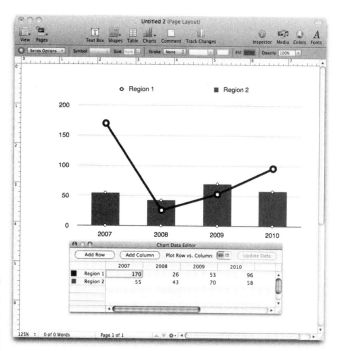

Figure 3-13:
Edit the
chart data.

If you've chosen a three-dimensional chart, you get one more item: a controller for the chart's position in three-dimensional space. The controller is shown in the upper left of Figure 3-14. As you drag the arrows up and down or right and left, the chart rotates (but the controller stays still). Notice that as you move the chart in space, its shadow adjusts appropriately.

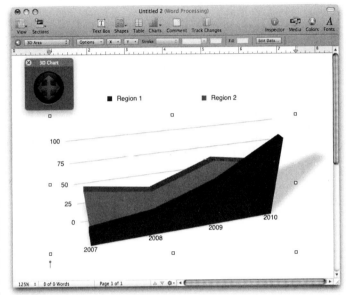

Figure 3-14:
Control
three-
dimensional
charts.

Including Comments

You can add comments to your iWork documents by clicking the Comment button on the toolbar or by choosing Insert➪Comment. You can then show or hide those comments using the View button on the toolbar or the View menu.

Customizing the Toolbar

The last point to notice about toolbars is that you can customize them, as shown in Figure 3-15. You open this dialog by choosing View➪Customize Toolbar or by Ctrl-clicking (or right-clicking) anywhere on the toolbar to bring up the contextual menu for the toolbar, from which you can choose the Customize Toolbar command.

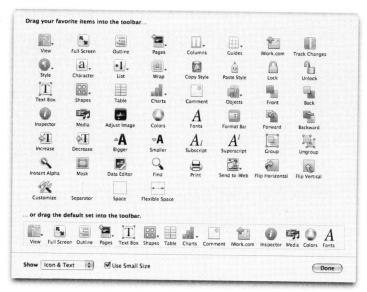

Figure 3-15:
Customize
your toolbar.

Drag icons into or out of the toolbar. The existing icons will move aside (or move together) as necessary. Notice that you have some special icons, such as the spaces at the bottom of the set of icons. You can use those or separators (vertical lines) to organize your toolbar. In the lower left, you can choose icons and text, text only, or icons only as well as the size of the icons. It's your toolbar, so make it comfortable to use.

You can also command-click the toolbar button to cycle through two sizes of text only and two sizes of icons only as well as the combination of text and icons.

All toolbars on Mac OS X have one additional feature: You can always move the default icons as a single group by dragging them from the bottom of the customization dialog.

Chapter 4

Inspecting the Inspectors

*I*nspectors let you inspect and adjust settings for whatever you've selected in the current document: a paragraph, an image, or the entire document. They compress a large amount of information and functionality into a small and well-organized tool.

Using Inspectors

One icon that is always present on the toolbar is the Inspector icon, towards the right. Click it to open an Inspector window. You can also choose View⇨ Show Inspector. Figure 4-1 shows a typical inspector used with a Business Card template in Pages.

The Business Card template has a number of identical parts so that you can print multiple business cards on a perforated sheet that you buy in an office supply store. Because this is a page layout document, you can move the individual card images around so that they align properly with the perforated sheet. You select a part by clicking it.

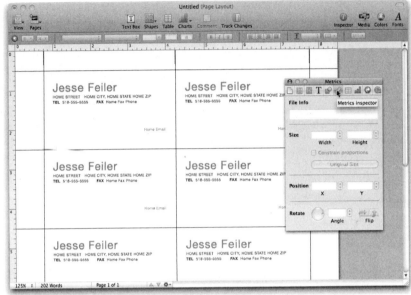

Figure 4-1:
Use inspec-
tors to view
settings for
an iWork
document
and its
contents.

An inspector is always up-to-date, showing information about the current selection in the active window of the application. If you switch from one document to another or select another item, the inspector's data is updated, as you can see in Figure 4-2. In Figure 4-1, the document as a whole is selected; in Figure 4-2, a single part of the document (a single business card) has been selected, and you can see its location in the X and Y coordinates. (Details of this inspector are described later in the chapter in the section, "Check and set positions with Metrics Inspector.") If you've selected multiple items in a document, inspector displays composite information about all of them.

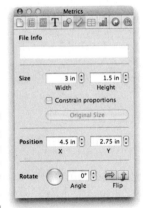

Figure 4-2:
Inspectors
are auto-
matically
updated.

An Inspector window is an efficient way of presenting information about a selected object in an iWork document. Across the top of the Inspector window, buttons let you select specific inspectors that the Inspector can show. For example, clicking the T button causes the Inspector to display Text inspector. If you hover the pointer over any button or other control in the Inspector window, you'll see a description of what it does.

Inspectors present a remarkable amount of information in a small space. The information varies depending on which application you're using and what is selected. The inspector for page layout documents has about 125 separate settings in its ten inspectors, which you access with the ten buttons at the top of the Inspector window. Many of the settings are described in this section and in later chapters for each of the applications. As you use the Inspector window, feel free to explore any of the settings that interest you. Inspectors for Numbers and Keynote documents have their own inspectors with their own settings.

In Figure 4-2, the inspector is shown for a Pages page layout document. Most of the buttons across the top are used in the other iWork applications, although they are sometimes in a different order, and some applications have additional buttons. From left to right, these are the buttons in Figure 4-2 and the inspectors that they display in the Inspector window:

- **Document inspector:** This is the leftmost inspector in all cases; it contains information about the document. For Pages and Numbers documents, it lets you set margins. For all documents in all applications, it lets you set a password for the document.

- **Layout inspector:** Only for Pages documents, this inspector lets you set columns and page numbering.

- **Wrap inspector:** This inspector lets you control how text wraps around the selected object in the document.

- **Text inspector:** The Text inspector is where you can control spacing in paragraphs, alignment, tabs, and other text settings. It controls just about everything involving text except the selection of fonts and styles such as bold or italics. (Those are set with the Fonts window.)

- **Graphic inspector:** Set graphic borders, fills, shadow, and opacity with Graphic inspector.

- **Metric inspector:** Use Metric inspector to set size, rotation, and absolute position.

- **Table inspector:** Table inspector lets you format tables, add or delete rows, and sort data.

- **Chart inspector:** Use Chart inspector to set everything from the light source to the color of the chart. Also use it to edit the chart's data.

✔ **Link inspector:** Use Link inspector to establish hyperlinks in your documents. (In Pages, it also controls merge fields.)

✔ **QuickTime inspector:** QuickTime inspector controls embedded QuickTime movies.

In some cases, you want to see information about several aspects of the selected object. You can do that by opening multiple Inspector windows. Simply hold down the Option key while clicking the Inspector button on the toolbar or choose View⇨New Inspector. You can have as many inspectors open as you want.

All inspectors always display information about the current selection in the active window. The selection can be an object such as a picture or a paragraph, a word, or even a single character that you have selected with the mouse.

Formatting Text with Text Inspector

Before you can format text, you first open Text inspector. Here's how to do that:

1. **Select the text you want to format.**

2. **Open an inspector if necessary.**

   If no inspector is open, open one by choosing View⇨Show Inspector or by clicking Inspector on the toolbar.

3. **Click the T button in the top row to open Text inspector.**

4. **Click the Text tab, as shown in Figure 4-3.**

Figure 4-3: The Text tab in Text inspector is the same for all applications.

Text inspector settings control text in the environment of a document (or part of a document). Any fonts and font settings you've already set in the Fonts window or may set in the future aren't involved in these settings. The sole exception is text color, which can be set in both the Fonts window and Text inspector.

Colors & Alignment settings

The first section of the Text pane in Text inspector controls the colors and alignment of the selected text. The first button opens the same Colors window you saw in Chapter 3.

Next, a set of five buttons lets you handle the horizontal alignment (called the *justification*) for the selected text. From the left, the buttons set the alignment to:

- ✔ **Left**
- ✔ **Centered**
- ✔ **Right**
- ✔ **Fully justified:** Adds small spaces between characters so that the left and right margins are the same for all lines
- ✔ **Text/Number alignment:** If available, aligns text in a table cell to the left (normal position) and aligns numbers in a table cell to the right (normal position)

The final set of alignment buttons aligns text vertically within a container such as a shape or a text box. (It doesn't apply to Pages word processing documents themselves because the document itself isn't within a container.) The choices are top, center, and bottom.

Spacing settings

You can adjust spacing between characters horizontally, between lines of text vertically, before or after paragraphs, and between the text itself and the boundaries of its container (if any — Pages word processing documents don't have containers).

All of these settings use variations on the same interface shown previously in Figure 4-3. The value for each setting is a number: a percentage in the case of character spacing, a number of lines in the case of line spacing, and points in the case of the other three values. You can set these numbers in three ways:

- Use the horizontal slider to increase or decrease the value.
- Use the stepper (the arrows) to increase or decrease the value by 1.
- Type the value you want to use into the box.

The defaults for each type of spacing and the reasons for changing them are listed here:

- **Character spacing:** This is expressed as a percentage. Its default value is 0, which makes the font look as it was intended to look in most cases. Character spacing is also known as *tracking*. In some large font sizes, the spaces between the characters look too big; often, tracking is reduced for such cases.

  Other times you may be tempted to change character spacing because it looks peculiar. Before you change the tracking, check out other techniques for solving the issue. For example, in some fonts you can use ligatures — special spacing for pairs of specific adjacent letters such as *fi*. In the case of fonts with a typographic option, turn on ligatures in the Fonts window if certain pairs of characters appear too far apart. Conversely, if a pair of characters appears too close, consider turning ligatures off. If a particular pair of characters (such as *fi*) always looks wrong, it's probably a ligature issue.

  Another situation to consider is fully justified text when the lines of text are short. In the case of a typical line of text in a book, full justification works well because there are several inches of text to work with. Narrow columns (such as a newspaper column), however, may not have enough text to work with. This effect is exacerbated if the line of text contains several long words. You can solve this by adjusting tracking, by turning off full justification, or by rewording.

- **Line spacing:** In the old days of typewriters, line spacing choices were single, double, or occasionally triple spacing. Because the typeface was fixed, the height of the line needed to display the tallest character was known. These choices are still available, as shown in the pop-up menu in Figure 4-4. But today you can change fonts, typefaces, and font sizes within a line, so the height of a line of text is no longer so easy to calculate. In the menu in Figure 4-4, Single and Double basically have their classic meanings; Multiple simply means that the line space isn't an integer, for example, 1.5 line space.

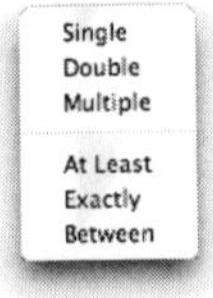

Figure 4-4: Enhance other line spacing options.

Single
Double
Multiple

At Least
Exactly
Between

The system calculates the height of the line from the top of characters to the bottom of descenders. *(Descenders* are those parts of characters such as *g* and *y* that extend below the *baseline,* which is the bottom of characters such as *e* and *x.)*

The three other settings for line spacing follow:

- **At Least:** iWork uses your line spacing setting unless a large character in a line of text would overlap the preceding line, in which case additional space is used. Less space than specified will never be used.

- **Exactly:** No exceptions are made to the settings you have selected no matter what the result looks like.

- **Between:** The line spacing you indicate provides a blank space between lines. For example, triple spacing will produce a line height three times the normal line height. If you choose the Between option, the line height will be standard but a space the size of two standard-size blank lines will lie empty above that single line's height.

✔ **Before/After Paragraph:** These settings specify the size (in points) of the space before or after a paragraph. These numbers aren't additive. If you specify a space of 72 points after a paragraph (72 points = 1 inch) and a space of 144 points before the next paragraph (144 points = 2 inches), the space between those paragraphs will be 2 inches: the higher, not the sum, of the two values. The space before the first paragraph is always 0; the space after the last paragraph is also 0.

✔ **Inset Margin:** For a paragraph that you place within an object such as a text box, this is the inset from each side. You cannot specify separate values for each side.

Formatting Graphics with Graphic Inspector

As you can see in Figure 4-5, Graphic inspector has five main sections. Not all of them are available for selected graphic objects. For example, a graphic object that doesn't contain an image cannot be shown with an apparent mirror reflection of the image. The five sections of Graphic inspector let you adjust the following attributes of objects:

✔ **Fill:** You can fill selected objects with solid colors, images, gradients, or combinations of images and colors.

✔ **Stroke:** You can set the attributes for a line object or the line that borders an object. The attributes you can set are color, the line width, its endpoints (arrows), and its appearance (solid, dashed, and so forth).

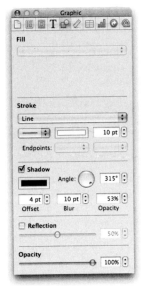

Figure 4-5:
Use Graphic
inspector.

✔ **Shadow:** Set a shadow for the selected object. The settings are the same as for text shadowing, described in Chapter 3, except instead of using the outline of text characters for the shadow, you select a color from the Colors window to shadow the exact shape of the selected object.

✔ **Reflection:** If an object contains an image, this setting automatically produces a reflection of the image outside the object with greater or lesser opacity. It is generally best to use either a shadow or a reflection; using both produces peculiar results.

✔ **Opacity:** This setting lets you choose whether the object hides anything behind it (100%), is totally transparent (0%), or is somewhere in between. Note that the setting is for the entire graphic object; you can separately set opacity for its border (using Stroke settings) or its center (using Fill).

Beyond the general settings described here, you can do some simple tasks with Graphic inspector, such as

✔ Fill an object with color

✔ Create a gradient fill

✔ Place an image inside a graphic

✔ Use a tinted image fill

✔ Choose stroke settings

I describe each of these processes next.

Filling an object with color

The settings for shadows, opacity, and reflection are similar to settings you have already seen for text in Chapter 3. Here's how to fill an object with a color:

1. **Select the object you want to fill with a color.**

2. **Display an inspector.**

3. **Click the Graphic button to display Graphic inspector.**

4. **Select Color Fill from the Fill pop-up menu.**

   A color well appears.

5. **Use the color well to select the color you want.**

6. **If you want to adjust the opacity, use the Opacity setting.**

Creating a gradient fill

In iWork a *gradient* is a pattern that changes from one color at one side to another color at the opposite side. Gradients can provide elegant effects in your documents, but they also can lead you astray. If your document will be printed, test the gradient effect on a printer as early in the process as you can. Different types of printers handle colors in different ways. What appears as a smooth gradient transition on your screen may have ugly bars and be not at all smooth or elegant on some printers — particularly those designed for black-and-white printing.

To create a gradient fill, follow these steps:

1. **Select the object you want to fill with a gradient.**

2. **Open or create an Inspector window.**

   Choose View➪Show Inspector, View➪New Inspector, or click Inspector on the toolbar.

3. **Click the Graphic button to display Graphic inspector.**

4. **Select Gradient Fill from the Fill pop-up menu at the top of Graphic inspector, as shown in Figure 4-6.**

5. **Use the color wells to select the colors to start and end the gradient. (The top color well is the starting color.)**

   If you select a color with an opacity of less than 100 percent, it appears with a diagonal bar through it in Graphic inspector. On the screen or when printed, the opacity effect is generated and the bar is not shown.

Figure 4-6:
Fill the
object with
a gradient
fill.

6. **In the Fill area, select the angle of the gradient.**

You have three ways to select the angle. The right-pointing arrow automatically selects 0 degrees; the downward-pointing arrow selects 270 degrees. Use the wheel to select any other angle, or use the text box to enter the angle.

Placing an image inside a graphic

One of the most common tasks is to fill a graphic object with an image. There are many reasons for placing an image inside an object rather than just inserting the image (or pasting it) into the document itself. First, inside an object, the image can be framed or highlighted by the object itself. Second, if your images are of different sizes, you can place them inside objects of the same size, shape, and orientation to make your document look cleaner.

Here's how to place an image inside a graphic:

1. **Select the object you want to fill with an image.**

2. **Display an inspector.**

3. **Click the Graphic button to display Graphic inspector.**

4. **Select Image Fill from the Fill pop-up menu, as shown in Figure 4-7.**

Figure 4-7:
Use Image
Fill.

5. Click the Choose button and select an image file to insert into the graphic object.

A small version of the graphic appears in the Inspector window.

You've seen a color well; the similar looking object in Figure 4-7 that contains the image is called an *image well*. Once Graphic inspector is open, you can drag a file from Finder into the image well rather than clicking the Choose button.

6. Scale the image.

A small pop-up menu (set to Tile in Figure 4-7) is now available. These are the possible settings, as shown in Figure 4-8.

Figure 4-8:
Scale the
image.

- **Scale to Fit:** If the image and the object have the same dimensions, the image simply is placed in the object. If the dimensions are different, the image is resized as best as possible. In some cases, part of the object may not be shown. Scale to Fit is a quick way to scale an image in which the center is the most important part and it doesn't matter if you can't see some of the edges.

- **Scale to Fill:** In this case, the image is kept as large as possible, but all of it is shown. In some cases, this may leave fairly large sections at the top or sides. This is a good choice if you want to make certain that the entire image is shown.

- **Stretch:** The image fills the object. If they're different shapes, the image is distorted as necessary. This sometimes works well with images when you don't care a great deal about the detail. If you stretch an image of a pine forest, the pine trees may turn out taller or wider than they are in the original image, but as long as the image and object are roughly the same shape, the trees in the image will still be recognizable as pine trees.

- **Original Size:** The image isn't resized. It may not all be visible in the object.

- **Tile:** This is like the Original Size setting, but if the image is smaller than the object, the image is repeated (at its original size) as many times as necessary to fill the object.

Using a tinted image fill

The last choice for filling an object is Tinted Image Fill, which combines an image and a color. Here's how to do that:

1. **Select the object you want to fill with an image.**

2. **Display an inspector.**

3. **Click the Graphic button to display Graphic inspector.**

4. **Select Tinted Image Fill from the Fill pop-up menu, as shown in Figure 4-9.**

5. **Click the Choose button and select an image file to insert into the graphic object.**

   A small version of the graphic appears in the image well, below the Fill menu.

6. **Scale the image.**

   For details, see Step 6 in the preceding section.

7. **Use the image well to select the color to use.**

   The Choose button selects an image file for the image well; clicking the image well brings up the Colors window so you can choose a color. The diagonal line in the image well indicates that the color isn't opaque. (If the color is opaque, you will not see the image and the entire process is pointless: Just use the Color Fill option.)

Figure 4-9:
Use Tinted
Image Fill.

The settings for shadows, opacity, and reflection are similar to settings you
have already seen for text in Chapter 3.

Choosing stroke settings

The only other item in the Graphic inspector to examine is the Stroke settings.
When you select a graphic object, you can set the stroke of its border — the
color, width, and type of line (solid, dotted, or dashed). In addition, certain
types of graphic objects are basically lines with a beginning and an end. For
those, you can set the type of endpoint as shown in Figure 4-10 if you have
chosen Line from the pop-up menu in the Stroke area.

Adding Images to Your Documents

You can add images to any iWork document. Use Insert⇨Choose to select the
file you want to insert. Once the file is inserted in your iWork document, you
can move and adjust it. You make some of these adjustments with Metrics
inspector or Graphic inspector; others you do by directly manipulating the
images.

Figure 4-10:
Set stroke
options.

Masking images with shapes

When you have a graphic in an iWork document, you can mask it with shapes so that only part of the image is shown. This replaces the cropping you may have performed in other applications. What appears is the part of the image that shows through the shape.

Follow these steps to mask an image:

1. **Select an image in an iWork document.**

2. **Choose Format⇨Mask to place a mask on top of the image.**

   You can also choose Format⇨Mask with Shape to use a predrawn shape such as a triangle or circle.

3. **Drag the handles at the corners of the mask until it is the size and shape you want.**

4. **Drag the image until the part you want to show is over the mask.**

5. **Use the Edit Mask slider below the mask to enlarge or shrink the image itself.**

   Figure 4-11 shows the process in action.

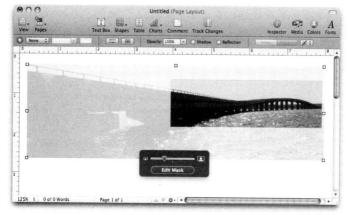

Figure 4-11:
Experiment
with the
mask and
the image.

6. **Repeat Steps 3–5 until you're satisfied. Then click out of the image.**

   What is shown is only the part within the mask, as shown in Figure 4-12.

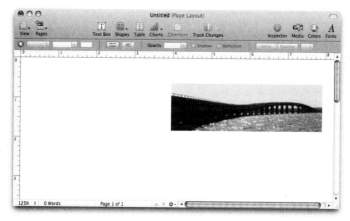

Figure 4-12:
The image is
masked.

Checking and setting positions with Metrics inspector

Metrics inspector, shown in Figure 4-13, lets you control the size and location of objects. For many people, the easiest way to arrange objects (including inserted graphic files) is by moving them around to the approximate position you want and then using the mouse to resize or reshape them. For finer control, however, you can specify exact coordinates for each object. iWork uses X/Y coordinates for the units you've chosen in Preferences. The origin (0,0) is the upper-left corner of the document.

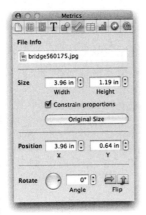

Figure 4-13:
Use Metrics
inspector
to position
objects.

You can flip objects. You can also constrain an object's proportions so that as you're resizing it with the mouse, you don't distort the image that it contains.

Adjusting images

Images can be used throughout iWork. You can use images as title graphics identifying chapters or other sections of a document, but they frequently are used as the content of a document itself. Nothing prevents you from creating a spreadsheet in Numbers that contains columns of information about items: prices, names, and images.

For example, a chapter about the history of Quebec City might have an image of the 400-year-old city walls next to the chapter and the title. Within a chapter on sixteenth-century architecture, an image of Quebec City might be placed beside an image or another walled city so that the reader can compare two or more styles of city wall construction.

Whether an image is used on its own or inserted into a graphic object, you can adjust the image inside iWork. The adjustments that you make apply only to the inserted image: The original image isn't changed.

The adjustments that you can make are common to image manipulation; you can make the same adjustments in iPhoto, Aperture, and Photoshop.

Follow these steps to adjust an image in iWork:

1. **Select the image in the iWork document.**

2. **Choose View⇨Show Adjust Image to open the Adjust Image window, shown in Figure 4-14.**

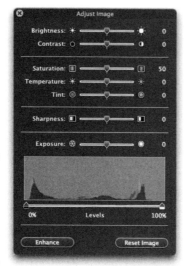

Figure 4-14:
Change
image
settings
in iWork
documents.

Using Media Browser

The basic media manipulation programs (iPhoto, iTunes, and iMovie) let you assemble images, audio, and movies into groups and categories. iWork Media Browser lets you browse these files in the categories you've created in the iLife applications. From Media Browser, you can drag media files into your iWork documents without worrying about where they're stored on disk.

To display Media Browser, choose View⇨Show Media Browser. The window shown in Figure 4-15 appears.

Once you've placed media files in your iWork documents, you can use QuickTime and other inspectors to adjust the appearance and behavior of the media files. In the case of images, you can place them inside objects as described previously in this chapter.

Adjusting Table Settings

When you create a table, Table inspector (see Figure 4-16) opens automatically. If you'll have to do something with an inspector to finish your current task, iWork opens it automatically, as is the case when you create a table. At any time, you can go back, open an inspector, and modify your settings.

Figure 4-15:
Use Media
Browser.

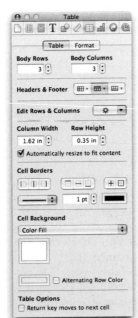

Figure 4-16:
Use Table
inspector to
modify table
settings.

Note the two tabs at the top of the window. You use the Table tab to control the general formatting of the table and the Format tab to control specific settings for each cell.

Setting cell and table properties

Table inspector handles general table formatting. Seven sets of settings are available:

- **Body Rows and Body Columns:** Use the steppers (arrows) or type numbers to set the number of rows and columns in the table.

- **Headers & Footer:** Three buttons let you set left, top, and bottom headers and footers. Each is a pop-up menu; you can select 0 to 5 rows or columns for each type of header and footer. The default value is 0.

- **Edit Rows & Columns:** To edit a row or column, first select a cell in the relevant row or column. Then click the action menu and make your choice (see Figure 4-17). To merge cells, you need to first select the cells to merge.

Figure 4-17:
Edit rows
and col-
umns with
the action
menu.

- **Column Width and Row Height:** Here's where you adjust the settings for the column and row specified by the currently selected cell. If you select the entire table with a single click anywhere in the table, these settings apply to all rows and columns. You can click column or row borders as shown in Figure 4-18 to select them so that you can change their settings (such as color or line width in Table inspector) or to drag them to resize the columns or rows. (Note the double lines and the double-headed arrows when the cursor is over a row or column.)

  In addition to setting column width and row heights, you can use the Automatically Resize to Fit Content check box in Table inspector for any selected cell, row, or column. iWork will adjust the table appropriately. This can leave you with different-sized cells, rows, or columns, but each one will be the right size for its data.

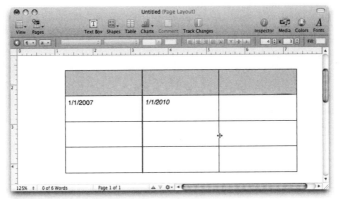

Figure 4-18:
Drag row or column borders to select them.

✔ **Cell Borders:** Select a cell or group of cells and adjust their borders here. You can also select a row or column border as shown in Figure 4-18 to format it using these controls. You can control the position of the borders (left, right, top, bottom, and so forth), the shape of the line (solid, dotted, or whatever), and its color by using the color well at the right of the Cell Borders section.

✔ **Cell Background:** The background for a cell can be set with the same options available for fills in Graphic inspector discussed previously in this chapter: none (the default), color fill, gradient fill, image fill, and tinted image fill.

✔ **Table Options:** You can let the Return key move to the next cell. If this option is turned off, the Return key functions simply to insert a Return within the cell so that you can create multiple lines or paragraphs within the cell.

Setting formats and formulas for cells

You use the Format tab in Table inspector to format selected cells. Basic cell formats for numbers, currency, date and time, and others are provided. When you choose a format, Table inspector changes to show the specific settings for it. Figure 4-19 shows the Currency settings.

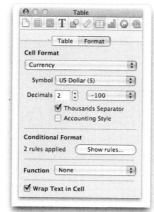

Figure 4-19:
Format
cells for
currency,
numbers,
and other
formats.

Setting a conditional format

In addition to setting a format for a cell, you can provide a conditional format that varies based on a condition you specify. Figure 4-20 shows an example of conditional formatting that you can construct for yourself to test. Conditional formatting has been applied to each cell in the Last Order column. The condition is simple: If sales have increased (that is, the last order is greater than the first order), make the Last Order cell background gray and display the text in bold and italic.

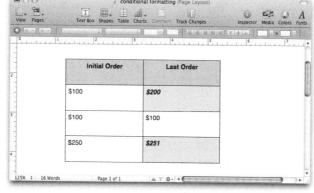

Figure 4-20:
Conditional
formatting
changes a
cell's format
based
on data
conditions.

Here's how to construct conditional formatting:

1. **Select a field in the Last Order column.**

2. **In the Format tab of Table inspector, click Show Rules.**

This opens the Conditional Format dialog shown in Figure 4-21.

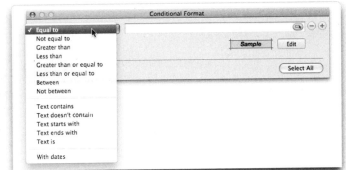

Figure 4-21:
The con-
ditional
formatting
rules dialog.

3. **From the pop-up menu, choose Greater Than, as shown in Figure 4-22.**

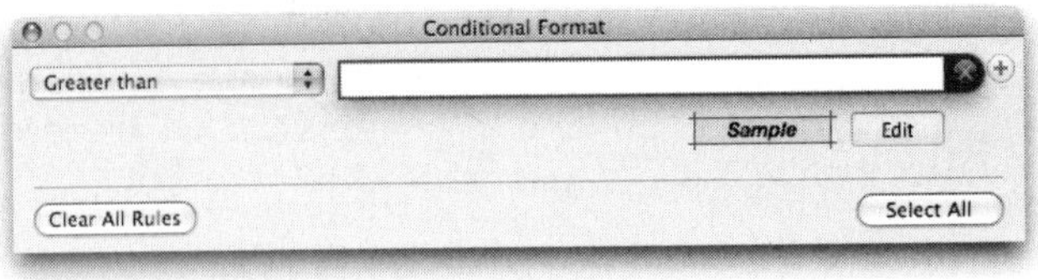

Figure 4-22:
Select a cell
to use in the
comparison.

4. **Select the cell or value to be used in the comparison.**

   If this cell or value is greater than the value in the Last Order field, the conditional formatting is applied. To use a specific value, type it in the value
   field to the right of the pop-up menu. To use the value in a cell for the comparison, click the blue oval to the right of the value field to open the cell
   reference field. Click the cell that contains the value you want to use.

5. **Click the Edit button to specify how the cell should be formatted if the
   condition is true.**

   As shown in Figure 4-23, you can set the text color; bold, italic, underline,
   or strikethrough formatting; and the fill color for the cell background.

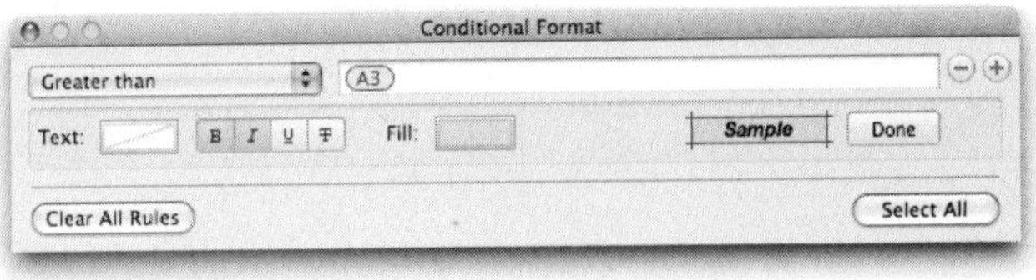

Figure 4-23:
Specify the
formatting
to use if
the condi-
tion is true.

The comparison value or cell is part of the rule. If you copy and paste cells, that comparison value will not be adjusted automatically.

Setting a formula

Although tables are not full-fledged spreadsheets, they have many spreadsheet features. For example, you can add a third column to the table shown in Figure 4-20 to display the order goal. A formula computes a 50 percent increase by multiplying the value in the Initial Order cell by 1.5. Here's how to do it:

1. **Create a new column.**

   You can click a cell in the Last Order column and choose Add Column After from the action menu in the Edit Rows & Columns section of the Table tab.

2. **Type Goal in the header of the new column.**

3. **Click in the first data cell of the Goal column.**

4. **From the Format pane of Table inspector, use the pop-up menu in the Function section at the bottom (see Figure 4-24) and choose Formula Editor.**

   If you want, you can choose any of the other formulas that are built into iWork.

Figure 4-24: Select a formula or use Formula Editor.

5. **In the formula reference field that opens above the selected cell, type your formula.**

   You can use a combination of text and mouse clicks in the fields you want to use. In this case, click in the Initial Order field and type *** 1.5** as shown in Figure 4-25.

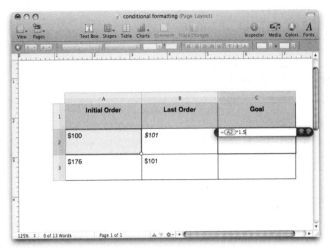

Figure 4-25:
Create the
formula.

6. **If the formula is correct, click the green check mark at the right to accept it.**

If you want to close the formula reference field without accepting the format, click the red X at the right.

7. **Choose Format⇨Table⇨Fill⇨Fill Down to fill the formula down the other cells in the column.**

Adjusting Chart Settings

When you create a chart, Chart inspector opens automatically; you can also open it by clicking the inspector's Chart button, as shown in Figure 4-26. Chart inspector provides you with detailed settings for your chart.

Figure 4-26:
Use Chart
inspector.

You'll probably use the following settings most often:

- ✔ **Edit Data:** Click this button to open Chart Data Editor, which is shown in Figure 4-27.

- ✔ **Show Title:** This is the name of the chart.

- ✔ **Show Legend:** This lets you identify which chart elements refer to which data sets.

There's more information on this topic in Chapter 15.

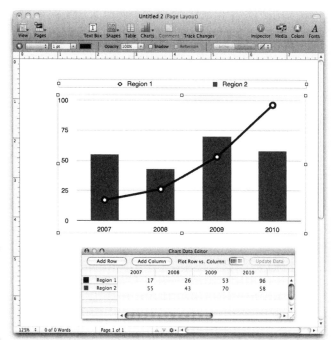

Figure 4-27: Use Chart Data Editor to edit the chart's data.

Managing Links

Link inspector always has a Hyperlink tab, as shown in Figure 4-28.

Select the object you want to serve as a hyperlink, select the Enable as a hyperlink check box, and then specify the type of link from the pop-up menu shown in Figure 4-29.

Figure 4-28:
Manage
links
with Link
inspector.

Figure 4-29:
Select the
type of link.

Perhaps the most important setting in Link inspector is the check box that allows you to make all hyperlinks inactive. You must do this to edit the links; otherwise, every time you click a link and try to edit it, it will be active and will take you to the link itself.

Setting QuickTime Options

The last inspector button lets you open the QuickTime inspector for a selected QuickTime object. You can set where the movie starts and stops, what the key frame is, how the movie repeats, and the movie's volume.

Part II
Turning the Page with Pages

The 5th Wave   By Rich Tennant

"They won't let me through security until I remove the bullets from my Pages document."

In this part . . .

Pages is two applications in one: It lets you create word processing documents in much the way that you do with Microsoft Word, but you can also use it to create page layout documents much as you would do in Adobe InDesign or Quark Xpress.

Pages provides you with advanced tools such as automatic creation of tables of contents as well as controls over page numbers in various sections of your documents. As with all the iWork applications, you can add graphics, QuickTime movies, charts and tables, and hyperlinks to your documents.

You see how in this part.

Chapter 5

Getting to Know Pages

For each of the three iWork applications, you'll find that the basic tools described in Part I come into play. For example, although tables and charts in Numbers spreadsheets can be more complex than tables and charts in Pages and Keynote, the basics are the same.

Pages is the word processing application (and, in fact, it's two word processing applications).This chapter and the others in Part II provide an introduction to the features, tools, and technologies you find in Pages.

The basics of Mac OS X as well as of iWork apply to each iWork application, including Pages. For example, there's nothing special about printing with Pages: It's the way you print in any Mac OS X application. But before you relax completely, keep an eye out for printing in Numbers (see Chapter 16). Some Numbers-specific features reflect the fact that Numbers deals with spreadsheets that can be much, much larger than individual pages.

Two Faces of Pages Documents

Pages lets you work with two different types of documents: word processing documents and page layout documents.

Word processing documents

A *word processing* document in Pages (as in any word processing program) lets you type what you want without worrying about page breaks and line breaks. If you type a sentence that is longer than the page is wide, Pages automatically breaks the sentence where necessary and continues on the next line as you type. This is known as *wrapping* the line. Likewise, when you come to the bottom of the page, Pages creates a new page and continues your text on that page. This process continues for all your text as well as for any tables, pictures, or graphics that you add to it. Everything flows along from line to line and from page to page and even from column to column within multicolumn documents. Figure 5-1 shows a word processing document in Pages.

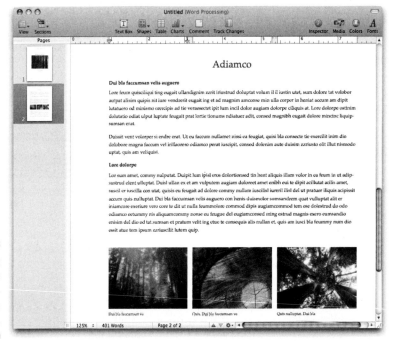

Figure 5-1:
A Pages word processing document.

You can manually control how Pages wraps text. You can use the Return or Enter key to start a new line. Likewise, you can insert a *page break* wherever you want to force Pages to begin a new page.

Other formatting techniques you can use for word processing documents are discussed in Chapters 6 and 7.

Page layout documents

A *page layout* document lets you design a page using objects that don't move. The objects can be the same tables, pictures, and graphics that you can add to a word processing document, but they don't flow. They stay where you place them. Figure 5-2 shows a page layout document.

Figure 5-2:
A Pages
page layout
document.

As you can see in Figures 5-1 and 5-2, graphics can appear in both types of documents. In fact, you can't tell by looking at a document which type of document it is. But when you open the document in Pages, you can tell immediately which type it is. If you were to type a new paragraph at the top of Figure 5-1, the graphics in the middle of the page would move down as that paragraph was inserted. If you were to type more text into the page layout document in Figure 5-2, the graphics wouldn't move.

Text boxes

Everything on the page in a page layout document (such as the page shown in Figure 5-2) is a self-contained object that contains text or graphics and remains where you put it. A special kind of object is a *text box*. You can type text in a text box, and the text will flow and wrap just as it does in a word processing document. Although it flows and wraps, it never extends beyond the text box, so the text box itself stays where you place it.

You can link text boxes so that text will flow automatically from one to the other. They're particularly useful in newsletters and brochures where you might want to have several text boxes on the first page, each of which is linked to other text boxes later in the document that provide the continuation of the text.

You can use text boxes in both word processing and page layout documents. If you place a text box within the flow of text in a word processing document, the text box provides a second set of flowed text within the main text flow. As you will see in Chapter 7, you can set options so that the text box itself stays put or flows as a single entity with the text in which it is embedded. Furthermore, you can place objects inside text boxes, so the text box can contain flowing and wrapped text and graphics that will never extend beyond the boundaries of the text box. And if you want, you can place a text box inside a text box, but that is likely to produce a very strange looking document.

Document types

Choosing the right document type isn't difficult. Each document type can contain the same objects (text, tables, shapes, and images); the main difference is whether the objects move as you type.

If you're creating a letter, report, or novel, you probably want a word processing document. You don't want to worry about page breaks except when you manually insert them at the end of a chapter or section. If you add graphics, you probably want them to flow with the text.

On the other hand, if you're creating a flyer or brochure, you generally want things to stay where you place them. A one-page flyer must stay on one page. You can achieve this effect with a word processing document by watching how much text and other information you add to the document, but it is generally easier to use a page layout document.

In the cases of brochures and newsletters, you may want a distinct difference in the layout of the first and second pages. By using linked text boxes, you can type the text on the first page and let it flow automatically to a text box with a different format on a later page. Once you have set up the text boxes, Pages will take care of everything as you add or delete text: You don't have to worry about the format.

You won't find a Pages Police to tell you what type of document to use. Apple has given you the tools to achieve your goals in many ways. If you're more comfortable working in word processing documents, you can make them look like page layout documents, although it will probably entail more work. If you're more comfortable working in page layout documents and graphics programs, you can make them look like word processing documents. (You can even use Numbers to type letters and memos if you're happier working in spreadsheets.)

Choosing Basic Templates

Throughout iWork, Apple provides you with templates for documents, spreadsheets, and presentations. These provide starting points for your own work. You can always start with a blank page and do everything yourself, but many people like to use a template either as-is or customize it. This section provides an introduction to the Pages templates.

Word processing templates

As you can see in Figure 5-3, Pages provides templates for a variety of types of word processing documents. The list of template types gives you an indication of the kind of documents that are usually created as word processing documents rather than page layout documents. The first category consists of blank documents that you can work with as you see fit. One is vertically oriented (portrait) and the other is horizontally oriented (landscape).

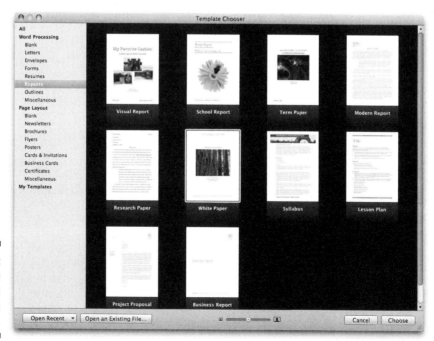

Figure 5-3:
Browse the word processing templates.

When you select a category, Pages shows you the first page of the various templates available so that you can get an idea of the design. When you move the pointer over the first page, you see an interior page. If you want to explore a template in more depth, simply select it and click the Choose button, or double-click it. Either way, Pages will create a document based on the template.

Page layout templates

The page layout templates, shown in Figure 5-4, also begin with blank documents. Then you can see the types of documents that lend themselves to page layouts. As with word processing templates, you can get a preview of the documents and their design.

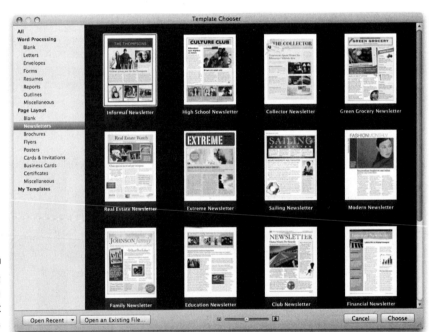

Figure 5-4: Browse the page layout templates.

Creating a Document

As you can see, the multitude of templates in Pages lets you quickly get started creating effective and attractive documents. Now it's time to begin creating your documents.

From a template

Creating a document from a template takes four simple steps:

1. **Choose File⇨New Document from Template Chooser or use the keyboard equivalent, ⇧-⌘-N.**

   This opens the Template Chooser dialog (refer to Figures 5-3 and 5-4).

2. **Select the template category you want to use for either a word processing or page layout document.**

   For example, in Figure 5-4, the Newsletters template category is selected.

3. **Select the specific template you want within the category.**

4. **Click the Choose button in the lower-right corner.**

   The Template Chooser closes and your document is created.

From a default template

By default, the New command in the File menu functions exactly like File⇨New Document from Template Chooser. However, you can set a preference to bypass Template Chooser and automatically create a new document based on the same document template each time you choose File⇨New. You do this with the Preferences window, which is shown in Figure 5-5.

Pages, like all iWork applications, lets you set preferences. These preferences apply to all documents you create and edit with the application. Here's how to set preferences for Pages:

1. **Open the Preferences window by choosing Pages⇨Preferences or pressing ⌘-, (comma).**

2. **Click the General button at the top of the window to show the General settings.**

3. **Click the Use Template radio button.**

   This opens Template Chooser.

4. **Select the default template you want to use for the New command.**

   From now on, the New command will use that template. To change the default template, simply repeat these steps.

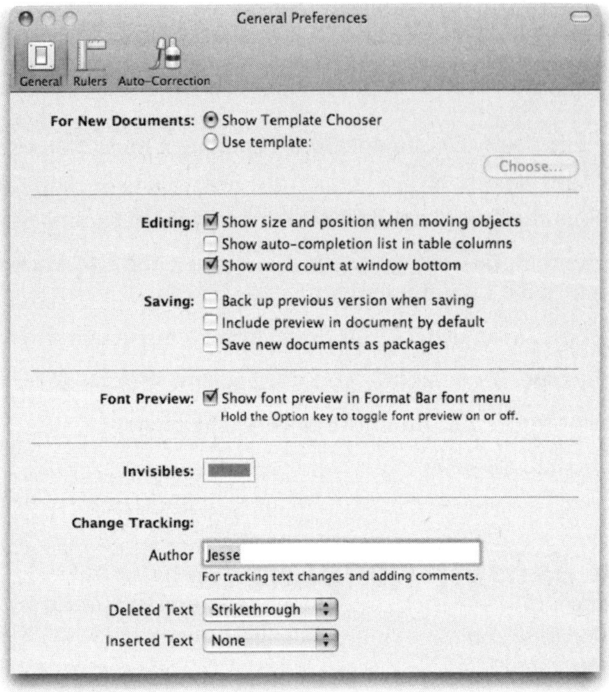

Figure 5-5:
You can set prefer-
ences for the behavior of all Pages documents.

From scratch

To create a document from scratch, use Template Chooser to create a blank word processing or page layout document as described in the "From a template" section. Alternatively, set the default template to a blank word processing document or a blank page layout document and choose File⇨New, as described in the "From a default template" section.

Setting Pages Preferences for All Documents

As you can see in Figure 5-5, you can set a number of other preferences that apply to all documents you open with Pages. If you change preferences and then open a document that you worked on previously with other settings, the new settings will apply. In general, *preferences* are for the application, and *settings* are for individual documents.

If you share your computer with other people, you don't have to worry about interfering with their preferences. Pages (like all applications on Mac OS X) stores preferences separately for each account on the computer.

When you open Preferences by choosing Pages⇨Preferences or pressing ⌘-, (comma), you can select any of the three sets of preferences by clicking the appropriate button at the top. The default is General preferences. If you've opened and then closed Preferences while Pages is open, it reopens to the preference you last viewed during that session.

General preferences

The General Preferences pane has six sets of preferences:

- ✔ **For New Documents:** The first preference lets you choose the behavior of the File⇨New command, as described in the preceding section.

- ✔ **Editing:** These preferences help you as you're editing the document. They are particularly useful in making Pages behave like other word processing applications you may be accustomed to (or making Pages not behave like other word processing applications whose features you detest).

  - You can control whether the size and position of movable objects are shown as you move them.

  - You can display an auto-completion list in table columns for partially typed words.

  - You can choose whether to have the document's word count shown at the window bottom.

- ✔ **Saving:** These preferences control options when you save a document.

  - You can automatically back up the previous version of a document as it was at the last save command; the file has BACKUP added to the name. Note that only one backup copy is saved. You can drag those old copies to a new location on your hard disk so that you can keep several older backups if you want.

  - You can automatically add a preview of the document to the file so that the preview is visible in Finder windows. You can override this preference with an option in the Save dialog for an individual file, as shown in Figure 5-6.

  - You can save new documents as a Mac OS X package that includes supporting files. (This is an advanced feature; you probably don't want to use it, but it can't do any harm unless you need to share your documents with someone else.)

Figure 5-6:
Choose
whether to
save a pre-
view image
with the
Pages
document.

✔ **Font Preview:** The format bar can list font names in a standard font or using the particular font for each font name. This gives you an idea of what the font will look like.

✔ **Invisibles:** Invisible characters such as tabs and returns normally aren't displayed in a document, but their effects are visible. You can use the View➪Show Invisibles command in any Pages document to display those characters. View➪Show Invisibles is a per-document setting, not a global preference for all documents. However, the color you use to display invisibles is a global setting, and you set it in General Preferences. Click the color well to open the Colors window, as described in Chapter 3.

✔ **Change Tracking:** The last settings control how change tracking is stored and displayed. This is the feature that keeps track of every change to the document with before-and-after versions, dates, times, and who made the changes. You can enter the name to be associated with the changes and control how deleted and inserted text is formatted.

Rulers preferences

The second set of preferences control the rulers you can display around your document. Click the Rulers button to display the following settings, as shown in Figure 5-7:

✔ **Default Zoom:** You can always adjust the window's zoom factor using the pop-up menu in the lower left of the window. By default, the window zooms to 125 percent. This reflects the fact that when a document is printed, smaller font sizes are generally used than when the document is displayed on a monitor.

✔ **Ruler Units:** You can choose inches, centimeters, points, or picas. You can also set the origin of the rulers. The origin is the 0,0 point — that is, the point that is 0 on both the horizontal and vertical rulers. You can place it at the upper left of the document, with numbers increasing to the right on the horizontal access and down on the vertical access. Or you can place it in the center of the document with larger numbers going to the right and smaller (even negative) numbers going down to the left margin. Instead of units, you can display a percentage. Finally, you can choose whether a vertical ruler is shown in word processing documents. (It appears in page layout documents at all times when rulers are shown.)

✔ **Alignment Guides:** The alignment guides help you position objects accurately. You choose the color of the guides from the color well. You can also choose whether to display them at the edges or centers of objects (or both).

Auto-Correction preferences

The Auto-Correction preferences let you configure Pages so that certain keystrokes are automatically transformed into specific characters and symbols. As with the General preferences, these apply to all documents — unless you change them. If you change them, the changes take effect from then on; nothing is changed in documents you have opened previously.

1. **Open the Preferences window by choosing Pages⇨Preferences or pressing ⌘-, (comma).**

2. **Click the Auto-Correction button at the top of the Preferences window to show the Auto-Correction Preferences pane, as shown in Figure 5-8.**

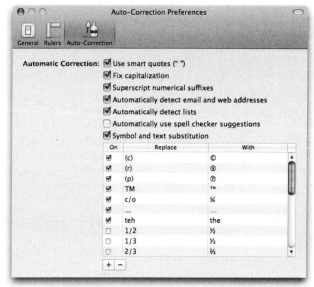

Figure 5-8: Set preferences for abbreviations, shortcuts, and corrections.

Basic Auto-Correction preferences

There are two sets of Auto-Correction preferences. The first six are check box choices that are common to many word processing applications:

✔ **Smart Quotes:** Smart quotes are sometimes called curly quotes. They look like " and " or, in the case of single quotes, ' and '. Your keyboard has straight quotes, " and " and ' and '. When smart quotes is turned on, Pages automatically converts straight quotes that you type to the appropriate smart quotes.

To know whether to use opening or closing quotes (" or "), Pages relies on spaces. If you type a space and then "Hello, how are you" and then another space, Pages recognizes the space before the first quote and turns it into an opening quote. Then it recognizes the space after the closing quote and turns it into a closing quote symbol. If you're using quotes in phrases where the spaces aren't in the standard positions, check that the substitution is what you want.

✔ **Fix capitalization:** This preference helps correct capitalization mistakes that occur if you're typing quickly and accidentally capitalize the first two letters of a word, such as *THis*. With this preference set, as soon as you finish typing the word and press the space key, Pages automatically corrects the word to *This*. This preference doesn't correct any other capitalization errors, and it doesn't refer to a dictionary or other source to determine whether a word should be capitalized. If you really meant to capitalize the first two letters, just retype the second letter as a capital and Pages will defer to your typing.

✔ **Superscript Numerical Suffixes:** This preference converts plain text to a superscript numerical suffix. If you type 1st when this preference is set, Pages will convert it to 1st.

✔ **Automatically Detect Email and Web Addresses:** Just as its name says, this preference converts text that appears to be an email address or a Web address to a hyperlink. You can then click the link and open your email program to begin typing a message or go to the Web address. See the next section for how to turn off this preference on a case-by-case basis.

✔ **Automatically Detect Lists:** The final basic preference comes into play when Pages thinks you're typing a list. If this preference is set, Pages begins to format the list according to the styles you've set. You can change the list settings (and turn the list back into plain text).

✔ **Automatically Use Spell Checker Suggestions:** Instead of just flagging a potential spelling error, Pages can make suggestions for a correction. In many cases, you can just click a suggestion and go on with your work.

Modifying auto-detected email and Web addresses

It's great to have hyperlinks in your Pages documents. You and the people with whom you share your documents can just click the link to go to a Web address or to open and address a new mail message. Having the ability to auto-detect email and Web addressees makes it even easier to add them to your Pages documents as hyperlinks.

There's only one problem: How do you edit the link and its text? If you click it, you're off to your browser or email program. Here's how to modify an email or Web address that's active in a Pages document:

1. **Scroll the page so that the link is in view, but don't click it yet.**

2. **If the inspector isn't shown, choose View⇨Show Inspector or click the Inspector button at the right of the toolbar.**

   Inspectors were discussed in Chapter 4.

3. **Click the Hyperlink tab, as shown in Figure 5-9.**

4. **At the bottom of the pane, select the Make All Hyperlinks Inactive check box.**

    Now you can edit any link in the document by clicking it.

5. **When you're finished, select the Make All Hyperlinks Active check box to clear the check mark.**

Setting symbol and text substitution

The second group of auto-correction settings controls symbol and text substitution. The bottom part of the Auto-Correction Preferences window consists of a table of substitution rules. A number of rules are installed automatically in Pages, and you can add your own. In addition, a check box at the left of each substitution rule determines whether that rule is turned on.

The default rules in Figure 5-8 handle different types of substitutions:

✔ You can create special characters such as $\frac{1}{2}$ by simply typing 1/2, without using modifier keys such as opt or ⌘.

✔ Common typos such as *teh* for *the* can be corrected automatically.

You can add your own rules easily:

1. **With the Auto-Correction Preferences window visible, click the + button, which is in the lower left, as shown in Figure 5-10.**

    A new line is added to the bottom of the scrolling list. The check box in the On column is set automatically, and the pointer is positioned in the next column (Replace).

2. **In the Replace column, type the text that you want to replace.**

3. **Using the mouse or the tab key, move to the next column (With) and enter the new text.**

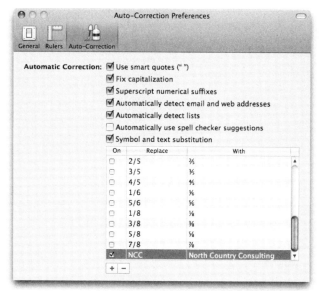

Figure 5-10:
Add a
new auto-
correction
rule.

You can use a similar process to remove a substitution rule. Scroll to the rule you want to remove, select it by clicking in the row, and then click the – button to remove it.

Rather than removing a rule, consider just turning it off. That way, if you change your mind, the rule is still there.

Saving Your Work

As with any Mac OS X application, you save your work using File➪Save to save the file with the last name you used or File➪Save As to rename the file. The basic Save As dialog is shown in Figure 5-11.

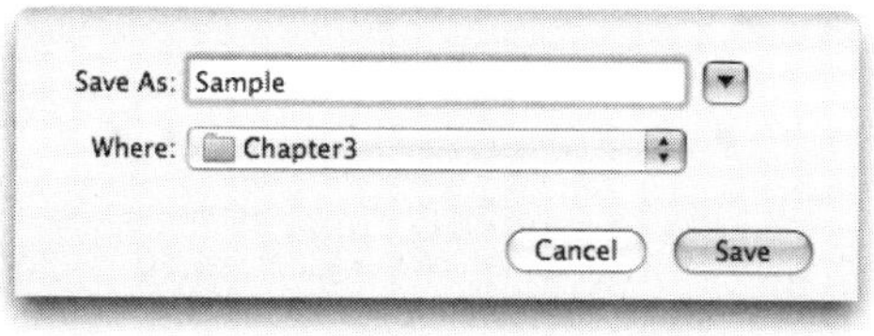

Figure 5-11:
Save your
work.

You can expand the Save As dialog by clicking the downward-pointing arrow next to the file name, as shown in Figure 5-12.

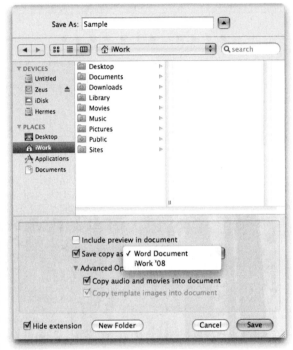

Figure 5-12:
You can specify additional options for the Save command.

The Pages-specific options in this dialog give you greater control over what is saved. Note, however, that each of these options can increase the size of the file:

- ✔ **Include Preview in Document:** This is a preview of the document's contents for display in Finder.

- ✔ **Save Copy As:** Pages formats have changed with new releases. You have an option to save a copy in the prior format. This is useful if you're exchanging documents with someone who doesn't have the latest version of Pages. If you're sharing files with people who are using Microsoft Word, you can also choose to save a copy in Word format.

- ✔ **Copy Audio and Movies into Document:** These files can be very large. If you're saving the document to send to someone who will print it, there's no reason to include these files.

✔ **Copy Template Images into Document:** The Pages document that you see on the screen can include images from its template as well as images you've inserted in the document. In some cases, the template images should be saved in the document so that it's complete. In other cases, the template images are just placeholders, so there's no reason to save them with the document.

Creating a Template from a Document

To create a template from a document, you use the same dialog and the same options as the Save dialog discussed in the preceding session. When you're ready to save your document as a template, choose File⇨Save As Template.

The only difference between the Save dialog and the Save As Template dialog is that by default the template is saved to a folder called My Templates inside your home directory. The path is <home>/Library/Application Support/iWork/Pages/Templates/My Templates. The newly created template will now show up in Template Chooser.

To remove a template, remove it from the folder in your home directory.

Chapter 6

Editing Word Processing Documents

*1*n Chapter 5, you saw how to create Pages documents — both word processing and page layout types of documents. When you find yourself looking at a blank word processing document or a document based on a template, this chapter tells you what to do next.

This chapter deals with the major entities in your word processing document, such as paragraphs, headers, and footers. Later, in Chapter 9, you see how to fine-tune both page layout and word processing documents. The format bar, which is discussed in Chapter 9, can be used for fine-tuning or for quick shortcuts.

One of the nice things about a word processing document is that you can just start typing. The text flows as you type; new pages are created as needed, and formatting is basically taken care of for you.

If your document is lengthy, however, page after page of type can become difficult to read. You can communicate your message more effectively if you use some of the tools described in this chapter. Even a short document can often benefit from organization.

Is iWork WYSIWYG?

WYSIWYG (What You See Is What You Get) isn't really the case on the computer screen. Myriad settings influence what you see. The display resolution changes the size of everything on the display, and system-wide settings such as Font Smoothing in System Preferences modify text on the screen in subtle ways. Inside applications, you can zoom in or out of a document. Look in the lower left of a Pages document and you will see that the default zoom factor is 125 percent: Text is larger on the screen (all other settings and options being equal) than it is on a printed page (although you can change the zoom factor for a printed page, too). You can change the default zoom by choosing Pages⇨Preferences and clicking the General tab.

The default zoom is 125 percent for a good reason. As a general rule, font sizes that are comfortable to read on a printed page are hard to read on a screen. You may have noticed this when you created text documents and then printed them. Depending on the font, a font size of 10 or 12 is comfortable for reading on the screen but looks right for a headline when printed. Pages has built-in styles that look good for printed documents. To make these styles more legible on the screen, the zoom factor is set to 125 percent rather than 100 percent.

Whenever you're creating an iWork document that will be presented on some device other than the computer you're working on, proofread the document on the device that will be used. That means doing the final proofreading of a document that will be printed by printing it and looking at the printed copy. If it will be printed on a specific printer, have a test run with the actual printer and paper that will be used. If you're preparing Pages documents or Keynote slides for a presentation, proofread the slides on the screen you will be using if possible. If the image is to be projected, check to see that it is sized properly and that the potted palm at the side of the platform doesn't obscure critical parts of your slides.

Managing Paragraphs

Your word processing document consists of paragraphs. (Technically, it could have no paragraphs but be made up of tables, images, and media files, but normally at least one paragraph exists.) In a word processing document, paragraphs flow one after the other by default. Pages inserts page breaks as needed. You can modify this default behavior in a variety of ways, such as by manually inserting page breaks (even within a paragraph) or by forcing Pages to handle pagination in special ways for given paragraphs. This section shows you the principal paragraph management settings.

Paragraph settings apply to the entire paragraph, for example, you might make a paragraph single-spaced or double-spaced. You can select the paragraph you want to apply settings to in two ways:

✔ Position the pointer in the paragraph and triple-click.

✔ Click anywhere in the paragraph. It doesn't matter where in the paragraph you click because the paragraph settings are the same for every location in the paragraph.

Setting vertical spacing

Three vertical spacing settings for paragraphs are available: the space between lines, the space before the paragraph, and the space after the paragraph. (The before and after spaces aren't additive — they're used to compute the actual space between any two paragraphs.)

Here's how to set vertical spacing for a paragraph:

1. **Click in the paragraph for which you want to adjust vertical spacing.**

2. **Open an inspector.**

3. **Click the T button at the top to display the Text settings.**

4. **Click the Text tab.**

   The inspector looks like Figure 6-1.

Figure 6-1:
Set vertical
spacing in a
paragraph.

5. **Set the line spacing using the slider, the stepper arrows, or the box.**

   You can also use the small pop-up menu below the text box. The default line spacing is one line. The height of the line is determined by the tallest font in the line; as a result it can appear that there are several different line spacing values for a single paragraph, but only font variations actually cause them.

6. **Set the space before and after the paragraph with the sliders, steppers, or text box.**

   Pages automatically handles potential conflicts between interparagraph spacing settings as follows:

   - **First paragraph:** There is no space before a first paragraph regardless of the setting.

   - **Last paragraph:** Likewise, there is no space after a final paragraph.

   - **Conflicting settings:** If the space after a paragraph and before the next paragraph is the same, that's the space that's used. If they differ, the larger space is used.

Setting indents with an inspector

The preceding section showed you how to set vertical spacing. This section and the one that follows deal with horizontal settings:

1. **Click in the paragraph for which you want to adjust horizontal spacing.**

2. **Open an inspector.**

3. **Click the T button at the top to display the Text settings.**

4. **Click the Tabs tab.**

   The window appears as shown in Figure 6-2.

5. **Click the stepper arrows or type in the boxes to set the first line indent, left indent, and right indents.**

Figure 6-2:
Set paragraph indents.

Indenting the first line of a paragraph is a common style. Other times, the first line of the first paragraph of a section is indented.

Make sure that your paragraph boundaries are visible. If the space between paragraphs is the same as the space between lines in a paragraph, and the paragraph has no first line indent, the break between paragraphs is difficult to see.

If you need to group several paragraphs, use headings or subheadings, as I do in this book.

Setting indents with the ruler

You don't have to use Text inspector to set the indents for a paragraph. You can use the ruler instead:

1. **If the ruler isn't visible, choose View➪Show Rulers or click the View button on the toolbar.**

   The ruler is shown in Figure 6-3.

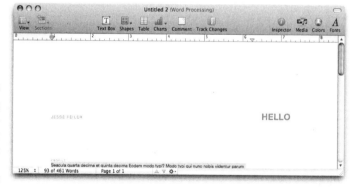

Figure 6-3: Set paragraph indents from the ruler.

2. **Drag the downward-pointing triangle on the left to set the left margin.**

   The first line indent marker is the rectangle right above the triangle. By default, the first line indent moves with the left margin. To adjust the first line indent, drag it separately, as shown in Figure 6-4.

3. **Drag the downward-pointing triangle on the right to set the right margin.**

The ruler and Text inspector work together. If both are visible, changes made in one are automatically reflected in the other.

Using decorative caps

In addition to indents for the first line of a paragraph or the first line of the first paragraph in a section, you can use a decorative cap for the first character of a paragraph. Typically this technique is used at the beginning of a chapter or section. The first character uses a distinctive font and a much larger size than the text of the rest of the paragraph. This is a good place to use very elaborate letters. Explore the Fonts window to see what you can work with.

Figure 6-4:
Set the first line indent with the ruler.

Setting tabs

You can set tabs for a paragraph using Text inspector.

1. **Select the paragraph.**

2. **Open Text inspector and click the Tabs tab (refer to Figure 6-2).**

   If you need a new Inspector, choose View⇨New Inspector or View⇨ Show Inspector; you can also click Inspector on the toolbar if no inspector is visible.

3. **Click the + button beneath the list of tab stops in the lower left.**

   This creates a new tab. It will be located to the right of the previous tab at a distance set in the Default Tabs box.

4. **If you want to change the new tab, double-click the new value in the Tab Stops list and then change it.**

   For example, in Figure 6-2, the Default Tabs value is set at .5 inch, so all new tabs are in increments of .5 inch. I started with tabs at 0.5, 1, and 1.5. In the figure, the 1.5 tab is being edited to move it to 1.75.

5. **Select the type of tab from the Alignment list, at the right.**

   The most common tab is a left-aligned tab. This will produce a column with an aligned left side. Right- and center-alignment function similarly. Decimal tabs align the column based on a character that you set in the Decimal Tab Character box. Most often, the Decimal option is used to align numbers on their decimal point.

6. **If you want, choose a tab leader.**

   Tab leaders can improve readability when there is a fairly long distance between the text and the next tab. For example, in this book's table of contents, dots are used as leaders between the chapter titles and the page numbers.

Setting pagination

Finally, you can set options for the interaction of pagination and paragraphs. These settings are available in Text inspector in the More tab, as shown in Figure 6-5.

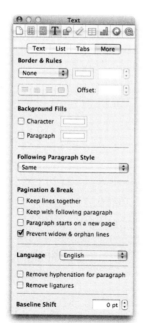

Figure 6-5:
Set
pagination
preferences.

The pagination settings are in the Pagination & Break section of the inspector. Turn any setting on or off to get the effect that you want.

In the case of a preference such as Keep Lines Together, Pages will do its best, but if the paragraph has five pages of text in it, there is no way Pages will be able to fit it onto a single page.

The only setting that is guaranteed to take effect is Paragraph Starts On a New Page. Pages can easily do that.

The last setting, Prevent Widow & Orphan Lines, generally is turned on because it makes the document look better. Widow and orphan lines are single lines at the top or bottom of a page, respectively. If the line is short (perhaps a single word), a widow or orphan can look peculiar. Forcing the previous line down so you have at least two lines at the top or bottom of the page generally looks better.

Using Headers and Footers

You can improve the appearance of your documents by using headers and footers, which are special sections of text at a page's top and bottom, respectively, for information such as page numbers, dates, titles, and author names. When Pages inserts a page break, it places the appropriate footer at the bottom of the page and places the appropriate header at the top of the next page.

Headers and footers can contain constant text such as the document name or certain variable information such as a date. Most documents that are more than one page long benefit from headers and footers.

Constructing a header

Most of the Pages templates have headers and footers, but many of them aren't filled in. Choose View➪Show Layout to show all the layout elements on a page. Figure 6-6 is the Modern Report template with the layout shown. The page header is at the top.

Even without displaying the layout, you can click where you know the header is to activate it.

To construct a header, type it as you would normally type any paragraph, but keep your text to a single line (two or three lines at the most). The longer the header and footer, the less room on the page for your text.

Figure 6-6:
Show the
layout.

In the past, teachers assigned reports by page count. The advent of word processors and headers and footers allowed innovative students to fulfill the page count with a remarkably small amount of text and a remarkably large amount of header and footer information. Today, most teachers assign reports by word count, not page count, so the header/footer trick no longer works.

You can also insert special markers that will be used during pagination. These are all in the Insert menu:

- ✔ Date & Time
- ✔ Page Number
- ✔ Page Count

Figure 6-7 shows a typical footer that combines text with some special symbols. At the left, the actual footer is

> Page <page number> of <page count>

By default, footers and headers contain a right-aligned tab, so if you press the Tab key after inserting something at the left, whatever you type will be placed at the right. You can set additional tabs if needed.

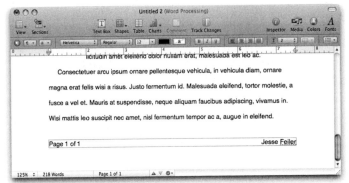

Figure 6-7:
Create a
footer.

Moving headers and footers

You can turn headers on and off and move them, as follows:

1. **Click in the section of the document you want to modify.**

2. **Open an inspector and click the Document button at the left.**

3. **Click the Document tab, as shown in Figure 6-8.**

Figure 6-8:
Place
headers
and footers.

4. **Use the check boxes in the Document Margins section to turn the headers and footers on or off.**

   If you turn a header or footer off, its content is removed. If you subsequently restore it with the check box, it will be blank.

5. **To place the header or footer below the document's top margin or above its bottom margin, use the stepper arrows or text box.**

   This moves the header or footer down or up, leaving more blank space at the top or bottom of the page.

Using section headers and footers

Pages word processing documents are composed of sections. You can set separate header and footer options for any section:

1. **Click in the section you want to modify.**

2. **Open an inspector and click the Layout button at the top** (it's the second from the left).

3. **Click the Section tab, as shown in Figure 6-9.**

Figure 6-9: Specify a special first page.

4. **Select the First Page Is Different check box.**

   The header and footer on the first page are removed. You can create new ones there. If you already created a header or footer, it continues to appear on pages after the first page.

Using the Sections Menu to Add and Reuse Sections

A document *section* is one or more pages that are treated as a unit. You can adjust headers and footers for each section; you can also control whether page numbers restart at the beginning of a section (refer to Figure 6-9).

For now, it's important to know just these basics and that most of the Pages word processing templates come with several sections defined for the document even if they aren't shown. You find out more about sections and how to create them in Chapter 11.

To select a section to insert into a document, click the Sections button on the toolbar or choose Insert⇨Sections. Figure 6-10 shows the sections for the White Paper template. The sections are well named and include a variety of pages. Experiment by adding various sections to your document to see what they look like. One of the advantages of using sections is that you can create a common look for different types of pages in your document.

Figure 6-10:
Use
template
sections.

Navigating through a Document

When you have a document with many pages, a fast way to navigate through the document is to use thumbnails of the pages. To do that, follow these steps:

1. **Show page thumbnails by clicking the View button on the toolbar or by choosing View⇨Show Page Thumbnails.**

   A page thumbnail for each page in the document appears in the Pages pane on the left of the screen, as shown in Figure 6-11.

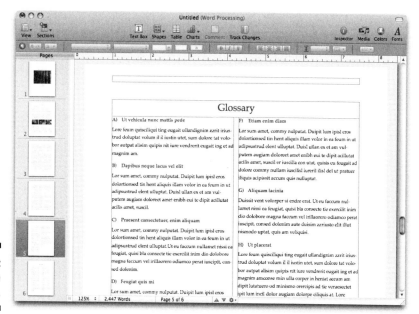

Figure 6-11:
Show the thumbnails.

2. **To rearrange the sequence of pages, drag the thumbnails up or down.**
3. **To delete a page, select it its thumbnail and press the Delete key.**

Chapter 7

Editing Page Layout Documents

In This Chapter

▶ Creating a one-page flyer

▶ Setting a big title

▶ Adding an image

▶ Creating tear-off tabs

*W*ord processing documents tend to be fairly simple: They consist of words that are built into sentences and paragraphs. You can add graphics and other elements, but most of the time you're typing one word after another.

Page layout documents generally have a range of objects, such as text boxes, graphics, and even movies and hyperlinks. You need to identify the components, know how to create and edit them, and put them all together.

As always with iWork, the easiest and fastest way to get started is to begin with one of the built-in templates. In this chapter, you create a document from a template. Then you explore what you've created, seeing how each component is created and how it can be customized. You can apply these steps to any page layout document, whether you construct it from a template or a blank document.

Analyzing the Templates

The Page Layout templates are divided into nine categories:

- ✓ **Blank**
- ✓ **Newsletters**
- ✓ **Brochures**
- ✓ **Flyers**
- ✓ **Posters**

✔ **Cards & Invitations**

✔ **Business Cards**

✔ **Certificates**

✔ **Miscellaneous**

Each template comes with built-in styles, and many of them have placeholder text and pictures, which you replace with your own text and pictures. As with word processing documents, as well as Numbers and Keynote documents, the templates not only provide a jumping-off point but also can give you ideas for the documents you want to create. These ideas can be specific, such as the types of information you should consider putting into a brochure, or general.

Open Template Chooser by choosing File⇨New From Template Chooser. As you click the various categories in Template Chooser and look at the thumbnails of the various templates, you get an excellent basic lesson in graphic design (something the people at Apple know from top to bottom). Figure 7-1 shows some newsletter templates.

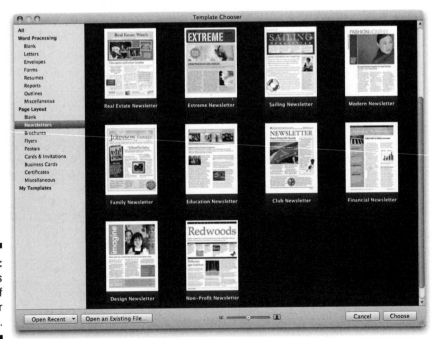

Figure 7-1:
iWork has
a variety of
newsletter
templates.

To see a particular template full-sized, simply create a document from the template. When you've finished viewing the template, close it without saving it.

It's easy to spot the title in each template, even when the templates are thumbnail-sized. If you want to become an iWork pro, start training yourself to analyze what you're seeing. What makes the titles stand out from the rest of the elements on the template? Here are some of the ways in which the designers at Apple have done this:

- **Titles are large.** Here's where you can go to town with a distinctive font and a large font size.

- **Titles are brief.** If a designer has to work with a long title, such as *Sailing Newsletter,* one solution is to make *Sailing* much larger than *Newsletter.*

- **Backgrounds can help a title stand out.**

    - Large type for the title with plenty of white space around it can help the title stand out.

    - A color or an image behind the title can also help it stand out. If you use this technique, the color or the main color in the background image should not be used extensively elsewhere on the page.

Starting with a Simple Template

The built-in flyer templates are some of the simplest page layout documents. Generally, they are a single page, although a few of them have alternate page layouts (such as one version with tear-off slips for phone numbers and another one with no such tear-off slips). Because the flyer templates are usually a single page, they're a good place for us to start exploring exactly what goes into a page layout.

To create a template-based document, in this case a flyer, follow these steps:

1. **Choose File⇨New Document from Template to open Template Chooser.**

    You can also use ⌘-N if you've set General Preferences to open Template Chooser.

2. **In the Page Layout group at the left of the window, click the Flyers category to show the templates for flyers.**

    Figure 7-2 shows you the range of choices for flyers in iWork.

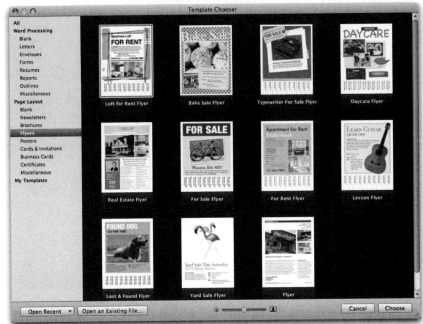

Figure 7-2:
Select a
template for
your
document.

3. **Double-click the For Sale template (the one with a large photo of a bike) to create a document based on it.**

   You can also select it with a single click and then click the Choose button in the lower right. Your new document opens in its own window, as shown in Figure 7-3.

The first step in exploring a document is to know what you have in the document. Everything on a page in a page layout document is some kind of object, such as an image, a text box, a shape, a table, or a chart. Information (including colors and images) is always located within an object. Objects sometimes are grouped either with the Pages Arrange➪Group command or conceptually in your mind and the minds of your users.

Here's what you should be able to identify in your new document:

- ✔ **Title:** The title is *For Sale* on a solid red background.

- ✔ **Image:** The image in this case is the bike. This is a placeholder image that you replace with whatever you are selling.

✔ **Description:** The description of what's for sale includes the name of what's for sale and its price in large text. It is followed by placeholder text. If you look closely, you may see your own phone number at the end of the text! You'll see later in this chapter how Pages can pick up information on request from your Address Book and your Me card.

✔ **Tear-off tabs:** Ten identical tear-off tabs at the bottom have the name of the item for sale and the phone number for people to call.

Figure 7-3:
View your
new
document.

Modifying the Title

Depending on what you're going to use the flyer for, you may or may not have to modify the title. Perhaps it will read *Free* or *Best Offer* rather than *For Sale.* Even if you're going to leave the text unchanged, you may want to alter other aspects of the title such as its font or size. In this section I show you how the title is constructed in the template and how you can modify it. (You can also use this information to create your own title on a blank document or another template.)

The title consists of bold text on a red background. Here's an important iWork design note: The text on the red background is icreated with two objects. See Figure 7-4, in which both objects are selected. Look for the two outlines: one around the red box, and the other around the text box within the red box.

Figure 7-4:
The title
consists of
two objects.

Here's how to make changes to the title:

✓ **Change the text:** Double-click the text to select it all. You can then type replacement text. Alternatively, you can click where you want to make a change; then type the new text or delete the text you don't want.

✓ **Change the text formatting:** Double-click the text to select it all. Then do one of the following:

• Use Text Inspector to change the font, color, and other attributes (for more information on these tasks, see Chapter 3).

• Use the Fonts window to change the font, color, and other attributes (for more on the Fonts window, see Chapter 2).

✓ **Change the background shape or color:** Click to select the background shape, and then drag the handles of the background shape to change its size and shape. Change its color using the Fill section in Graphic inspector (see Chapter 3) or the Colors window (Chapter 2).

Changing the Image

You'll want to use your own image unless you happen to be selling a gray-and-yellow bike. In this section we look at how the image has been placed on the flyer. Then you can simply replace it with your own image or change the settings for the image such as its angle on the page. If you just replace the image, your own image will appear tilted slightly to the right just as the place-holder image is.

Here's another design tip incorporated into this template. The photo of the bike is tilted a bit, just enough to draw your attention. Note too the light gray shadow behind the image. It's subtle, but it helps to draw your attention to the image. Both techniques are used extensively throughout the iWork templates and in other examples of good design.

You can change the formatting of any image. If you insert a new image in a document, it will be inserted in its original orientation, but you can change it. If you're working from an image that has already been inserted and manipulated (such as this one), you can make further adjustments to it. Here's how to make the adjustments to an image such as the one in the For Sale flyer:

1. **Click the image to select it.**

   You can zoom in or out using the Edit Mask slider that appears below the image, as shown in Figure 7-5.

Figure 7-5:
Use the Edit Mask slider below the image to change the zoom factor.

2. **If an inspector is not visible, click the Inspector icon on the toolbar to show the inspector.**

   You can also choose View➪Show Inspector.

3. **Click the Graphic button at the top of the inspector.**

   Graphic inspector appears, as shown in Figure 7-6.

4. **Adjust the Stroke settings to change the border around the image.**

   You can change the width of the border, its shape, or its color. The template has the Stroke settings set to an unbroken, white, 10-point line. Figure 7-7 shows the image if you change the Line setting to None (no border).

Figure 7-6:
Use Graphic
inspector to
adjust the
image.

Figure 7-7:
Use Graphic
inspector to
change the
border.

5. **Adjust the Shadow settings.**

You can turn the shadow on or off with the check box. The Shadow settings are increased in Figure 7-8 to make the shadow bigger and more prominent. Compare this image to Figure 7-5, which shows the results of the default settings (shown in Figure 7-6). For Figure 7-8, they were changed to Offset (24), Blur (30), and Opacity (100). Experiment to see what looks best to you, but remember not to go to extremes.

A subtle shadow with a suggested light source at the upper left is usually best, providing a slight 3-D effect and drawing attention to the image.

Figure 7-8:
You can change the shadow.

Setting the Main Text

You adjust the text and its characteristics just as you adjust text in a word processing document. Because this is placeholder text, you can't edit it. If you begin to type, you will simply replace it. That doesn't matter because the placeholder text is meaningless and you must replace it. To edit the text, just click in the text box, as shown in Figure 7-9, and type away.

Figure 7-9:
Edit the text
in the text
box.

Automatically Inserting Your Phone Number in the Flyer

iWork provides the ability to merge data from Address Book with your documents. Several templates use the feature to automatically insert your phone number. For this to work properly, you must have your own card in Address Book. Then you insert a Sender field in your document. Although the Flyers template has already completed the second step, this section walks you through both.

Creating a Me card in Address Book

Here's how you create a Me card:

1. **Launch Address Book.**

2. **Choose Card⇨Go To My Card to go to your card.**

   Congratulations! You have a Me card and you don't have to create a new one unless the Me card is not yours. This can happen if you're using someone else's computer. Get their permission before proceeding with the next step.

3. **Type your name in the search field at the upper right of the window.**

   You don't have to click a button: Address Book finds any cards with the name you type.

4. **If there's no card with your name, create one by choosing File⇨New Card and filling in your data.**

5. **With your card visible, as shown in Figure 7-10, choose Card⇨Make This My Card.**

   A small *me* appears in the lower left of your card image.

Figure 7-10:
Make
certain your
Me card is
visible.

Using the Merge or Sender field

Two types of fields that interact with your Address Book data can be added: Merge and Sender fields. You can see them both at work in templates for letters. The Merge fields in a letter contain information about the person you're writing to; the Sender fields in a letter contain your information.

These fields are already placed in many of the templates. The Sender fields pick up data from your Me card. The Merge fields pick up data from the appropriate Address Book record. Simply drag an address card from Address Book into your document, and the data for that person automatically appears in the Merge fields.

The Flyers template has a Merge field that picks up data from a selected Address Book card. This section shows you how to delete it and create a new Sender field that picks up your own work phone number from your Me card:

1. **Delete the existing Merge field by selecting it and pressing Delete.**

    In the For Sale flyer, the Merge field is the phone number at the end of the placeholder description text. Leave the placeholder text.

2. **Place the cursor at least one space after the placeholder text.**

3. **Choose Insert⇨Sender Field⇨Phone⇨Work Phone, as shown in Figure 7-11.**

Figure 7-11:
Insert a
Sender field.

In the document, the Sender field you've inserted appears as shown in Figure 7-12 with the data from your Me card. If it doesn't appear, check the following:

- Do you have a Me card?

- Do you have a work phone on the Me card?

- Have you finished editing the Me card? If you've just created it or just typed your work phone, try going to another card so that your update is captured.

Figure 7-12:
The Sender
field is
inserted.

The Me card is used by default for a Sender field, but sometimes you don't want that. Perhaps you're preparing this flyer for a friend and you want to use her card instead of your Me card. Simply drag her Me card from the Address Book to the Sender field, and the Sender field automatically picks up the information from that card and retains it until you change it again.

Changing the Info on the Tear-Off Tabs

At the bottom of the Flyers template are tear-off tabs that people can take with them to contact you. Each one is its own text box, which you can see if you click one. As always happens when you click a text box that has been rotated, it immediately returns to a horizontal state, as shown in Figure 7-13.

Figure 7-13:
Each
tear-off tab
is its own
text box.

As you hover your cursor over the text box, you can see that the phone number is a Sender field. If you have changed the Sender field in the main text to your work number, you should change it here as well.

Chapter 8

Using Text Boxes

*W*ord processing documents let text flow from page to page, with new pages added automatically as they are needed. In page layout documents, the only items that appear on pages are objects. The objects can contain text, but the size and shape of the object limits the amount of text that can be shown.

Text boxes are objects that you place on a page and that can contain text. They can appear in both page layout and word processing documents. A text box can be used to highlight a small section of text; it can be used also to display part of a lengthy run of text that may continue in another text box on the same or another page. Although the main purpose of text boxes is to contain text and allow it to flow from one text box to another, they can also contain objects such as graphics, shapes, and charts. Their handling of text flow distinguishes them from other objects in iWork.

Think of a newspaper's front page, which typically displays a number of articles. Most of the articles are incomplete, and they end with a note such as "Continued on Page A14." That's an example of text boxes in action: The first text box is on the front page, and the second is on page A14. When the newspaper is laid out, the text boxes are linked. If an editor adds or deletes a paragraph in the text box on the front page, the text reflows between that text box and the text box on page A14. Once the text boxes and the link are set up, you can edit the flowing text just as you would in a word processing document.

This chapter shows you the various permutations and uses of text boxes.

About the text in this chapter

Demonstrating how Pages handles text sometimes requires a lot of text. Formatting the text at the top of a For Sale flyer requires a mere seven letters and one space. In some ways, that's trivial. Many of the tools and techniques you use to format *For Sale* are the same that you use to format a hundred pages or more of text, but when you deal with a large text document, some special problems (and solutions) arise.

To demonstrate some of the issues involved in large documents, this chapter sometimes uses text from *The Pickwick Papers* by Charles Dickens. With about 300,000 words, the novel is just under 800 pages long in a standard paperback edition or when displayed in Courier 12. That's enough text to demonstrate text-handling capabilities in Pages. And it's one of the greatest and funniest novels ever written.

You can download the Pages word processing text from the author's Web site as described in the Introduction.

Creating a Simple Text Box

The easiest way to start learning about text boxes is to create one and work with it. Experiment with a document that has a good deal of text in it to see the results of inserting a text box and adjusting its settings.

The text box created in this section is actually a *floating text box.* By default, all text boxes you create are floating text boxes; also, they are the only kind of text box you can create in a page layout document. The other kind of text box, an *inline text box,* is described in the following section. It can be placed only in a word processing document.

Creating the text box

You can create a simple text box by clicking the Text Box icon on the toolbar. In both word processing and page layout documents, a simple text box is created, as shown in Figure 8-1.

You can resize or reshape the text box with any of the eight handles. You can also drag it around by clicking and dragging the interior of the box. If you double-click in the text box, you can type text or paste it in.

Position the text box where you want it on the page. The text that's already on the page will flow around the box if needed.

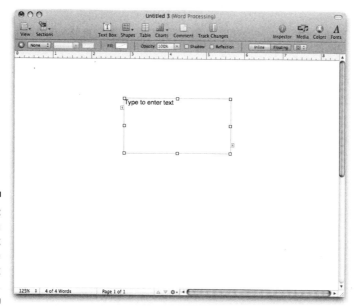

The text box contains text, but the box itself behaves like a shape. This means you can customize your text box using two sets of tools. Figure 8-2 shows a text box with text that is centered horizontally and vertically. The text box itself has a line border and a background gradient as well as a shadow.

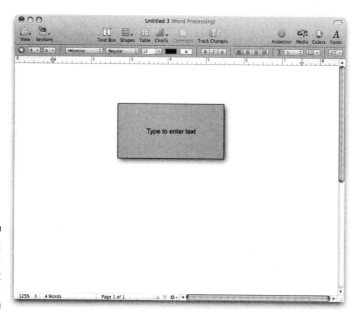

Modifying the text box

You can modify text in a text box with the following two inspectors:

- ✔ **Text inspector:** Select some or all of the text in the text box and style it with Text inspector. The Text inspector settings are shown in Figure 8-3.

- ✔ **Graphic inspector:** You can set the fill, stroke, and opacity for the text box using Graphic inspector. Use the Stroke setting to show the border of the box, and select the Shadow check box if you want to add a shadow. The Graphic inspector settings are shown in Figure 8-4.

Figure 8-3:
Change the text settings with Text inspector.

Customizing the text box

Figure 8-5 shows how the text box appears if you create it in *The Pickwick Papers* word processing document.

As you can see in Figure 8-5, just putting a text box into a default position in a document can make the existing text look peculiar. You can make things look better in three basic ways. You will probably use a little bit of each of them, as you experiment with the best size, shape, and position for the text box:

- ✔ **Resize the text box.** Click the text box to show its eight handles. Resize it as you want. (A single click selects the text box; a double click lets you edit the text.)

- ✔ **Move the text box.** Notice that as you move the box the text will wrap around it. Often this is what you want.

✔ **Use Wrap inspector to change how text wraps around the text box.**
Wrap inspector is shown in Figure 8-6 and is described in the following section. Note that you can turn off text wrapping by deselecting the check box shown in Figure 8-6.

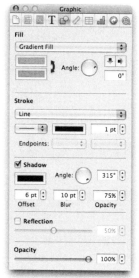

Figure 8-4:
Change the text box settings with Graphic inspector.

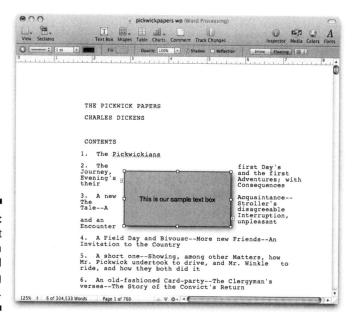

Figure 8-5:
Add a text box to a word processing document.

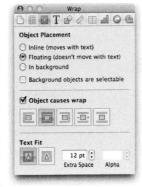

Figure 8-6:
Use Wrap
inspector
to integrate
the text box
with the text
around it.

Wrapping around the text box

As shown in Figure 8-6, Wrap inspector has three sections. The Object
Placement section of Wrap inspector is disabled for floating text boxes,
which is the type of text box you create in this section.

The principles of wrapping text around a text box are the same as wrapping
text around any shape.

The issue of wrapping text around something in a word processing document
or a page layout document is tricky in any program. Usually when you set
options and settings for text, a shape, or anything else, those options and
settings govern the object's appearance and performance. In the case of
wrapping, the options govern the appearance and performance of objects
next to the text box.

What's the best way to wrap text?

There is no single answer to the question of
the best way to wrap text. However, you can
consider some general issues that apply to text
boxes and any other objects around which text
is wrapped.

You may choose to have embedded objects
placed at the left of your document (using wrap
right or wrap larger). This provides a consistent
look and can make the text easier to read.

Another choice applies particularly to documents that will be bound like a book. On pages

that will appear on the left side of the book
(generally even-numbered pages), place the
embedded objects at the left. For pages on the
right side of the book (generally odd-numbered
pages), place the embedded objects at the
right. When the book or booklet is bound, it will
be easier to see the embedded objects or text
boxes if they are closer to the edge of the page
than if they are closer to the binding, where you
might have to stretch the book flat to see them.

Pages implements wrapping in a simple yet powerful way. Refer to Figure 8-5 to see what happens when you insert a text box into a section of text. The existing text moves to accommodate the text box. Wrap inspector lets you specify how and if that existing text will move and wrap. The settings are for the text box (or for any object inserted into the existing text), but those settings affect the existing text, not the text box. (There is actually a bit of interplay because the inserted text box and the existing text interact, but basically the existing text adjusts itself based on the text box's settings.)

Setting how the text box causes wrapping

Use the Object Causes Wrap check box to turn wrapping on and off. When the option is turned on, you then click whichever of the five wrapping techniques you want to use. From left to right, they are as follows:

- **Wrap left:** Text flows to the left of the object; there is no text to the right of the object. Usually if you use wrap left, you place the text box at the right side of the document. Figure 8-7 shows how you can do this with the document shown previously in Figure 8-5.

- **Wrap both sides:** This is the default setting; you can see the result in Figure 8-5. Text flows on both sides and the text box is centered. This option works well if the text box is relatively narrow and the page is relatively wide, but most of the time this is the worst choice because you wind up with very short sections of text on the two sides.

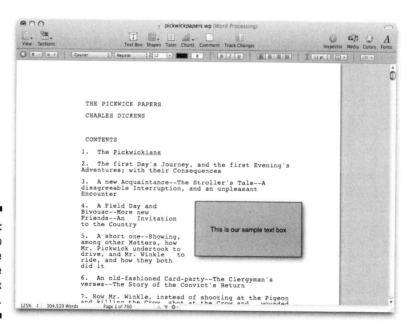

Figure 8-7:
If you wrap text to the left, place the text box to the right.

✔ **Wrap right:** This is the reverse of wrap left. If you do this, generally place the object at the left.

✔ **Wrap larger:** This option wraps text on one side or the other depending on which side is wider.

Use wrap larger instead of wrap right and wrap left. Move the text box to the right or left and the text will automatically flow to the other side. The result is the same as carefully setting wrap right and wrap left. As an added benefit, if you edit the document, perhaps adding other text boxes, you just need to reposition the text boxes to one side or the other and the document's text will flow the way you want it to: to the side opposite the text box.

✔ **No wrap:** Text doesn't wrap around either side of the text box but continues below the text box.

Setting how the text box causes text fitting

The last set of options on Wrap inspector handle text around irregularly shaped objects. You can also specify the distance between the text box and the text that is being wrapped around it.

With all of these settings, experiment with the results in your document.

Creating an Inline Text Box for a Word Processing Document

A floating text box is fixed to a place on the page. It floats in the sense that because it is fixed to a place on the page, the text that is next to it floats as you add or remove text in the document. When you do everything properly, the reader doesn't notice the difference between a floating text box and an inline text box. But a mistake is easy to spot. In this section I show an example of how you can get into trouble and how to prevent it.

In Figure 8-8, a floating text box has been placed in a word processing document. The text in the document references the text box as being to the right of the paragraph.

In Figure 8-9, some text has been added at the beginning of the document. The text reflows to incorporate the added text, but the floating text box stays where it is on the page. The reference to the text box being at the right of the paragraph no longer makes sense because that sentence has flowed down the page and is now below the text box. (That's the floating part — the text has floated past the text box.)

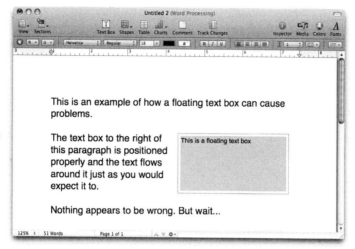

Figure 8-8:
A floating
text box
doesn't
move on the
page.

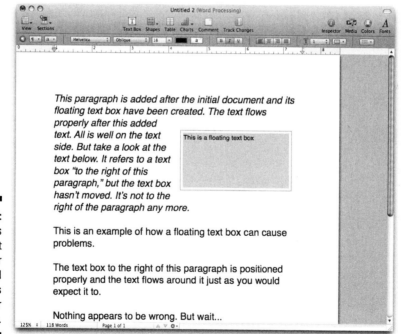

Figure 8-9:
References
to the text
box or other
embedded
shapes
no longer
match up.

Something worse can occur. Instead of text referring to a text box at the right of a paragraph, there might be no reference to the text box. That can puzzle the reader who now has to try to figure out why that text box is next to that paragraph.

Word processing documents allow you to change floating text boxes to inline text boxes. Inline text boxes are tied to a specific place in text rather than to a specific place on the page. You can create inline text boxes in two ways:

✔ **Use Wrap inspector to change the Object Placement setting to Inline rather than the default Floating.**

✔ **Place the cursor where you want the text box to appear and choose Insert⇨Text Box.**

Figure 8-10 shows an inline text box next to the paragraph that refers to it. When the text box is selected, an insertion point appears in the text. As you move the text box, the insertion point moves. The text box will stay at that point in the text, although its specific positioning is set by the Object Causes Wrap settings in Wrap inspector.

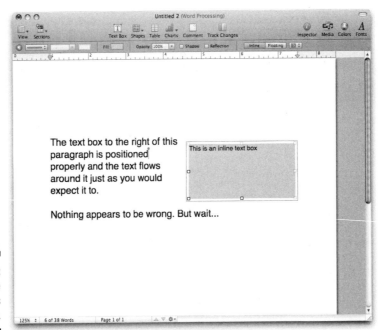

Figure 8-10:
An inline text box is fixed to text.

If text is added at the beginning of the document, as shown in Figure 8-11, the text reflows and the inline text box moves with its accompanying text.

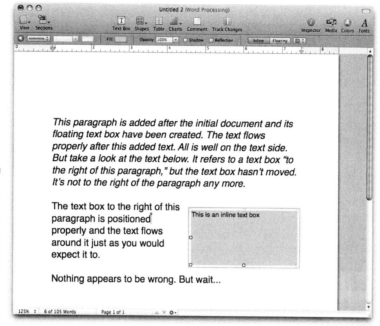

Figure 8-11:
You can
safely add
or delete
text without
disturbing
the inline
text box's
link.

Flowing Text between Text Boxes

Sometimes you want to put more text in a text box than will fit in it. If you are working with a floating text box in either a word processing or page layout document, you can flow text between several text boxes. You do this for several reasons:

- ✔ **To flow text in a page layout document:** Although word processing documents automatically flow text from page to page as you add it, in a page layout document the only way to flow text is from one text box to another (and, perhaps, another and another . . .).

- ✔ **To handle page jumps:** When a story begins on the front page of a newspaper and is continued inside the paper, the inside continuation is referred to as the *jump*. (On Web sites, articles sometimes have a few lines of text followed by a link that says Click Here to Read More. That, too, is called a jump.)

Creating a text flow link

Here's how you flow text between text boxes:

1. **Create a text box.**

   If you are in a word processing document, it must be a floating text box; in a page layout document it will automatically be a floating text box.

2. **Type or paste the text into the box.**

   In Figure 8-12, the entire text of *The Pickwick Papers* has been pasted into the text box. (Yes, all 300,000 words. Pages and your Mac are very powerful!) The clipping indicator in the center of the bottom of the text box indicates that there is more text than is shown — it's the square with the plus sign in it. The triangle indicators at the near top-left and near bottom-right let you specify the flow of the text, as explained in the next steps. If there's no more text, there's no clipping indicator.

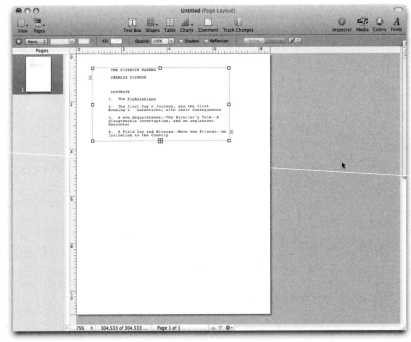

Figure 8-12:
Text in a floating text box that overflows shows a clipping indicator.

3. **Click the right arrow box at the lower right of the text box to begin the link.**

   You can link to a text box on any page of your document:

- To link to an existing text box, click the existing text box.

- To link to a text box that will be automatically created, click in the document at the approximate location for the new text box. Figure 8-13 shows the link to a text box on the next page of the document. Note that there is still more text to be flowed because the clipping indicator in the center of the new text box still contains a + symbol.

When the link is created, the right arrow box becomes a solid blue box.

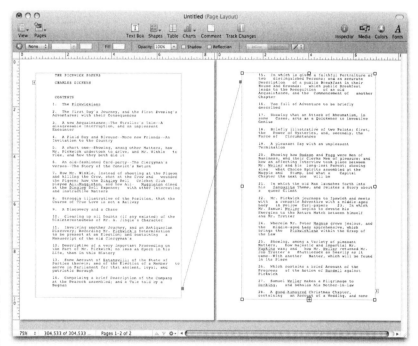

Figure 8-13:
You can link
text boxes.

You can link any number of text boxes, and you can resize each one as you want. To remove a link, drag the solid blue box for the link you want to break off the text box. The link will disappear and the blue box will revert to being an arrow, as shown previously in Figure 8-12.

Joining two text boxes

You can use the procedure in the preceding section to join two text boxes, each of which has its own text. Link them, and the text becomes a single flow. As you resize the text boxes, you will see that the text flows from one to the other.

Adding Objects to Text Boxes

You can insert objects into text boxes, as shown in Figure 8-14. They behave as inline text boxes do: You position them relative to the text in the text box, and they stay in that relative place.

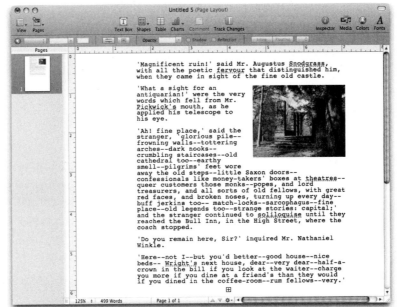

Figure 8-14:
You can add other objects to text boxes.

Here's how to add a graphic to a text box. The same technique works for other objects, such as tables and charts:

1. **Select the text box.**

2. **Click to set the insertion point approximately where you want the graphic to be.**

3. **Insert the object using the Insert menu.**

   • For a graphics file, choose Insert⇨Choose.

   • For a table, choose Insert⇨Table.

   • For a chart, choose Insert⇨Chart.

   • For a shape, choose Insert⇨Shape.

   You can't insert a text box into a text box.

Chapter 9

Fine-Tuning Your Pages Documents

. . . .

In This Chapter

▶ Formatting text from the format bar

▶ Managing styles

▶ Searching for text

▶ Navigating with thumbnails

. . . .

*T*his chapter explores some of the Pages tools that improve your productivity and make your documents look better. You might think of some of these tools as advanced features in the sense that you can manage to produce fine Pages documents without using them. But if you think *advanced* means *complicated,* you're wrong. They can save you time — sometimes a lot of it — and make your documents easier to read and much, much easier to reuse.

Using the Format Bar

One of the features of iWork that makes it so easy to use is that there are usually many ways to accomplish something. If you want to change a font, for example, you can use the Fonts window, a style (discussed later in this chapter), the format bar, or Text inspector. The format bar brings together formatting controls from many places in iWork; it resembles toolbars in other programs such as Microsoft Word.

You decide whether or not you want to display the format bar. When shown, it appears across the top of the window below the toolbar. Figure 9-1 shows the format bar with the toolbar hidden (so that you can concentrate on the format bar). As you can see, the format bar is only one row of controls, buttons, and icons. That is part of a compromise: Tools such as inspectors and the Fonts window have more space to allow you more control over formatting features, but the format bar brings many formatting features together in one place.

Figure 9-1:
The format
bar is at the
top of the
Pages
window.

The format bar has the following six sections (from left to right):

- **Styles:** The first section lets you manage styles for paragraphs and characters. For more control over styles, use the Styles drawer (described later in this chapter).

  - The round ¶ icon shows and hides the Styles drawer.

  - The ¶ pop-up menu lets you select a paragraph style for the current paragraph.

  - The *a* pop-up menu lets you select a character style for the currently selected text. If no text is selected, the character style will be applied to the next characters you type.

- **Font formatting:** The next five controls manage basic font formatting for the current selection. For more control, use the Fonts window (described in Chapter 2).

  - Use the first pop-up menu to choose a font family.

  - Click the next menu to choose the typeface (such as regular, bold, or italic).

  - The third pop-up menu lets you choose the font size.

  - Click the color well to choose a color for the font.

  - Click the color well containing the letter *a* to choose the background color for the selected text.

- **Character styles:** Use the next three buttons — which represent bold, italics, and underline — to turn styling on or off for selected text. For more control, use Text inspector (described in Chapter 3).

- **Paragraph alignment:** The next four buttons let you choose the paragraph alignment as follows: flush left, centered, flush right, and justified. For more control, use Text inspector (described in Chapter 3).

✔ **Line spacing and columns:** The next two pop-up menus let you adjust vertical line spacing and columns. For more control, use Layout inspector (columns) and Text inspector (vertical line spacing).

✔ **Styles:** The last pop-up menu lets you choose a list style for a selected list (or to convert text into a list). For more control, see the List pane of Text inspector.

Formatting Text with Styles

Word processing applications let you format text with underlining, italics, boldface, and many more features. With Pages, all you have to do is select the text in question and open the Fonts window (Format➪Font➪Show Fonts) or use Text inspector. You're finished.

It's easy to get carried away with text formatting. When used properly, it increases the readability of a sentence. When used in the wrong way, it really not only *doesn't* **help** but can ACTUALLY make a sentence much ***harder*** to read.

Styles let you set one or more formatting instructions and give them a name of your own choosing. You might do this for two reasons:

✔ **Consistency:** Particularly when it comes to formatting such as underlining and italics, a style can help you be consistent. For example, you can construct several styles that serve specific purposes in your document. You could create a style called Emphasis that you use for anything that you want to emphasize. If you set the style to boldface and the font color to red, all emphasized words would be shown that way. Also, you wouldn't have to go back to figure out what you decided you would use for emphasis: Just select the text and use the Emphasis style. If you were to print the document on a printer that doesn't support color, you could change the style to use, say, italics instead of boldface and red; the one change would affect all the uses of the style.

✔ **Simplicity:** Styles can be complex. It is typical for a style for a paragraph to include its margins, the spacing between lines, and sometimes even a border. You can construct a style and give it a name so that you can then apply all those settings at once to any given paragraph.

Styles can be copied and pasted. You can modify a style either for all its occurrences or on a case-by-case basis when you want to vary a single section of text or a paragraph. Creating a style in Pages is simple: You style some text or a paragraph, and then you create that as a style that you name.

Styles can be created for characters, paragraphs, and lists. They're easy to create, but the Apple developers of iWork are several steps ahead of you: Styles come with every iWork Pages template. You can modify them, delete them, or add more, but you always start with some styles.

Showing the Styles drawer

The *Styles drawer* helps you create, manage, and use styles. Even the simplest templates (the blank documents for both word processing and page layout) come with styles. To see your document's styles, you display the Styles drawer using one of the following methods:

- ✔ Choose View⇨Show Styles Drawer.
- ✔ Click the View icon on the toolbar, and choose Show Styles Drawer, as shown in Figure 9-2.
- ✔ In the format bar, click the ¶ icon all the way at the left, as shown in Figure 9-3.

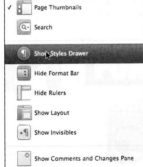

Figure 9-2:
Display
the Styles
drawer from
the toolbar.

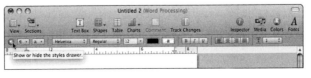

Figure 9-3:
Display
the Styles
drawer from
the format
bar.

Figure 9-4 shows the styles that come with the blank templates.

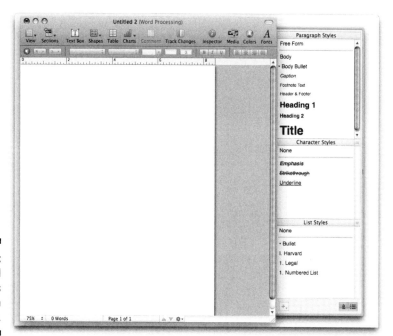

Figure 9-4:
All
templates
come with
styles.

iWork has no such thing as a totally blank document. The closest you can come to a blank document is a document based on one of the blank templates.

Templates have styles that help implement their look and feel. For example, the For Sale flyer template is shown in Figure 9-5 with its styles. Notice how the styles are displayed using some of their characteristics. For example, look at the Heading style and match it to the text *Mountain Bike $500* in the flyer. The styles shown at the right of Figure 9-5 are displayed in a *drawer*.

Drawers are a feature of Mac OS X. They slide out from the main window. As you resize the window vertically, the drawers automatically resize. You can drag the edge of the drawer to pull it farther in or out. Give it a bit of a shove with the mouse, and it will slide back into the window. (You can also use the Hide Styles Drawer command on the toolbar and in the menu bar; it replaces the Show Styles Drawer command when the drawer is open.)

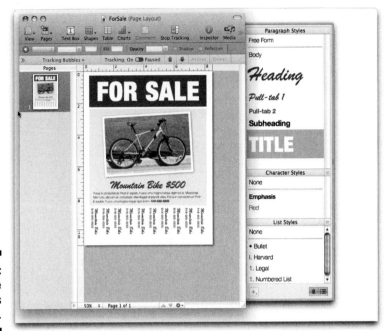

Figure 9-5:
The For Sale
flyer has its
own styles.

Using the Styles drawer controls

The Styles drawer has a lot of power. The Styles drawer has three sections: paragraph styles, character styles, and list styles. These sections can be manipulated as follows:

- ✔ **Resize sections:** You can resize the three sections by dragging the double-bar to the right of the heading for character and list styles. If you drag the double-bar to the right of the character styles up, for example, you enlarge the character styles section at the expense of the paragraph styles section.

- ✔ **Show and hide sections:** You can show or hide the character and list styles sections using the buttons in the lower right of the Styles drawer. The button with the letter *a* on it controls the character styles section; the one with the bulleted list on it controls the list section. The paragraph styles section is always shown.

To use an existing style, select the text you want to style. Then do the following:

- ✔ **Paragraph styles:** Click anywhere in the paragraph you want to style and click the style to use in the Styles drawer.

- ✔ **Character styles:** Select the character or characters to style and then click the style to use in the Styles drawer. If no characters are selected, the style will be applied to all the characters that you type starting with the next character.

  One of the most common problems using styles in any application is not selecting characters to style. The new style will affect the next characters you type, but nothing changes on the screen until you type a new character. If you have accidentally not selected any characters, but are expecting a word to be changed to another color or font size, this can be frustrating.

- ✔ **List styles:** Select the entire list and then select a list style. Note that list styles are associated with paragraph styles, so selecting a list style will modify the associated paragraph style on a one-time basis.

Handling style changes

At the right of each style name is a downward-pointing triangle (a *disclosure triangle*) that you click to open a menu. This menu (see Figure 9-6) is where you control individual styles.

Figure 9-6:
Use the
contextual
menu in
the Styles
drawer
to control
styles.

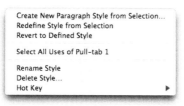

The downward-pointing triangle has another important function. It normally is gray, but if you override any of the styles' settings, it turns red.

Changing style on a one-time basis

As you are editing your document, you can change font sizes and colors, margins, and all the other attributes of text. You always have some basic paragraph style even if it's the catchall Free Form style. As you make your formatting changes, the currently selected style will show a red triangle next to its name instead of the standard gray one. The first three items in the menu shown in Figure 9-6 let you decide what to do with the changed style:

🖙 **Create a new style:** If you have deliberately made a change to the style, you can save it as a new style. For example, maybe you've decided that you would sometimes like the Heading style to be underlined. You can select a paragraph that uses the Heading style and underline it. The red triangle will appear, and you can choose to create a new style named, for example, *Underlined Heading*. The style will now appear in the Styles drawer.

• You're asked to provide a name for the new style, as shown in Figure 9-7. By default the style has the name of the existing style with a number after it. It's a good idea to give it a more meaningful name right away. You also can choose whether to apply the style on creation. That means that as soon as it is created it will be applied to the current selection. If you deselect this box, the style will be created and added to the list, but it won't be applied until you select some text and choose the style.

• If you're creating a character style, you can use the disclosure triangle to see which character attributes have been set, as shown in Figure 9-8. You can turn any of them on or off. If a character attribute isn't set in the character style, basic formatting (usually specified in the paragraph style) is used. The Select Overrides button in the lower right displays only the character style changes you've specified.

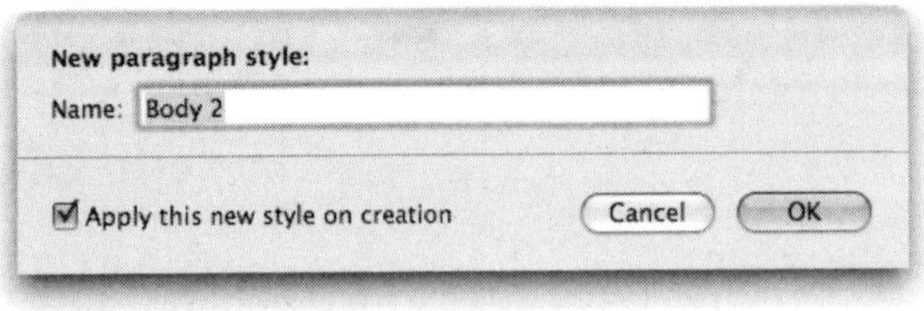

Figure 9-7:
Create a
new style
and name it.

New paragraph style:

Name: Body 2

☑ Apply this new style on creation   (Cancel)   (OK)

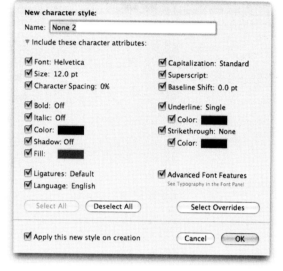

Figure 9-8:
Specify
character
attributes
for a
character
style.

✔ **Redefine the style:** If you decide that the Heading style would look better underlined, for example, select a paragraph that uses it and underline the paragraph. Then, in the contextual menu, choose Redefine Style from Selection. This changes the style. Now you have only one style, but it is the redefined one. All Heading paragraphs are now changed.

✔ **Revert to the defined style:** If you make a mistake or change your mind about the underlining or other formatting, choose Revert to Defined Style and your change is ignored. You are back to the original style without your modification.

✔ **Do nothing:** You don't have to do anything about that red triangle. If you made a formatting change and you meant to do it, so be it. Just move on. (There's no menu choice for doing nothing.)

Managing styles

Whenever you select a paragraph, a list, or some characters, the style name is highlighted. The name is also highlighted as you move the mouse over the style names in the styles list. You can use the downward-pointing triangle to open the menu shown previously in Figure 9-5 whether you've changed the style or not. Menu commands let you rename or delete the style. You can also associate a function key from F1 to F8 (at the top of the keyboard) with that style. That way, you can just select a paragraph, a list, or text and press the function key to apply the style.

Searching for Text

iWork has a powerful search feature. You display the search tool shown in Figure 9-9 by choosing View⇨Search or by clicking the View icon at the left of the toolbar (refer to Figure 9-2).

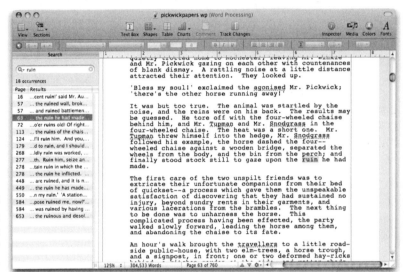

Figure 9-9:
Use search
to quickly
find text.

Type some text into the search box and Pages will quickly find every occurrence in your document. In the search area, you see page numbers as well as the search string in context. Click an item in the list and you immediately go to that occurrence in the document.

iWork indexes the text very quickly. And it indexes all the text. It will find your search string in a word processing document, in a text box, and even inside an object if you've typed text there.

The search list is updated as you modify the document.

Navigating with Thumbnails

iWork can provide thumbnails of your pages in sequence. Even though the thumbnails are small, you can often get a sense of what page you're looking at, particularly in a page layout document. You display thumbnails by choosing View➪Page Thumbnails. Just click a thumbnail to go to that page, as shown in Figure 9-10.

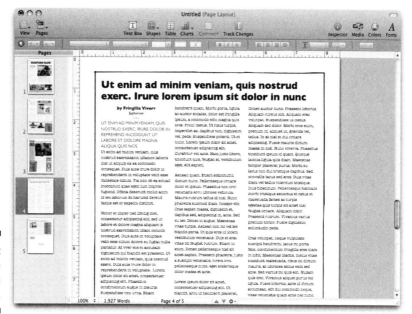

Figure 9-10:
Navigate
with page
thumbnails.

Chapter 10

Improving Your Documents

- -

- -

*T*he tools described in this chapter help you improve your documents by using features of iWork as well as comments and suggestions from other people. iWork has a variety of tools that make it easy for people to work together on documents.

These tools are available in Numbers and Keynote as well as in Pages. They have the same overall functionality in all the applications, but they have slightly different interfaces.

iWork.com implements the commenting and track changes functionalities through the Web so that multiple people can work on the same documents at the same time. See Appendix A for details.

Using Comments

Whether you're working by yourself or with others, you frequently need to make comments on your work. Sometimes comments are reminders; sometimes they're questions. For example, Figure 10-1 shows a typical comment questioning whether the date 1600 is the specific year or an approximation. You might leave this comment for yourself or add it to someone else's document. Either way, the comments need to be dealt with.

If you're reviewing a document (perhaps you're a teacher), comments may not require action — you might write "Good!" or "You really understand why black ice is so dangerous."

Either way, the point is that you want to be able to comment on a document without your comment appearing in the document. If you insert a comment into the document itself, not only can it appear when you print the document, but its presence can change the flow of the document, perhaps adding several pages to the uncommented document.

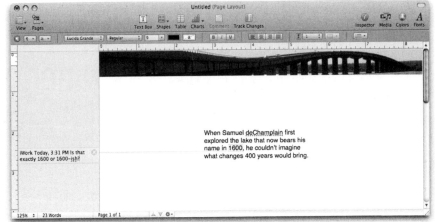

Figure 10-1:
The
Comments
pane
displays
comments
and links
them to
highlighted
text.

Showing and hiding the Comments pane

Comments are shown in the Comments pane, which appears at the left of a Pages document (refer to Figure 10-1).

To show or hide the Comments pane:

- Choose View⇨Show Comments or View⇨Hide Comments on the toolbar.
- Click the pop-up View menu on the toolbar and make your selection.

There's another special way to display the Comments pane: Simply create a comment, and the Comments pane appears automatically.

Creating a comment

To create a comment, first select what it applies to. That can be a word, a paragraph, or even a page; it can be an object, a text box, or an image. If you can select it, you can comment on it.

Highlighting one or two characters is possible, but it can make the comment hard to find. If you have a question or comment about one or two characters in a word, highlight the entire word and make it clear that the comment applies only to those characters.

When you've highlighted the subject of the comment, the next step is to create the comment. You have two choices:

- ✔ Choose Insert➪Comment.
- ✔ Click the Comment icon on the toolbar.

If necessary, the Comments pane is shown. If appropriate (such as words within a stream of text), the subject of the comment is highlighted. In all cases, a line is drawn from the comment subject to the Comments pane, where a *comment bubble* appears. The comment bubble is placed at the end of that line with the current date and time. Click in the bubble to type your comment. If your comment is emphatic, feel free to italicize it. Use bold text if you want to drive your point home. Your Pages text-editing tools work in comments as well as in the body of your documents.

Your comment is now linked to the document. The comment moves around the document as you move objects in the document. You can always hide the Comments pane if you don't want to see the comments. If you want to remove a comment, click the X in the upper-right of the bubble and it will be removed. Note that I said removed, not hidden.

Printing a comment

You can print comments along with your document. This is particularly useful if you're sharing a document with several people who may have to review it and act on the comments. Pages makes it simple to print comments. If the Comments pane is displayed, comments are printed, as shown in Figure 10-2.

Figure 10-2:
Comments
can be
printed.

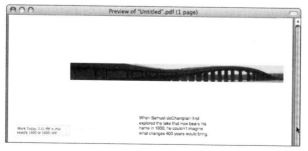

If the Comments pane is not displayed, comments are not printed, as shown in Figure 10-3. If you compare Figures 10-2 and 10-3, you see that the entire page image is made a bit smaller to allow for comments. This means that if you have a multipage document with comments only on some pages, all pages will be printed in the reduced size.

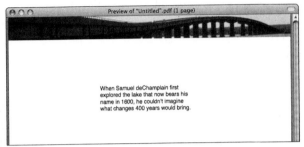

Figure 10-3:
Comments
can be
hidden in
a printed
document.

Tracking Changes

One of the best features of Microsoft Word is its ability to track changes. When Track Changes is turned on, Word keeps track of every change to the document whether it's adding or deleting text, changing the format, or inserting page breaks. It has several ways of displaying the changes, each of which is identified with its date and time as well as who has made the change. If several people are working on a document, you can see all their changes together.

Pages has implemented Track Changes functionality. It does almost everything that Microsoft Word does — and it handles Microsoft Word track changes documents. Figure 10-4 shows a Pages document with Track Changes turned on. In fact, the document was created in Microsoft Word. It started with one sentence: This is a document without track changes turned on. Track changes was then turned on, and I changed *without* to *with*. That counts as two changes: the deletion of *without* and the addition of *with*. The document was saved in Microsoft Word, and it was opened in Pages. When Track Changes is on, the tracking bar appears below the format bar, and the changes are shown at the left in *change bubbles*.

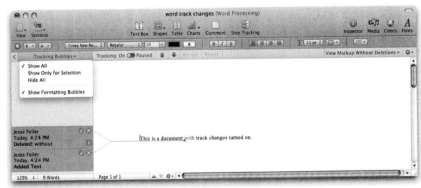

Figure 10-4:
Track
Changes
lets you
trace your
document's
history.

Pages tracks changes to text and formatting, but it also tracks changes to objects in both word processing and page layout documents, as shown in Figure 10-5.

Figure 10-5:
Changes in page layout documents are tracked.

Setting up Track Changes preferences

Preferences for Track Changes are set in General Preferences. Just choose Pages⇨Preferences, and click the General tab, as shown in Figure 10-6.

At the bottom of the window is the Change Tracking section. The first item is the name that will be used for your changes. The name, like all the preferences here, applies to all your documents. Below your name, you can set preferences for how deleted and added text is displayed. This, too, applies to all your documents.

Inside your Pages documents, the changes are stored with all their details, including whether text has been added or deleted. Your preference determines how additions and deletions are shown on Pages documents on your computer. If you choose Strikethrough for deleted text, for example, that's how it will appear. If you give that document to someone else who has chosen Underline as the indicator for deleted text, that's how it will appear for them. Track Changes stores the action; your preferences (and your friends' preferences) determine how the changes are displayed.

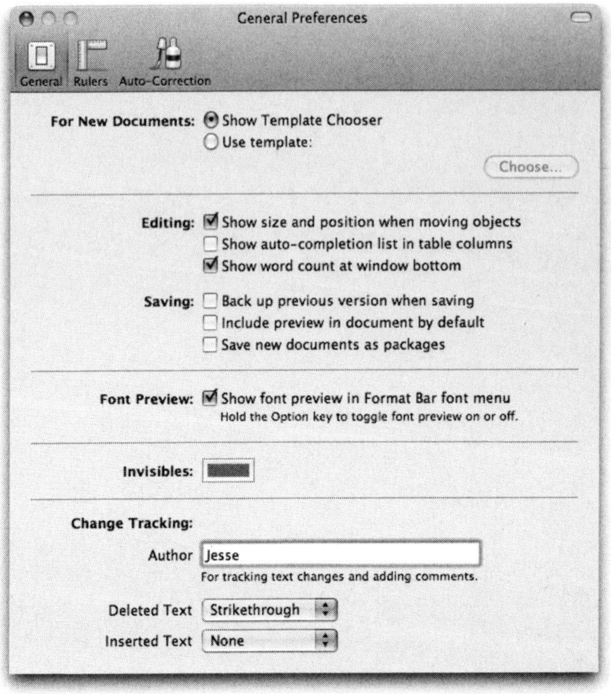

Figure 10-6:
Set up Track
Changes
prefer-
ences.

Starting and stopping Track Changes

The tracking bar appears when Track Changes is turned on for a document. You turn on Track Changes (and show the tracking bar) by clicking Track Changes on the toolbar. The Track Changes icon immediately changes to a Stop Tracking icon.

After you have turned on Track Changes, changes from that point on are tracked as you make them — unless you pause tracking as described later in this section. Each change is identified with your user name and the date and time of the change. In addition, as shown in Figures 10-4 and 10-5, each change has a check mark and an X in the upper right of its bubble. The check mark lets you accept a change, and the X lets you reject it.

When you accept a change, the change bubble disappears and the change is permanent (unless you change it again). When you reject a change, the change bubble disappears and the change is undone.

Track Changes stores its changes with the document each time you save it. If you have changes that have not been accepted or rejected, you can't turn Track Changes off. If you try to stop tracking with unresolved changes, you see the dialog shown in Figure 10-7.

Figure 10-7:
You must
resolve all
changes
before
stopping
Track
Changes.

All changes must be accepted or rejected to turn off Change
Tracking.

Click Accept All Changes to keep the current version of the document. Click Reject
All Changes to reject all tracked changes.

Cancel   Reject All Changes   Accept All Changes

Viewing (and not viewing) changes

Although you can't turn off Track Changes with unresolved changes, you
don't have to see them. You can accomplish this in several ways:

- Show or hide the Comments and Changes pane by choosing
  View⇨Show/Hide Comments and Changes Pane or by clicking the View
  menu on the toolbar. You can also click the double-arrow at the far left
  of the tracking bar. Changes will still be tracked, but you won't see them.

- Use the Tracking Bubbles menu at the left of the tracking bar to show or
  hide bubbles, as Figure 10-8 demonstrates. The bubbles disappear, but
  the Comments and Changes Pane is still visible.

- If Page Thumbnails are shown, the changes are highlighted on the
  thumbnails. This lets you quickly see which pages contain changes. You
  can click the thumbnail to go to that page immediately and deal with the
  change.

- Finally, if you hover your mouse over something that has been changed,
  you see a summary of the change, as shown in Figure 10-9. This can
  occur even if the change bubbles are not visible. This is particularly
  useful with text. Deleted and added text is highlighted in the document
  as it is changed, but the summary of the change adds the information of
  who did it and when.

Figure 10-8:
The
Tracking
Bubbles
menu
controls
change
bubbles.

✓ Show All
Show Only for Selection
Hide All

✓ Show Formatting Bubbles

Figure 10-9:
Hover your
mouse over
a change to
see details.

Pausing Track Changes

Although you can't turn Track Changes off with unresolved changes, you
can use the tracking slider next to the Tracking Bubbles pop-up menu in the
tracking bar to pause Track Changes and to turn it back on. This keeps Track
Changes active (and keeps the tracking bar visible), but you can work for a
while without your changes being tracked.

One reason for pausing Track Changes is if you are about to do a series of
changes that will generate a number of change messages, each of which
needs a response. Rearranging paragraphs in a lengthy document is an example of this: Each paragraph is marked as changed when it is deleted and then
marked as changed when it is inserted in its new location.

Accepting and rejecting changes

You can accept and reject changes in several ways:

- For a given change, click the check mark (accept) or X (reject) button
  in the upper right of the change bubble. The change is accepted or
  rejected and the bubble disappears.

✔ Highlight a particular change bubble and click Accept or Reject at the center of the tracking bar.

✔ Use the up and down arrows in the center of the tracking bar to move to the previous or next change, respectively. The arrows are deliberately placed next to the Accept and Reject buttons so that you can quickly navigate through the changes and deal with them.

✔ Accept or reject all changes with a single command from the Action menu at the far right of the tracking bar, as shown in Figure 10-10.

Figure 10-10:
Use the
Action menu
for more
tracking
commands.

Printing a clean copy without changes

The Action menu contains another useful command: Save a Copy as Final. This command saves a copy of the document with all changes accepted. Your original document still has the changes for you to accept or reject, but you have a copy that you can print or send to someone.

Chapter 11

Advanced Word Processing Techniques

In This Chapter

▶ Formatting columns

▶ Paginating your document

▶ Creating a table of contents

Your word processing documents are already set up by Pages with a number of optional features: headers and footers, automatic page numbers, various margin controls, and the ability to create footnotes and to automatically update tables of contents (yes *tables* — you can have several in one document). These tools are valuable for all your documents, but they are particularly important for large documents.

Large documents — large Numbers spreadsheets and large Keynote presentations as well as large Pages documents — require special handling so that your readers don't get lost (and so that you don't get lost as you're writing the document!). The challenges of a large spreadsheet are different from those of a large presentation or a large word processing document.

Working with Sections for Improved Formatting of Long Documents

Word processing documents consist of words, paragraphs, and pages. They also contain *sections*. Just as you can format words, paragraphs, and pages, you can also format sections. A section can be as small as part of a page or many pages long. In the case of a book, a section is usually a chapter.

Each section can contain its own formatting. Sections also may contain text that is either placeholder text you can replace or text that remains unchanged.

When you create a document from a template, all of the template's sections are available, but not all of them are inserted into the initial version of the document. For example, the Project Proposal template, which is in the Reports section of templates, has the sections shown in Figure 11-1 built into the template. In a document created with the Project Proposal template, only the Cover and Executive Summary are used; you need to add any other sections that you want.

Letter

Cover

Table of Contents

Executive Summary

Budget

Schedule

Contact Information

Figure 11-1:
Templates
come with
at least one
section
already
defined.

Adding a section to a document

Here's how to add a section to a document:

1. **Position the cursor where you want to insert the section.**

   Most sections in the templates automatically begin on a new page. You can change this setting for individual sections after you've inserted them.

2. **Insert the section:**

   - Choose Insert⇨Section to display a submenu of the document's sections (refer to Figure 11-1). Choose the one you want to insert.

   - Display the same menu by clicking the Sections icon on the toolbar.

Rearranging sections

If you have page thumbnails displayed, you can use sections to improve your navigation. Figure 11-2 shows page thumbnails in a document that has two sections. The first section contains one page, and the second section has two pages. The second section is selected, as you can tell by the yellow border around its pages.

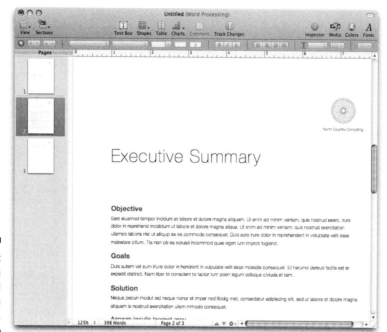

Figure 11-2:
Pages can be grouped into sections.

You can move a section by dragging it in the page thumbnails. As soon as you start to drag a page that is inside a section, the section collapses into a single page image with a number in the lower right showing you how many pages are in the section. Figure 11-3 shows what happens as you drag the two-page section in Figure 11-2.

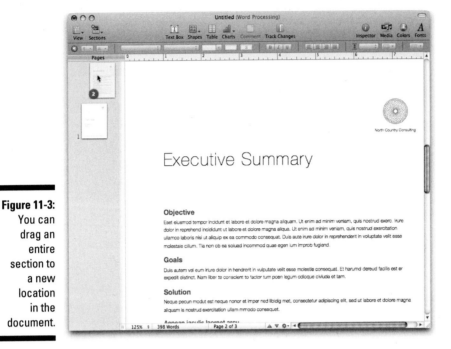

Formatting Your Document and Sections

Sections exist in every document. A page layout document in Pages has one section for each page. By default, a blank word processing document has a single section. As you add pages, they are added to this section. You are never without a section in a Pages document, whether you know it or not.

The fact that you always have a section in a Pages document matters because many of the format settings you use actually apply to sections. In the basic case of a word processing document with all the pages in one section, there is no practical difference between settings for the document and the section. But as soon as you have two or more sections in the document, those section settings become important.

When you're formatting text, you select whatever you want to format and use commands or the inspector to format the selected text. When you're formatting sections, you click anywhere in the section to format it using the inspector. If you're formatting a document, you do not need to click anywhere; as long as the document is open in your window, your inspector settings will apply to it. The only time you really have to worry about carefully selecting text to format is when you're working with part of a section. Otherwise, a click anywhere in the section will let you format the entire section, and a click anywhere in the document will let you format the entire document.

If the inspector is not visible, open it using one of these techniques:

✔ **Choose View➪Show Inspector to open the inspector.**

✔ **Click the Inspector icon, at the right of the toolbar.**

If you already have an inspector open, you can choose View➪New Inspector to open another inspector. If more than one inspector is open, clicking the Inspector icon on the toolbar closes all of them. You can also use the close box in individual inspectors to close them.

Most of the settings described here use Document inspector (the leftmost icon in the Inspector window) and Layout inspector (the next icon in the Inspector window).

Setting document information

Document inspector, shown in Figure 11-4, has three tabs:

✔ **Document:** This controls document settings such as margins.

✔ **TOC:** This controls the table of contents.

✔ **Info:** This displays the statistics for the document (the number of words, for example) and lets you enter a title and an author. This information is available as part of the file; it is not automatically displayed in the document itself.

Setting the document information is a good idea so that you can discover a year from now why you created the document. If you're working with a specific document length in mind (perhaps for a school assignment), Document inspector is where you check how close you are to your goal.

Setting document margins

Use the Document tab of Document inspector (see Figure 11-5) to set the document's basic margins.

If you're using a standard paper size, you can usually use the default settings. If you need to change the paper size, click the Page Setup button at the top of the inspector to open the standard Mac OS X Page Setup dialog.

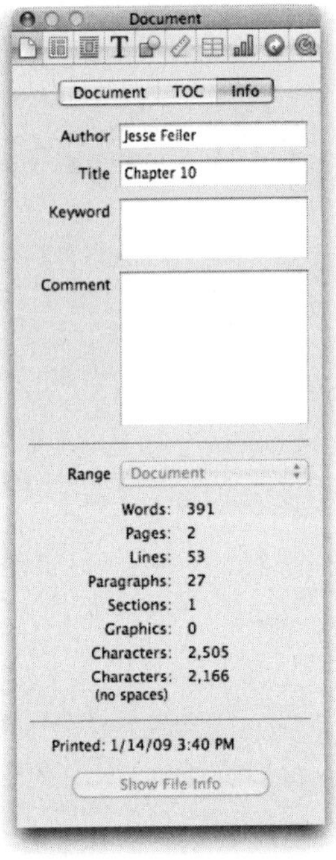

Figure 11-4:
The Info
tab of
Document
inspector
lets you
describe the
document.

Figure 11-5:
Set
document
margins
here.

The Facing Pages check box lets you create margins for a document that will be printed on both sides of the paper and prepared like a book. The left and right margins are changed to Inside and Outside, respectively. Visualize a book open to two facing pages. On the left page, the inside margin is the right margin (nearest the binding) and the outside margin is the left margin. On the right page, the opposite is true: The inside margin is the left margin and the outside margin is the right margin. Pages keeps track of which margin is which on different pages. That is, neither page is inside or outside. Each page has both an inside margin and an outside margin.

If you're planning to use facing pages, you have to help Pages by inserting blank pages where necessary. For facing pages to work, each part of the document must have an even number of pages. Fortunately, if you're working with sections, these blank pages are inserted for you automatically.

Setting multiple columns

One of the reasons for using sections is so that you can apply formatting to an entire section. In the cases of margins and columns, you may want to apply formatting to only part of a section; to do so, you create *layouts.* This section shows you how to set multiple columns for a layout.

Sometimes an entire section or even an entire document is presented in columns. Other times you have columns in only part of a document — perhaps only on part of a page.

You always have at least one layout in your document. If you want another layout, position the cursor where you want the new layout to begin and choose Insert⇨Layout Break. Now you'll be able to change the formatting of either layout independently. If you want a section with columns such as the one at the front of this book, you would have your initial layout for the one-column text, then you'd insert a layout break to be able to format a two-column layout, and after that you'd insert a layout break to be able to format the remaining text as one column.

The most basic layout has a single column. You need to add new layouts only if you want to change to multiple columns (or back to one) or to change the margins just for that layout.

Use Layout Inspector, shown in Figure 11-6, to set the column settings for each layout. Note that you can force a layout to begin on a new page; this command is available for every layout except the first one, which already starts on a new page.

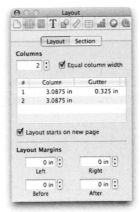

Figure 11-6:
Use Layout
inspector to
set columns.

Paginating your document

Use the Section tab of Layout inspector to control pagination of your document. You can number each section separately or number all the pages of the document together, as shown in Figure 11-7.

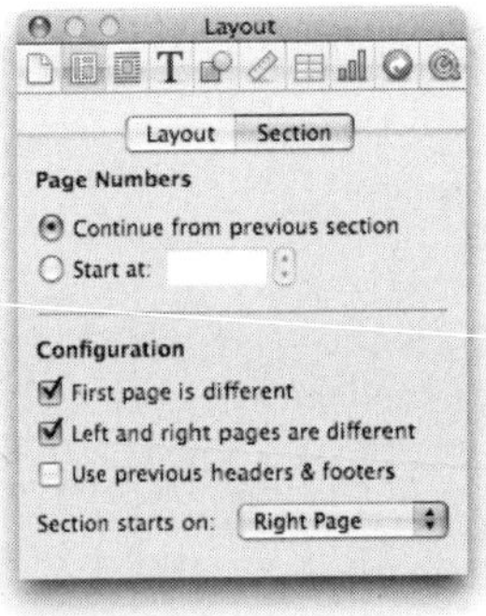

Figure 11-7:
Control
pagination
from Layout
inspector.

Here's a practical example of how you can use sections and automatic Pages tools to format a lengthy document such as *The Pickwick Papers* document, which you can download from the author's site as described in the Introduction.

With the document still in one section, the section settings are shown in Figure 11-7. Insert a page number in the footer by choosing Insert⇨Automatic Page Numbers, which opens the dialog shown in Figure 11-8. Note that Pages provides you with the option to align numbers at the left, right, or center as well as at the inside and outside margins.

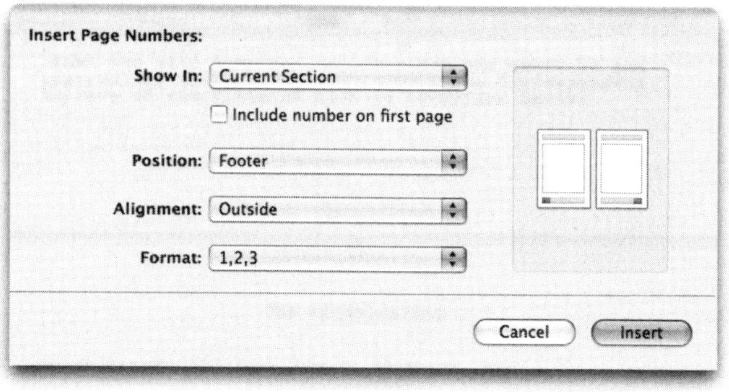

Figure 11-8:
Insert
automatic
page
numbers.

Now, break the document into chapter sections. You do this by positioning the cursor just before the start of each chapter (before the *C* in Chapter), and choosing Insert⇨Section Break. It's important to do this after you have formatted the unbroken section containing all the pages, because when you insert the breaks for each chapter, the settings from the previous section are carried forward. You can change each section, but in this case, you want each section to have the same type of formatting.

Sometimes making the first page different lets you add special formatting to it; other times, you want to add special formatting to the other pages. In our example, the first page is marked as being different, as shown in Figure 11-7. Type the name of the chapter into the header on the second page, and the chapter name will appear in the header of every page except the first one (which already contains the chapter title). Because the first page is marked as being different, if you type a header for this page, the header text will appear only on the first page.

If you indicate that each section should begin on a right-hand page, Pages will insert blank pages if necessary to force the first page of each section to be a right-hand page.

Creating and Updating Tables of Contents

Particularly when it comes to long documents, a table of contents is a great tool for your readers. Pages can automatically create a table of contents for you. It does this by relying on the styles you use in the document. You don't mark items to appear in the table of contents; instead you use a specific style for the table of contents items (there can be more than one), and that style is automatically picked up by Pages.

You don't have to use the styles that Pages provides: Any styles that you use in your document can be in a table of contents. However, you must use the styles consistently. For example, if you want each chapter title to be placed in the table of contents, the chapter title should always use a unique style. If you want headings placed in the table of contents, those, too, should use a unique style.

Here's how to create a table of contents:

1. **Create a table of contents page or section in your document.**

   • If you're using a Pages template, look for a section called Table of Contents. Position the cursor where you want to insert the table of contents, and then either choose Insert⇨Sections⇨Table of Contents or click the Sections menu on the toolbar. This is the easiest method.

   • Position the cursor where you want the table of contents and choose Insert⇨Table of Contents. This inserts the table of contents code into your document as part of an existing section rather than as a separate section.

2. **Specify the table of contents.**

   Open Document inspector to the TOC tab, as shown in Figure 11-9, to set up your table of contents. All of the styles you've used in the document are shown. Select the check box to the left of each style that you want to appear in the table of contents.

   You can use the check box on the right to make the page numbers for entries into links that take you from the table of contents to the page in question. (Obviously, this works only with the online version of documents.)

3. **Create the table of contents by clicking the Update Now button.**

   The table of contents will be automatically updated in the future whenever you save the document, but you can always regenerate it using the Update Now button.

   If the Update Now button is dimmed, chances are you forgot Step 1, creating the table of contents section in your document. Pages will have nowhere to place the table of contents so it can't generate it.

4. **Format your table of contents.**

   Go to the newly generated table of contents and open the Styles drawer, (Choose View⇨Show Styles Drawer or use the View menu on the toolbar) as shown in Figure 11-10. The styles in the table of contents are named after the styles used for table of contents entries, but the style names are preceded by *TOC*.

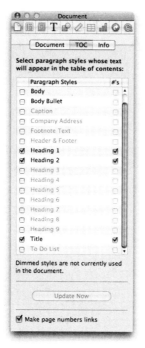

Figure 11-9:
Create a
table of
contents.

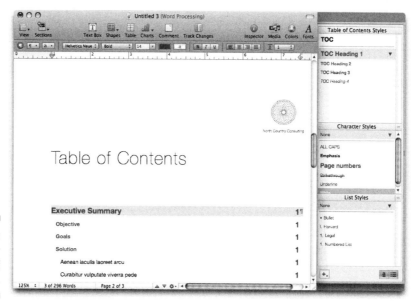

Figure 11-10:
Format your
table of
contents.

5. **Select the table of contents and click the Tabs pane of Text inspector, shown in Figure 11-11.**

One of the most common formatting changes for a table of contents is to add dots or dashes, called *leaders,* between the entry and the page number. As you see in Figure 11-11, a single tab stop is defined for each TOC style. Select that tab stop and choose the type of leader you want. The entry you selected changes immediately. If you don't like the look, try another leader character.

You can change other formatting as well. For example, you may want to indent subheadings in the table of contents beneath chapter or section titles. If you do so, you may want the subheading page numbers indented from the right.

Figure 11-11:
Reformat a
table of
contents
entry.

6. **Update the style.**

Click the downward-pointing arrow next to the style name in the Styles drawer, and choose Redefine Style from Selection, as shown in Figure 11-12. The formatting is applied to every entry that uses this style.

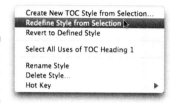

Figure 11-12:
Change the
style.

Your table of contents takes shape before your eyes. And Pages remembers your style changes, so the TOC styles appear the same whenever you update your table of contents.

Part III
Counting on Numbers

The 5th Wave   By Rich Tennant

"I've used several spreadsheet programs, but
this is the best one for designing quilt patterns."

In this part . . .

Numbers is the most recent addition to the iWork suite of applications. To call it a spreadsheet doesn't do it justice; it's like no other spreadsheet you've probably ever seen. Sure, you can create enormous sheets of rows and columns, but Numbers makes it easy to create useful and understandable spreadsheets. If you want to mystify people with your ability to throw hundreds (or thousands) of numbers on a page, you may want to look for another spreadsheet application. But if you want to use the iWork features to clarify your data and demystify all those numbers, Numbers is for you.

Chapter 12

Getting to Know Numbers

*Y*ou've never seen a spreadsheet like a Numbers spreadsheet. Something about spreadsheets turns even the most imaginative and creative person into a zombie wandering through a maze with an infinite number of rows and columns. Well, in most cases it's not infinite — in Microsoft Excel, somewhere around 1 million rows and 16,000 columns give you 17 billion cells you can use in your spreadsheet.

Numbers can be described in many ways, but one of the most direct is this: Numbers gives you every tool and technique the people of Apple could think of to help you manage your data without getting lost in 17 billion cells on a single spreadsheet. This chapter gives you an introduction to Numbers, starting with the basic design that tames spreadsheets and continuing with a guide to the features and functions in the Numbers window.

Taming the Spreadsheet Jungle with Tables

In 1979, at the dawn of the personal computer era, the VisiCalc spreadsheet program, written for the Apple II, was one of the most popular programs. It was a fair representation of large accounting sheets with rows and columns that could accept any kind of data you entered. One spreadsheet was one file.

People quickly started bumping up against that limitation, and two changes came about over time:

✔ **Tables within spreadsheets:** Even though early spreadsheets were smaller than today's models, they still had almost unlimited rows and columns. People quickly learned that they could use a few rows and columns for a specific purpose, creating subspreadsheets or tables on that vast grid of cells. This made sense because within a single spreadsheet, it is possible to easily connect one set of cells to another. This means that these subspreadsheets and tables could automatically be updated if only one number was changed.

✔ **Linked spreadsheets:** There were issues with dumping multiple tables into a single spreadsheet. People clamored for the ability to have one spreadsheet automatically update and respond to updates in other spreadsheets in other files. Microsoft addressed this by creating documents called *workbooks;* each workbook can have a number of spreadsheets, all of which can communicate with one another. Today, when you create a Microsoft Excel document, you get a workbook with three sheets to start with.

The people at Apple took this decades-long history and designed Numbers in a radical, new way: It's designed not the way software designers think people should use a spreadsheet, but the way people have been using spreadsheets for three decades.

Adding tables to spreadsheets

When you create a Numbers document, you have three things to work with:

✔ **A Numbers document:** This is the container for everything. It's similar to a Microsoft Excel workbook.

✔ **One of more sheets:** You have one or more spreadsheets (*sheets* in the Numbers world of simplicity).

✔ **Zero or more tables:** The subspreadsheets or tables that people have been creating in Microsoft Excel and other spreadsheets exist in Numbers as formal structured tables. Numbers gives them a specific name: *tables.* (And, yes, you can have a Numbers document with no tables, you have to have at least one sheet.)

The simple idea of making tables into an actual part of the Numbers application rather than letting people create them any which way leads to a major change in the way you can use Numbers when compared to an old-fashioned spreadsheet.

Working with tables

Now that tables are part of the software, Numbers can provide tools for managing them in ways that were not possible before (because tables as such never existed before for most people). You can see this in documents created from the Numbers templates such as the Travel Planner, which is used in this section.

Selecting tables

Because a table is a Numbers object, you can select it. This is not the same as selecting the cells in a subspreadsheet table. You don't have to worry about accidentally including or excluding cells that you don't want in the subspreadsheet table. A Numbers table has defined boundaries.

To select a table, move the pointer over the border of the table until it changes to a black cross, as shown in Figure 12-1. You can also click the table in the Sheets pane to the left of the window. (You find out more about the Sheets pane later in this chapter.)

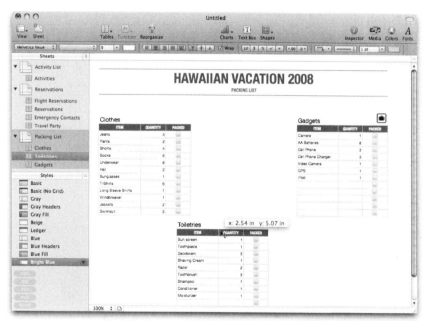

Figure 12-1: You can select tables.

Numbers tables or iWork tables?

If tables are so important, and if Pages and Keynote both support them, why not just live your life with tables in Pages and Keynote? Until iWork '08 and the debut of Numbers, that's just what many people did. But many others found that although the tables in Keynote and Pages were powerful, they did not have all the features needed for spreadsheet development. Adding all that functionality to the basic iWork table structure would have added complexity to all iWork applications.

We now have the best of both worlds. If you want high-end spreadsheet tools, you can use Numbers, which has basic iWork shapes, text boxes, and media content features just like the other iWork applications. And if you want basic table functionality, you can use Keynote or

Pages with the standard iWork tables. Just as the distinction between page layout and word processing documents depends in many cases on an individual's preferences, the choice of tables in Pages or Keynote or tables in Numbers often is a matter of personal preference.

If you are accustomed to using spreadsheet applications, Numbers is probably a good choice for you. Although it goes dramatically beyond applications such as Microsoft Excel, it still has a more "spreadsheety" feel. If spreadsheets give you a headache, try Numbers anyway, because it may cure that headache forever. If it doesn't, rest assured that you can do sophisticated table management in Keynote and Pages.

Moving and resizing tables

The sheet in Figure 12-1 has three tables. You can select a table and move it. As you drag it, you can see its current location (this is a preference you turn on and off).

Also, when a table is selected, the same eight handles you see on any selected shape in any iWork application are available so that you can resize the table.

Selecting table cells

You can select a cell in a table by clicking the cell. When you do, *reference tabs* appear at the top and sides of the table, as shown in Figure 12-2. The reference tabs have row numbers and column letters — just like old-fashioned spreadsheets.

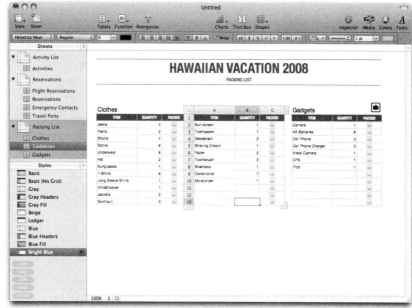

Figure 12-2:
Reference tabs appear in tables when cells are selected.

When the reference tabs are displayed, small arrows appear as you move the pointer over them. If you click one of the small arrows, you bring up a *reference tab menu,* as shown in Figure 12-3.

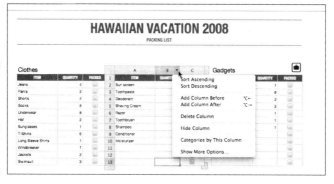

Figure 12-3:
Reference tab pop-up menus act on a row or column.

Creating a Numbers Document

The best way to get an overview of Numbers is to create a document and explore it. This section provides a high-level view. Later in this chapter and in the other chapters in Part III, you explore Numbers documents in more detail.

Creating the document

As with all iWork applications, we begin by creating a document from a template, as shown in Figure 12-4. Choose File⇨New Document from Template in Numbers to open this window.

Figure 12-4:
Create a
document
from a
Numbers
template.

As you browse through the templates, remember that moving the pointer over a template's thumbnail image lets you see additional pages in the template. Explore the templates to get an idea of what you can do with Numbers. For most of this chapter, the Travel Planner template is used.

Create a document based on the Travel Planner template by double-clicking the Travel Planner template or by selecting it and clicking the Choose button in the lower right of the window. Your screen will look like Figure 12-5.

Exploring the Travel Planner document

The window shown in Figure 12-5 has six sections. The template has other sections, but this is the initial display. I go over each section in turn.

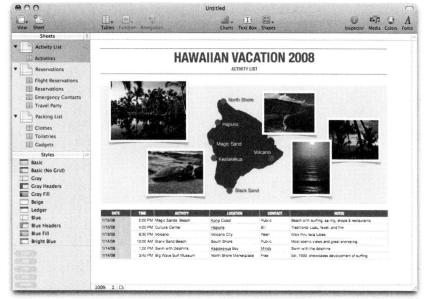

Figure 12-5:
Create a
document
from the
Travel
Planner
template.

Sheet

The main part of the window displays a sheet from the document. The *sheet* can contain tables as well as other iWork objects such as shapes, text boxes, and media. You insert them from the toolbar or the Insert menu, as in any iWork application. This is a major difference between Numbers and other spreadsheet applications.

Choose Edit⟶Select All to select all the objects in the document. Figure 12-6 shows that the sheet has one table plus a text box for the title, a background shape for the title's background, a colored background for the center part of the sheet, five photos, a shape that is the map, and round shapes along with text boxes for the place names on the map. These objects are placed on the sheet, not inside a table or table cells.

Toolbar

At the top of Figure 12-6, you see the Numbers toolbar. It contains buttons that are specific to Numbers as well as many that are common to other iWork applications, such as View, Charts, Text Box, Shapes, Inspector, Media, Colors, and Fonts. These buttons function as they do in the other applications. (The Inspector window has customized Numbers panes, as you will see.) Tables, Functions, and Reorganize are unique to Numbers.

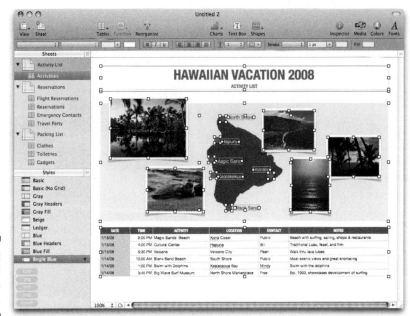

Figure 12-6:
Select all
the objects
in the sheet.

Format bar

The format bar is shown just below the toolbar. Like the toolbar, it can be
shown or hidden. It has Numbers-specific features.

Sheets pane

At the left, you see the *Sheets pane.* It looks somewhat like the Page
Thumbnails pane in Pages and the Slides pane in Keynote. Unlike those, however, the Sheets pane cannot be hidden, but you can resize it by dragging the
divider between it and the sheet canvas to the left or right.

The Sheets pane shows the structure of the document. As you can see in
Figure 12-6, there are three sheets — Activity List, Reservations, and Packing
List — each of which contains tables (such as Activities, Travel Party, and
Gadgets).

When you select a sheet or any table within a sheet, the sheet and all of its
tables are highlighted. You can use the triangle to the left of a sheet name to
collapse it, as shown in Figure 12-7.

Sheets can contain not only tables but also charts. Tables include data shown
in rows and columns; charts are graphs based on the tabular data.

At the bottom of the Sheets pane are the Styles pane and the instant calculations.

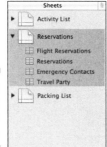

Figure 12-7:
You can
collapse
sheets.

Styles pane

Each table can have its own table style. Templates come with styles designed
specifically for that template; you can add your own styles and modify the
styles in your document. When you select a cell in a table, the Styles pane
reflects the style for that table, as shown in Figure 12-8.

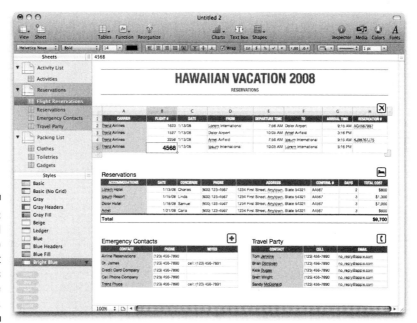

Figure 12-8:
Select a cell
in a table to
highlight
the table's
style in the
Styles pane.

If you want to change the table's style, just click another style in the Styles
pane, as shown in Figure 12-9.

Much as in the Pages Styles drawer, a triangle appears next to the selected
style. You can click it to open the menu shown in Figure 12-10.

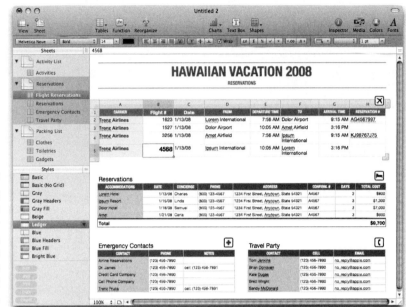

Figure 12-9: Click another style in the Styles pane to change the current table's style.

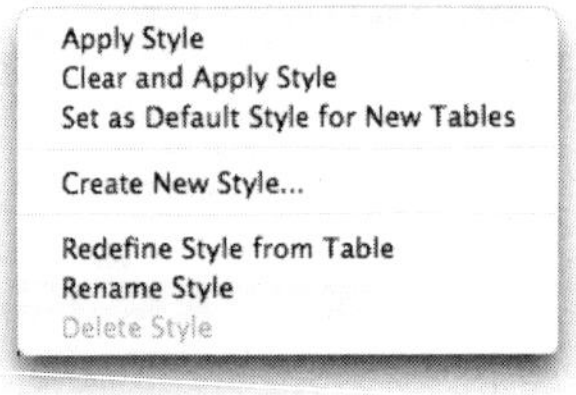

Figure 12-10: Use the Styles menu to modify table styles.

Apply Style
Clear and Apply Style
Set as Default Style for New Tables

Create New Style...

Redefine Style from Table
Rename Style
Delete Style

If you've modified a table's style, the Styles menu is where you can decide whether to change the style in every table that uses it or to create a new style.

Instant calculation results

One of the most useful Numbers features is the set of instant calculation results at the bottom of the Styles pane. In Figure 12-11, a column of numbers has been selected in the second table. (To make the numbers easier to read, they've been enlarged and are shown in bold.)

The instant calculation section automatically displays the results of a calculation using any selected cells. The selected cells can be a row, a column, or part of a row or column as well as noncontiguous cells selected by ⌘-clicking cells within a single table. The calculation results are sum, average, minimum value, maximum value, and count (the number of nonblank entries). You don't have to do anything for instant calculations to appear. They appear whenever your selection permits it.

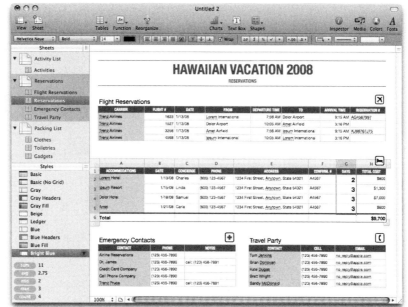

Figure 12-11:
Use instant
calculations.

Chapter 13

Creating and Editing Numbers Documents

Sometimes you can use an iWork template without any changes: Just type your text into a newsletter layout in Pages, use Keynote slides with no changes except for your text, or use a Numbers template just by typing your data. Other times, you want to customize the template in various ways, such as providing custom formatting for cells and creating your own headers for rows and columns. This chapter gets into the structure of Numbers documents, focusing on sheets and tables as well as basic formulas and common procedures such as sorting and filtering data.

Creating Sheets and Tables

Unless you're using a template without structural changes, such as adding new sheets, charts, or tables, you'll find yourself creating these objects. Chapter 15 is your resource for charts; this section shows you how to create new sheets and tables.

Creating sheets

You use sheets to organize your tables, charts, and other iWork elements such as shapes, text boxes, and media. Sheets are often designed to be printed, so iWork provides a print view so you can see what the sheet will look like when printed.

You can put all your charts and tables into a single sheet, or you can put one chart or table into each sheet. Most of the time, you decide which tables go into which sheets by taking into account what is most logical and how you need to print your data (if you need to print it at all). Most people make a case-by-case decision based on their way of working and the complexity of the data.

Here's how to create a sheet:

1. **Click Sheets on the toolbar to add a sheet or choose Insert➪Sheet.**

   The sheet is named with a default name such as Sheet 1, Sheet 2, and so forth.

2. **Double-click the name of the sheet in the Sheets pane and type a descriptive name.**

   Alternatively, display Sheet inspector by opening an inspector and clicking the Sheet button (the second from the left in Figure 13-1). Figure 13-1 shows both methods of changing a sheet's name: changing the name in the Sheets pane and changing the name in Sheet inspector.

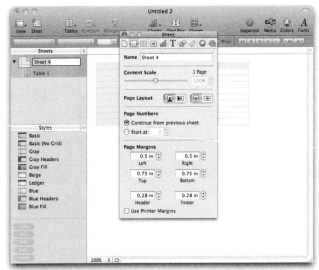

Figure 13-1: Provide a meaningful name for sheets as soon as you create them.

Creating tables

When you create a sheet, you automatically create a table within it. You can add charts or more tables to the sheet along with shapes, text boxes, and media. You can delete any of these objects to create an empty sheet, but by default, each new sheet contains a table.

You can create six types of tables:

- ✔ **Headers:** Creates a table with headers for the rows and columns.

- ✔ **Basic:** Has headers only for the columns.

- ✔ **Sums:** A basic table that also has a row at the bottom with summary functions that add the numbers in each column. You can always delete sums for any column you don't want summed. Numbers handles nonnumeric values appropriately so that text is not added in some mysterious manner to a numeric summary if you happen to type text such as *N/A* for a cell's value.

- ✔ **Plain:** The most basic table; it has no headers and no sums.

- ✔ **Checklist:** Has a header for columns and a column of check boxes at the left of the table.

- ✔ **Sums Checklist:** This combines a checklist and sums, with a header for each column, a check box at the left of each row, and a sum calculation at the bottom of each column.

If you want to create a new table, here's what you do:

1. **Select the sheet that the table will be placed in.**

   Select the sheet in the Sheets pane either by clicking the sheet name to select the sheet and all its contents or by clicking a chart or table within the sheet. The Sheet and all its contents are selected.

2. **Click the Tables menu on the toolbar and select the type of table you want to create, as shown in Figure 13-2.**

   You can access this menu also by choosing Insert⇨Table.

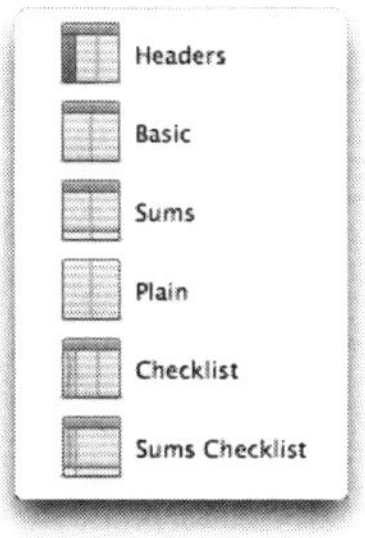

Figure 13-2:
Choose a
table.

- Headers
- Basic
- Sums
- Plain
- Checklist
- Sums Checklist

3. **Double-click the name of the table in the Sheets pane or in Table inspector, as shown in Figure 13-3, and type a meaningful name.**

   The check box to the left of the table name in Table inspector controls whether or not the table name is shown above the table on your sheet.

Figure 13-3:
Name the
table as
soon as you
create it.

Working with Headers

After you've created a table, you can change its headers and other settings, although you can't change one type of table (such as Sums) into another type (such as Checklist). One way around this limitation, however, is to change the separate settings for check boxes, sums, and headers.

Spreadsheets label columns with letters (A, B, C, and so on) and rows with numbers (1, 2, 3, and so on). Each cell within a table is uniquely identified with a letter and number: The cell in the upper left of a spreadsheet is A1. The Financials template (part of the Business category of Numbers templates) provides an example of how headers can work.

Figure 13-4 is the Income table in the Income Statement sheet for the Financials template.

The cell containing the word *EXAMPLE* is in column C and row 7; its identifier is C7. However, because the first row of the table is a header row and because the first column of the table is a header column, the text in those headers can also identify the cell: 2007 Depreciation and Amortization. In Numbers, you do not name cells. Instead, you name their column and row headers, and Numbers uses those to name each cell.

If Numbers can't find a header for a cell's row or column, it reverts to the old letter-and-number naming, such as C7. It also reverts to the old letter-and-number naming if you have duplicate header names. If, for example, you change the column for 2006 and type 2007 in its header, you'll have two 2007 header columns. In the case of such duplication, Numbers provides you with a reliable (but less user-friendly) letter-and-number name.

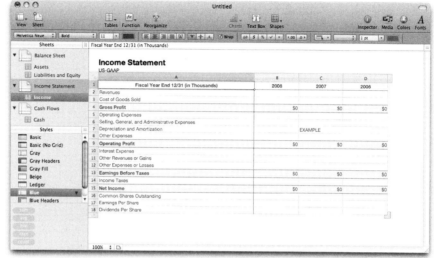

Figure 13-4:
Understand how Numbers uses headers.

Because Numbers is going to be using your header names to label cells, those names should be unique and descriptive. You only have to type them once. Numbers can handle duplicate names, but why complicate your life?

Numbers will revert to letter-and-number naming also if you don't have headers or don't have both row and column headers. Whenever possible, use both row and column headers, either by creating a table with both of them (the headers table) or by adding headers to your table.

Adjusting the number of header rows and columns in a table

Follow these steps to adjust the number of header rows and columns:

1. **Select the table.**

2. **Open Table inspector.**

   If you don't have an Inspector window open, open one by clicking Inspector on the toolbar. Then click the Table button (it's the third button from the left).

3. **In the Headers & Footer section, choose the number of rows or columns for each type of header and footer.**

   The three icons shown in Figure 13-5 let you set the number of header rows or columns for columns, headers, and footers (reading from left to right).

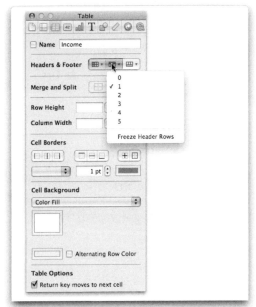

You can freeze header rows or columns (but not a footer row) using Table inspector. Freezing header rows or columns means that as you scroll through the table, the header rows or columns are always visible. If they're not frozen, you can scroll them out of sight.

Formatting headers and creating a new style

Because headers are so important, you may want to emphasize them in your tables. Some of the templates have styles that clearly show headers in contrasting colors; others are more subtle. You may want a dramatic formatting for headers while you are entering data and a more standard formatting when you're finished.

Here's how to change heading formatting and how to save it as a new style so that you can switch back and forth between the old and new styles of heading formatting:

1. **Select the header row (or rows) you want to format by clicking in the numbered label for the row at the left of the table, as shown in Figure 13-6.**

   The small triangle brings up a contextual menu that lets you add or delete header rows or columns. You don't need to worry about using it at this point.

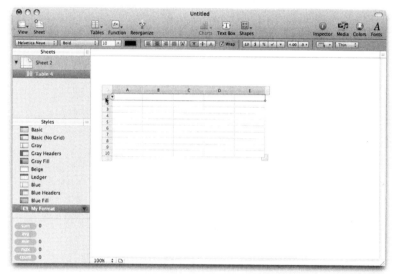

Figure 13-6:
Select a
header row.

2. **In Table inspector, make a selection in the Cell Background menu, as shown in Figure 13-7, and then select the color or image you want to use.**

   Your choices are Color Fill, Gradient Fill, Image Fill, and Tinted Image Fill.

3. **If you want a header column to be formatted, repeat Steps 1 and 2 with the header column.**

4. **In the Styles pane, click the arrow next to the name of the current style and choose Create New Style, as shown in Figure 13-8.**

5. **Name the new style.**

   The new style appears in the Styles pane and you can use it for any table in the document.

Figure 13-7:
Use Table
inspector to
select a cell
background
for the
selected
row.

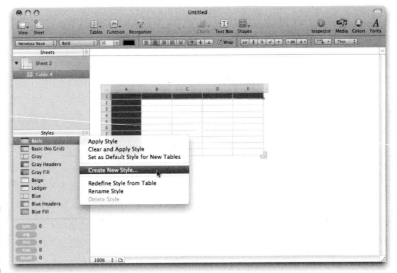

Figure 13-8:
Create a
new style.

You can switch back and forth between styles at any time. Select the
object to which you want to apply a style and then click the style name
from the list in the Styles pane. The style will be changed immediately
for the selected object.

Just as using styles can improve Pages documents, styles can improve Numbers documents and save time. Instead of adjusting various table settings each time you want a new look, combine the settings into a new style that you can select with one click. Having many styles in the document is not a problem as long as you give them descriptive names so you can remember what they represent.

Formatting Cells

Each cell in a table can have its own formatting. You use the format bar to set basic formatting such as fonts and alignment. Cells inspector lets you set the way data in the cell (or range of selected cells) is displayed with decimals, currency symbols, and so forth.

Using basic formats for cells

Figure 13-9 shows the Cells inspector window. The Cell Format pop-up menu (which is set to Number in Figure 13-9) determines the format. As you change its value, the middle of the Cells inspector window changes to provide additional settings for that format.

Figure 13-9:
Format cells
with Cells
inspector.

If one cell is selected, the formatting affects only that cell. If you select a number of cells, the formatting you set affects all those cells. If you select a number of cells that have different formatting, the Cells inspector pop-up menu is blank (it cannot display more than a single value). When you choose a new format from the pop-up menu, it is applied to all of the selected cells.

Figure 13-10 shows the various formats built into Numbers.

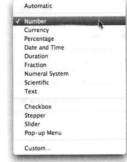

Figure 13-10:
Numbers
comes
with many
built-in cell
formats.

Many of the settings for cell formats appear in more than one cell format. Here are some of the settings that are available and the formats for which they can be set:

- **Thousands separator:** Most numeric formats let you choose whether or not to use a thousands separator. (You set this in ⌘⇨System Preferences using International and its Formats tab. For the United States, the thousands separator is a comma.) Available for Number, Currency, and Percentage.

- **Negative number formats:** Your choices are parentheses, the color red, or a minus sign. Sometimes a check box called Accounting Style is used for the option. Available for Number, Currency, and Percentage.

- **Decimals:** The number of decimal places to be used. Available for Number, Currency, Percentage, and Scientific.

- **Currency symbol:** With Cell inspector, you can change the currency symbol for specific cells in a spreadsheet. Available for Currency.

- **Fractions:** You can specify the amount of precision; examples are given such as 7/8 (one digit), 23/24 (two digits), halves, and quarters. Available for Fractions.

Using special formats for cells

Numbers has special formats that can make your tables much easier to use. These are standard Mac OS X controls that appear in a variety of applications such as iPhoto, Finder, and Bento:

- **Check box:** A check box is either checked or not. The first column of cells in the built-in checklist table consists of check boxes. Figure 13-11 shows a check box cell and the Cells inspector settings for it. The underlying value of the cell is either TRUE or FALSE depending on whether or not it is checked. You can prove this for yourself by formatting a cell as a check box and then using Cells inspector to change it to text or automatic formatting. The value of the cell is maintained when its formatting is changed (this applies to all types of cells, not just check boxes).

✔ **Stepper:** This is another quick form of data entry. As you can see in Figure 13-12, you can use Cells inspector to specify the range of values that the stepper supports. Steppers are useful for limiting input to certain values. The stepper itself is shown only when the cell is selected. When it is not selected, the value of the cell is displayed.

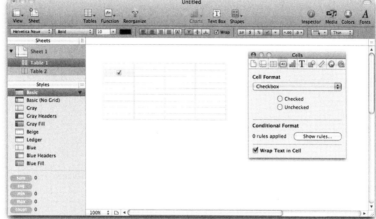

Figure 13-11: Check boxes provide on/ off or true/ false settings with the click of a mouse.

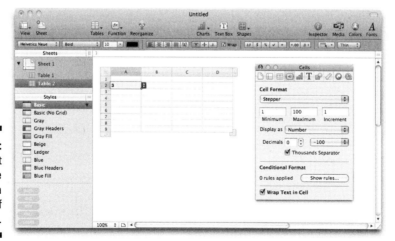

Figure 13-12: Steppers let you move through a range of values.

✔ **Slider:** A stepper lets you increase or decrease a value by a certain amount. A slider lets you move quickly across a range of values. As shown in Figure 13-13, you can also specify the range and the intervals that a slider represents. Like a stepper, the slider is displayed only when a cell is selected. At other times, the value is shown in the cell.

✔ **Pop-up Menu:** Pop-up menus work best for nonnumeric data, as shown in Figure 13-14. You start with three values. Double-click each row to type a new value. You can add or delete rows by using the + and - buttons at the lower left of the list of values.

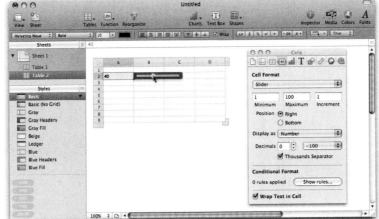

Figure 13-13: Sliders provide a fast way of changing values.

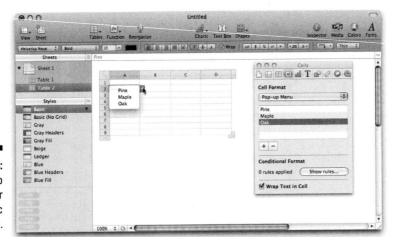

Figure 13-14: Use pop-up menus for nonnumeric data.

Chapter 14

Using Formulas and Functions

*O*ne of the most important features of any spreadsheet is the ability to place formulas into cells. Other spreadsheets, such as Microsoft Excel, offer functions and formulas — often the same ones you find in Numbers. Spreadsheet users expect to find a SUM function along with a TODAY function and all the other functions that they're accustomed to, particularly if they switch back and forth between spreadsheet applications or if they're sharing their documents. What sets Numbers apart is the ease with which you can create and manage formulas along with the large number of templates that implement sophisticated uses of formulas and functions.

Starting to Use Formulas

Formulas can contain specific values (called *constants* and sometimes *literals*); they also can contain references to cells in the spreadsheet. If a formula contains a reference to a cell, every time that cell's value is updated, the formula is reevaluated. A formula can contain a reference to a cell that itself contains a formula. There is no limit to the number of formulas in the chain of formulas for a given cell. Whenever the first value in the chain is changed, every formula is reevaluated. The only limitation to this chain of formulas is that it has to be a single path. You can't create what is called a *circular reference,* a formula that relies on evaluating a previous cell that contains a formula that includes the current cell. This would require that each cell be evaluated before the other one is evaluated — something that is logically impossible. One of them has to be first and one has to be second.

In addition to cell references and constants, formulas can contain *functions*, such as a function that sums a set of numbers. Formulas also can provide information that doesn't rely on values in the spreadsheet. For example, the TODAY function in most spreadsheets returns today's date. If you're working late and the clock strikes midnight, the TODAY function will return the date for the new day.

Using a formula to summarize data

Perhaps the most common formula is a summary at the bottom of a column, which is where most people place a summary when they work with paper and pencil. Summaries can also appear at the top of a column on the right or left of a row. Spreadsheets also make it easy to place a row or column summary in another location on the spreadsheet (perhaps a section of summary data in which all sums are shown for all relevant columns or rows). The built-in tables have built-in summary formats; the Sums and Sums Checklist tables have built-in summaries at the bottom of each column.

The example in this section uses the Financials template in the Business section of Numbers templates, as shown in Figure 14-1. Some test data has been entered for the figures in this section.

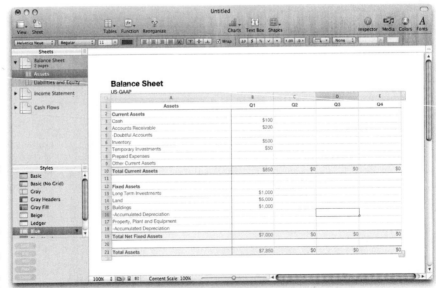

Figure 14-1:
Summarize data in columns and sections of columns.

If you experiment with the template, you'll see that the summary at the bottom of the table is not the sum of all the numbers in a column. Rather, the column has several sections, each of which is summed:

- ✔ **Total Current Assets ($850):** This is the sum of rows 3 through 9. It has distinct formatting to separate it from the detail lines above it.

- ✔ **Total Net Fixed Assets ($7,000):** This is the sum of rows 13 through 18.

- ✔ **Total Assets ($7,850):** This is the sum of Total Current Assets and Total Net Fixed Assets. If you added all the numbers in the column, you would get a column total that is exactly twice what it should be because it would include both the detail rows (3 through 9 and 13 through 18) and their subtotals.

Summarizing data that already includes subsummaries is one of the most frequent spreadsheet errors. Always do a reality check on your formulas. The arithmetic total of all numbers in the Q1 column in Figure 14-1 is 23,550. The total of all the detail lines is $7,850, which is the real total not including subsummaries.

In the Financials template, the correct summarization has all been done for you. If you had to work from scratch, here's how to do subsummaries such as Total Current Assets and Total Net Fixed Assets as well as the grand summary, Total Assets:

1. **Remove the formulas from the Financials template.**

   This lets you practice implementing the formulas for yourself. Select the cells that summarize data (B10 through E10 for Total Current Assets, B19 through E19 for Total Net Fixed Assets, and B21 through E21 for Total Assets). Then choose Edit⇨Delete. This deletes data values and formulas but leaves the formatting intact.

2. **Check that all formulas have been removed.**

   After you delete the formulas, the summary cells will be blank. If any cell displays $0, it means that a subsummary cell (such as Total Current Assets) has been cleared but the grand total (Total Assets) retains its formula. Except for the cells in which data is typed, you should not have any numbers in the main part of the table.

Creating formulas using the SUM function and a range of cells

The first summary to create is the Q1 summary of Total Current Assets. Then you can copy it to Q2, Q3, and Q4. Follow these steps:

1. **Begin to build the formula.**

   In cell B10 (Q1 Total Current Assets), type =. Typing = at the beginning of a cell starts to build a formula. Formula Editor opens, as shown in Figure 14-2.

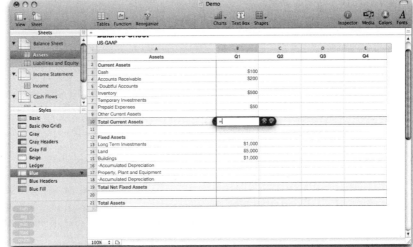

Figure 14-2: Open Formula Editor by typing = in the cell.

2. **Select the cells you want to summarize.**

   In this case, select cells B3 through B9 (Cash, Accounts Receivable, –Doubtful Accounts, Inventory, Temporary Investments, Prepaid Expenses, and Other Current Assets). Formula Editor displays the cells you're summarizing, as shown in Figure 14-3. By default, it uses the SUM function.

3. **Click the check mark to accept the formula and close Formula Editor.**

   The calculation is performed, as shown in Figure 14-4.

   Verify that the formula is working correctly by changing various numbers in the cells that are part of the formula; the result will change.

4. **Copy the formula from Q1 to the Q2, Q3, and Q4 cells.**

   The simplest way is to select the Q1 cell, where you've created the formula, and drag to add Q2, Q3, and Q4 to the selection. Choose Insert⇨Fill⇨Fill Right to fill the formula into the other selected cells.

   Note that you can fill right or down. The first cell in the selection must contain the formula you want to fill to the adjoining cells. If a formula uses other cells in its calculation, the filled formula cells will use the appropriate numbers. In other words, the Total Current Assets formula that is filled into Q2 will use the Q2 data values, not the Q1 data values.

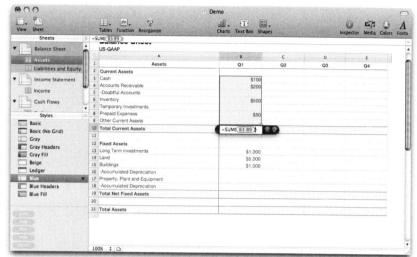

Figure 14-3:
Summarize
data.

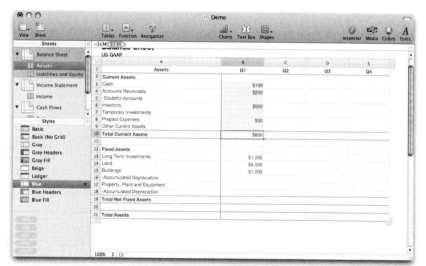

Figure 14-4:
The formula
is complete.

Create the subsummary formulas for Total Net Fixed Assets in the same way. SUM is the default function, but there are 250 built-in functions. The most commonly used functions are available from the Function menu on the toolbar. Select the cells you want to use in the function, then click Function on the toolbar and choose the function, as shown in Figure 14-5.

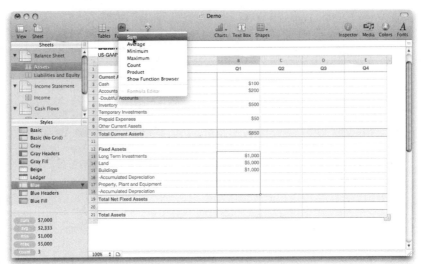

Figure 14-5:
Use other
functions.

Creating formulas by selecting individual cells

Sometimes you don't want to use a range of cells in a formula. That's the case for the Total Assets formulas for the bottom row in the sample table. It should summarize just two cells: the value for Total Current Assets and Total Net Fixed Assets.

Here's how to add the subtotals for Total Assets:

1. **Open Formula Editor by typing = in the Q1 Total Assets cell.**

2. **Click in the cells you want to include in the formula.**

   Click Q1 Total Current Assets and Q1 Total Net Fixed Assets. The cells are added to the formula, separated by + signs, as shown in Figure 14-6.

   If you've specified headers, Numbers attempts to use the cell names it generates from the headers. If it can't use them, it uses the cell letter and cell number names.

Editing formulas

When you select a cell that contains a formula, the *formula bar* appears. It's just below the toolbar in Figure 14-6. If you've chosen to show the format bar, it appears between the toolbar and the formula bar.

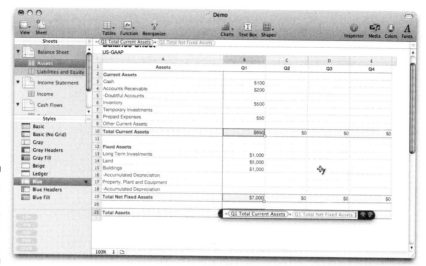

As you build a formula, it appears in both the formula bar and Formula Editor. You can click in the formula in either place and type additional text. If you select a cell or a range of cells, the cell or cells are added to the formula. You can also type the name of a cell by using the letter-and-number notation. By default, the + sign separates items in the formula.

You can use parentheses in complex formulas to indicate the order in which calculations should be carried out. Parentheses have the same meaning that they do in programming languages or algebra: Items within parentheses are evaluated first. Then the result of that evaluation is used to continue the formula.

Refining cell references

When you add a cell to a formula, either by typing its letter and number or by clicking it, that cell is referenced relative to the cell of the formula that is being built. For example, in building the subsummary for Q1 Total Current Assets, the range of cells above the Q1 Total Current Assets cell is selected. When you fill that formula to the right, the formulas in the cells for Q2, Q3, and Q4 Total Current Assets use the corresponding cells above them. This is also true if you copy and paste a formula. For example, if you copy and paste the formula from Q1 Total Current Assets anywhere else, it summarize the seven cells above it — whatever the values of those cells may be — just as it does in the original Q1 Total Current Assets formula.

Sometimes you don't want this behavior. When you want to refine a cell reference in a formula, using the formula bar or Formula Editor, place the mouse over the formula. When the small arrow in a circle appears, click to open the contextual menu shown in Figure 14-7.

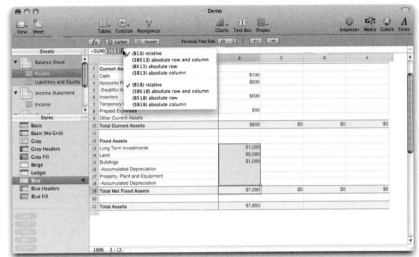

Figure 14-7:
Refine cell
references.

For each of the cell references in a formula, you can choose one of four options:

- ✔ **Relative:** This is the default setting. The cell reference is relative to the cell in which the formula is located. This is how the formula for cell Q1 Total Current Assets can be pasted or filled into Q2 Total Current Assets and still work.

- ✔ **Absolute:** By preceding the row and column indicators with a dollar sign, the reference is to that cell at all times. If you copy the formula to another cell, the reference to cell B10 or Q1 Total Current Assets always references that cell. The format you can choose is $B$10 or $Q1 $Total Current Assets.

- ✔ **Absolute row:** The reference for the cell is always in the chosen row, but the column reference varies depending on the formula cell.

- ✔ **Absolute column:** The reference for the cell is always in the chosen column, but the row reference varies depending on the formula cell.

If you're creating a what-if formula in which each row (or column) of data represents a different assumption, you might want to use absolute references for the items that don't change. You can also use unchanging values with absolute references for sales tax rates and the like.

Creating a multisheet and multitable summary

As is the case with all financial statements that follow Generally Accepted Accounting Principles (GAAP), the financial statement has three distinct sections:

- **Balance Sheet:** This summarizes assets and liabilities. A Balance Sheet contains separate tables for assets and liabilities.
- **Income Statement:** This statement combines income and expenses.
- **Cash Flow:** This shows the amount of money coming in and going out.

Each of these statements provides a different view on the operation of a business and each has its own summaries. It can be convenient to have a single overall summary of the summaries such as the one shown in Figure 14-8.

In this case, the summary simply brings together information from several sheets and tables; that information has itself been summarized, so we need to collect only the sums. Here's how to do it:

1. **Begin by creating a new sheet and table for the summary.**

   Click the Tables button on the toolbar and select the Headers built-in table. Name both the sheet and the table Summary.

2. **Set the header columns to the years you want to track.**

   Copy and paste (or type) the names of the rows you want to collect, such as Total Assets.

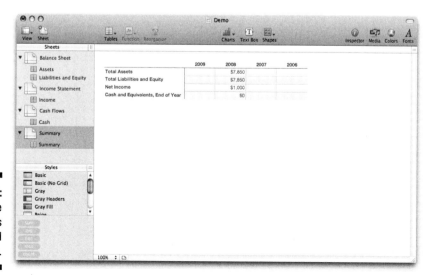

Figure 14-8: Summarize data across sheets and tables.

3. **Start to create a formula by typing = in a cell.**

   Format Editor opens, as shown in Figure 14-9.

Figure 14-9:
Begin the
formula.

4. **Navigate to the cell you want to reference (in this case Q1 Total Assets in the Assets table).**

   As you move to other sheets and tables using the Sheets pane, notice that Formula Editor stays in place. The sheets and tables appear to move beneath it. You can drag Formula Editor to a new location if you want to.

   Also at this time, the cursor changes to a function cursor, as shown in Figure 14-10.

5. **Click the cell you want.**

6. **Click the check mark to accept the summary.**

   Formula Editor closes and you return to the table where you started entering the formula. Repeat with any other cells you want to place on your one-page summary.

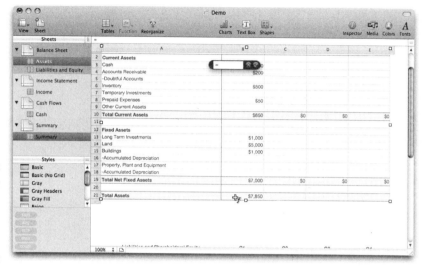

Figure 14-10:
Find the cell
to reference
in the
summary.

Using the format bar with formulas

If you show the format bar, you can use it as you're building a formula. When
you start to edit a formula, the format bar changes, as shown in Figure 14-11.
You have Cancel and Accept buttons, you can change the font size, and the
buttons on the right insert a line break or a tab in the formula. At the left, you
can click to open Function Browser.

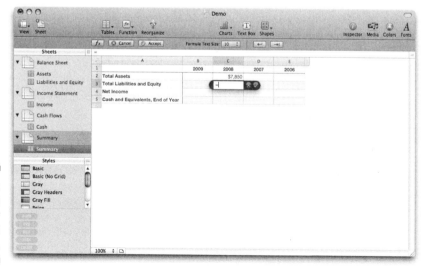

Figure 14-11:
Use the
format bar
as you build
formulas.

Using Formula List

You can show Formula List by clicking the View menu on the toolbar or by choosing View⇨Show/Hide Formula List. When Formula List is displayed, it appears at the bottom of each sheet, as shown in Figure 14-12.

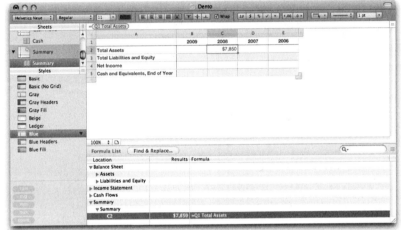

Figure 14-12:
Formula
List lets you
manage
your
formulas.

Formula List shows your sheets and tables; each sheet and table can be collapsed or expanded with the disclosure triangle next to its name. If you click a formula, you immediately go to the cell in which it is defined.

The Find & Replace button opens a dialog that lets you search for parts of formulas, such as a cell reference name, an operator, or a function. You can replace them if you want (for example, replace all references to 2010 with 2011). If you rename a header row or column, you don't have to worry: Numbers propagates the change appropriately. But if you want a wholesale replacement in various formulas, Find & Replace will do the trick.

Working with Functions

Numbers has 250 built-in functions, and you can even create your own functions. Click Function on the toolbar to open a menu from which you can select the most common functions — SUM, AVERAGE, MAXIMUM, MINIMUM, COUNT, and PRODUCT (the multiplied results of the items in the formula). You use the same menu to open Formula Editor in the selected cell and to open Function Browser.

Function Browser has the full list of Numbers functions. (The Function menu on the toolbar contains only the most common functions, but it also lets you open Function Browser.)

The vast majority of Numbers functions are common to most spreadsheets and, in fact, to many other applications. Most of these functions were around long before we even had computers. You'll probably use a small set of these functions, and that set will depend on the kind of work that you do.

The functions are divided into categories. You can open Function Browser, shown in Figure 14-13, in any of these ways:

✓ **Choose View⇨Show Function Browser.**

✓ **Click Function on the toolbar, and choose Show Function Browser.**

✓ **If you're editing a formula and the format bar is displayed, during the edit the format bar will change, as shown in Figure 14-11. Click the *fx* button at the left to show or hide Function Browser.**

At the left are the categories of functions. Selecting a category shows the functions within it at the right. At the top of the left pane you can choose to see all functions or just the ones you've used recently. Functions in the right pane are always displayed alphabetically.

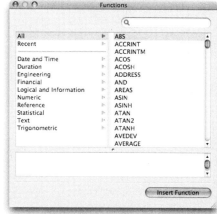

Figure 14-13: Use Function Browser to get complete function documentation and examples.

Click a function to see its full description, as shown in Figure 14-14.

Figure 14-14:
Find details
of each
function in
Function
Browser.

The format for these descriptions is always the same:

- ✔ **Function name.**

- ✔ **Brief description.**

- ✔ **Syntax:** This shows you how the function should be used. The name of the function is shown in dark gray. It is followed with parentheses that contain the *parameters,* or *arguments,* of the function. All functions have parentheses following the function name. The arguments must be in the same order in which they are shown in Function Browser. Some functions — such as TODAY() — do not have arguments.

  Each argument is described. If an argument is optional, it is identified as such in its description and appears at the end of the list of arguments.

  Arguments can be cell references or constants. Sometimes constants are numeric or text values with their own values (such as the number of months in a loan). Other times, the constants are specific instructions to the function about how it should operate. These arguments typically have values such as TRUE, FALSE, 1 (true), or 0 (false).

✔ **Usage Notes:** Sometimes there will be usage notes with suggestions and comments about how to use the function.

✔ **Example:** Finally, you see an annotated example of the use of the function.

You can use the Insert Function button at the lower right of Function Browser to insert the function in the current formula. The function is inserted with the placeholder arguments shown in the syntax section. If you don't replace them or if you make another mistake in the function, you see a red triangle and an error message, as shown in Figure 14-15. A yellow triangle is displayed for a warning. In either case, the formula containing the function is invalid, but in both cases, you can still save the Numbers document so that you can come back later and correct the problem.

Function Browser uses styled text with colors, italics, and various font sizes. None of this matters in the use of the function in your formula. Function names are often shown in CAPITAL LETTERS as they are in this book.

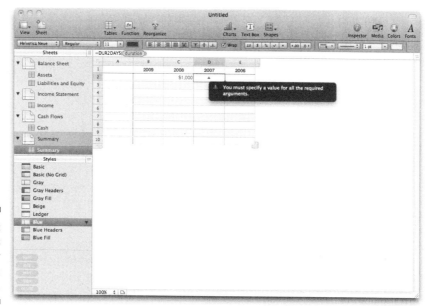

Figure 14-15:
Numbers
checks your
function
syntax.

Using Lookup Functions

Formulas and functions are not just about numbers. Some of the most impressive uses of formulas and functions have nothing at all to do with numbers. In this section we look at an example of the VLOOKUP function that is taken from the Grade Book template in the Education section.

Although this is an example from a Grade Book, the basic principle here —
looking up data from another table based on a value the user has typed in —
applies to many applications.

As shown in Figure 14-16, the first sheet is Student Data. It contains raw grade
scores as well as grades that are scaled using a curve. Everything in this
sheet is data.

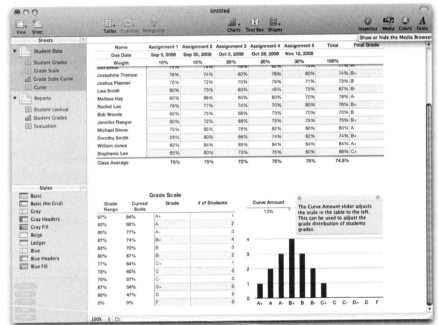

Figure 14-16: Student Data contains the data.

A separate sheet, shown in Figure 14-17, contains reports. This division
between data in one sheet and reports in another means you can change the
reports and the way in which data is displayed without any fear of corrupting
the data.

As the comment in Figure 14-17 suggests, you can type a student's name into
cell A3 and Numbers will retrieve that student's data. Try it with the Grade
Book example and you'll see how it works. What happens here is created
with the VLOOKUP function.

When you type a student's name in cell A3, data from Student Grades is
shown in cells B3 through H3 of the Student Lookup table in the Reports
sheet. The chart, Student Grades, is created from the data in Student Lookup.
That means if the data in Student Lookup changes — for example, if you type
another student's name, that student's data is placed in Student Lookup —
the chart is automatically redrawn with the new student's data.

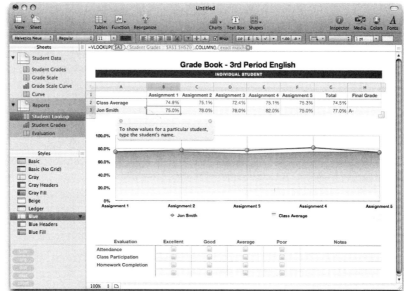

This mechanism works as long as cells B3 through H3 in Student Lookup are picked up from Student Grades. So, all you need is a formula to take the student name typed into cell A3 and retrieve the corresponding data from Student Grades.

The VLOOKUP function is the answer. It searches a range of cells for a matching value and then retrieves specific data in the row or column of that matching data. Here is the function as described in Function Browser:

```
VLOOKUP (search-for, columns-range,
          return-column, close-match)
```

The formula for cell B3, which contains the Assignment 1 grade, is

```
=VLOOKUP($A3,Student Grades :: $A$1:$H$20,COLUMN(),FALSE)
```

This function uses four arguments:

✔ **search-for:** This is what should be searched for. In this case, it's the value the user types into cell A3.

✔ **columns-range:** This is where VLOOKUP will look for the search-for value. In this case, it's the Student Grades table and the range of columns from A1 to H20. Refer to Figure 14-16, and you'll see that the range A1 through H20 is the entire Student Grades table.

✔ **return-column:** This argument tells Numbers which column from the selected row will be returned. In the example, the return-column argument itself is a function call: COLUMN(). COLUMN() returns the column number of the current column, that is, the column in Student Lookup. Because the columns in Student Lookup and Student Grades are identical, the formula in column 2 of Student Lookup will return the value of column 2 of Student Grades that matches the value of column 1 — the student name that has been typed into Student Lookup. For a mechanism like this to work, the columns must match.

✔ **close-match:** This argument takes a constant value that controls whether close matches are acceptable. If the value of close-match is TRUE (1) or if it is omitted, Numbers finds the row with the largest value that is less than search-for. For exact matches, you use FALSE (0) for this argument.

If you explore the cells in Student Lookup, you see that each cell from B3 to H3 has the same formula. Each includes the COLUMN() function, and each formula picks up the right data. Because you want each formula to search the entire Student Grades table, the rows and columns in Student Grades ($A$1:$H$20) are given absolute addresses. In that way, the entire table is always searched.

Because the entire table is always searched for a value that matches A3, you can type Class Average for the student name and retrieve the class average. If you do so, you'll have Class Average with identical data in the two rows of Student Lookup.

Now it's time to explain why the address for the first argument to VLOOKUP is column-absolute. It is always column A. If you add another row to the bottom of Student Lookup, you can copy the data from row 3 to row 4 and everything will work perfectly. The formula will still search the entire Student Grades table, and it will still use COLUMN() to select the column value based on the column in Student Lookup. And if you do copy row 3 to row 4, you'll see that the first argument to VLOOKP in row 4 is now $A4. That's because the column is absolute, and when you copied and pasted row 3's data into row 4, A stayed the same, but the row number changed.

The chart will still display data only from the first two rows.

Chapter 15

Working with Charts

. . . .

In This Chapter

▶ Creating charts

▶ Using Chart inspector

▶ Choosing chart types

. . . .

Some people have no problem looking at a table of numbers that fills an entire page and seeing the patterns right away. For other people, a chart can clarify your data, making it much easier to understand. If you are preparing information for several people to understand, you probably need to present both the raw data and a visual representation in a chart.

The same rules that apply to numeric data apply to visual data: Be clear and don't mislead.

For many people, using charts is a matter of trial and error. You usually start with the data, and then you prepare the chart and try it out on a test subject (yourself, to begin with). Does it clarify things? Does it help you understand? Numbers is a great tool to use for this experimentation because it makes it easy to both create charts and change their attributes.

 You can create charts in Keynote and Pages. Those charts are almost as powerful as Numbers charts and they look very much the same. Numbers charts can be pasted into Keynote and Pages documents, and they retain their relationship to your Numbers document where possible, unless you choose to unlink them. You see how to do this later in this chapter.

Creating a Chart

You create a chart in Numbers in two basic ways:

✓ **Start from the chart:** Create a chart. Numbers automatically creates an associated table with sample data in it. You can then modify, paste, or retype that data so that it flows into the chart.

✓ **Start from the data table:** Create a table that contains the data for your chart. Select the table or specific cells from that table, and then create a chart.

Every chart must have a table associated with it, whether it is a Numbers placeholder table or one that you have created.

Describing a chart

All spreadsheet tables serve as the basis for charts. Figure 15-1 shows a basic table. This table has row and column headers. The column headers are 2007, 2008, 2009, and 2010. The row headers are Region 1 and Region 2.

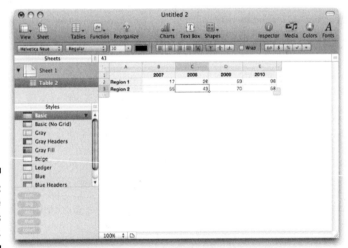

Figure 15-1:
Use a table as the basis for a chart.

Each type of chart has its own way of representing data, but the basic parts of a chart remain the same regardless of the chart type. Each value on a chart has three components:

✓ **Value:** This is the numeric value, such as a number of people, a temperature, or miles per gallon. Numeric values are usually plotted against the y-axis of a chart (the vertical line at the left). By convention, numeric values increase as you go up the y-axis. The selected cell in Figure 15-1 has a value of 43.

✔ **Category:** Each value is associated with a *category.* A category can be a date, a location, or any other attribute that applies to all values. Charts let you easily compare values for one category against another — for example, the temperature at one location with the temperature at another location. Categories can be text (such as place names) or numeric (such as dates, times, or altitudes). Categories are usually placed along the x-axis of a chart (the horizontal bottom line of the chart). If they are numeric (including dates and times), they are usually plotted so that they increase as you go to the right along the x-axis. The selected cell in Figure 15-1 is in category 2008.

✔ **Data series:** Each value is also associated with a *data series.* Like a category, a data series can be a piece of data, a region, or any other attribute that applies to all its values. You can compare values for one data series against another — for example, the temperature on one day with the temperature on another day. The selected cell in Figure 15-1 is part of data series Region 2.

Numbers makes it easy for you to switch a chart's orientation. In the scenario described here, the categories are years and the data series are temperatures. As you will see in the following section, you can click a button to change the categories to temperatures and the data series to years. Depending on your purpose and the data you're dealing with, one format rather than another will often make more sense.

Creating a chart from scratch

Follow these steps when you want to create a chart starting from a Numbers document:

1. **Create the Numbers document for the chart and its data.**

   Alternatively, open an existing Numbers document and select the sheet you want to use for the chart.

2. **Delete the table from Sheet 1.**

   A new Numbers document has a single sheet and a single table. Most of the time, you work inside a Numbers document that may have other tables or sheets in it, but by deleting any existing table, you can isolate the charting process to make it easier to see.

3. **Click Charts on the toolbar, and select a chart to create.**

   In this example, I chose a line chart. Numbers automatically creates the chart and an associated table, as shown in Figure 15-2. You can modify the table as you would any other table. Experiment with changing values and watch the chart change.

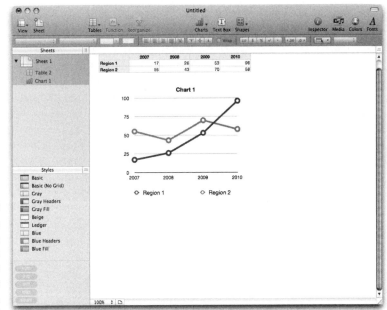

Figure 15-2:
Choose a
chart type to
create the
chart and its
table.

4. **Change the chart's series orientation.**

   Select the chart by clicking it. The table now has a dark frame, as shown in Figure 15-3. At the upper left, you can click the icon to change the chart's data series; in other words, the chart uses the table's rows instead of the table's columns as categories.

   When you change a chart's series orientation, you switch the categories with the data series. The values, which are plotted against the y-axis (the vertical axis at the left), are the same, but their representation (the color of their line, their dots, or their bars) changes.

Creating a chart from a table

Many times you create a chart from an existing table. It can be an entire table or part of a table. Figure 15-4 shows a table that lists reservations for a theater. Each cell in the table contains the number of reservations for a specific performance on a specific day. Many of the cells are empty: Not every type of performance is presented on every day.

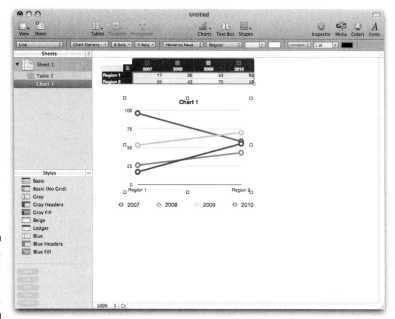

Figure 15-3:
Change the
chart's data
series.

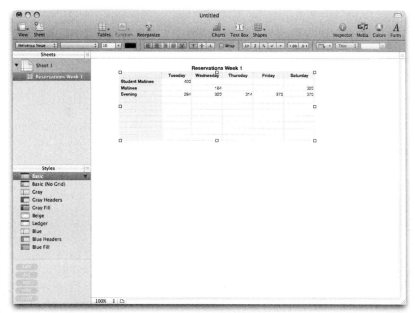

Figure 15-4:
Start from
a table of
data.

Here's how to turn the table shown in Figure 15-4 into a chart:

1. **Select the table, as shown in Figure 15-4.**

   Make certain that you select the table and not an individual cell. If you select a single cell by just clicking in the table, you'll chart that cell: a single value.

2. **Click Charts on the toolbar, and then choose a chart to create.**

   In this example, I chose a stacked horizontal bar chart. Numbers automatically creates the chart, as shown in Figure 15-5.

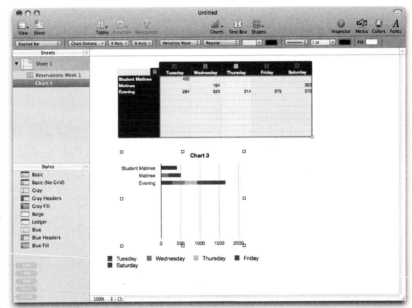

Figure 15-5: Numbers creates the chart from the table.

3. **Change the chart's series orientation.**

   Just as when you create a chart first and let Numbers create the associated table, you can change the chart's series orientation. Just click the Data Series button, and you get the result shown in Figure 15-6.

Creating a chart from part of a table

Both Figures 15-5 and 15-6 have space for the many empty table cells. You can remove these cells and clean up the chart in several ways. The simplest method in this case is to create a new chart based on part of the table — the cells that have data values in them.

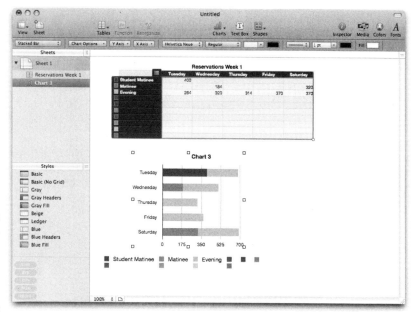

Figure 15-6: Change the chart's series orientation.

Begin by selecting the chart and deleting it. Now, select the cells from Wednesday to Saturday for matinees and evening performances. There are still some blank cells (there are matinees only on Wednesday and Saturday), but far fewer. With those cells selected, create a new chart by clicking Charts on the toolbar and choosing the same stacked horizontal bar chart. You will create the chart shown in Figure 15-7.

When you click in the chart, you'll see the dark frame around only the selected cells in the table. You'll also see that the data series button selects the rows as data series by default.

You can use the data series button to switch so that the rows (types of performances) are the data series, as shown in Figure 15-8.

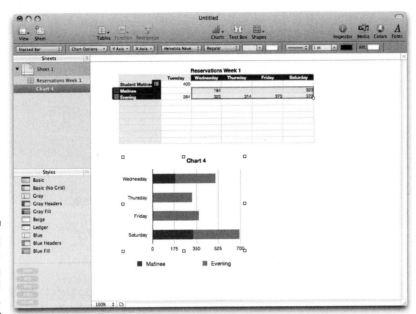

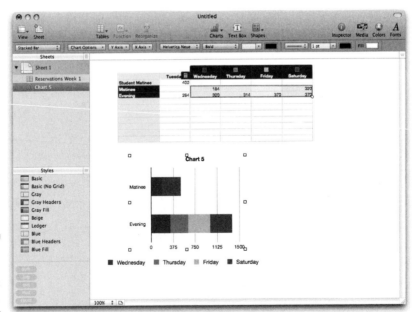

Modifying a chart's data

The chart looks much the same as the one created when the entire table was selected (refer to Figure 15-6), but there is a subtle difference. The legend at the bottom that matches the categories (Student Matinee, Matinee, and Evening) to specific colors has colors and blank names for the blank categories in the seven empty rows in the table. Unless you're planning to add more data in those categories, there's no reason to have the blank categories for the empty rows in the chart.

To change the data in the table that is included in the chart, first select the chart. This highlights the table with the dark frame around the selected cells. As shown in Figure 15-9, drag the corner of the frame (in this case the lower right) up or down or to the left or right until the correct cells are shown. In this case, as you drag the bottom up you remove the blank category rows. You'll see the chart legend change as the unneeded category boxes are removed.

You can also add or delete individual cells from the selected cells by ⌘-clicking cells to add or remove them. Use Shift-click to add or remove cells that are immediately adjacent to the selected cells.

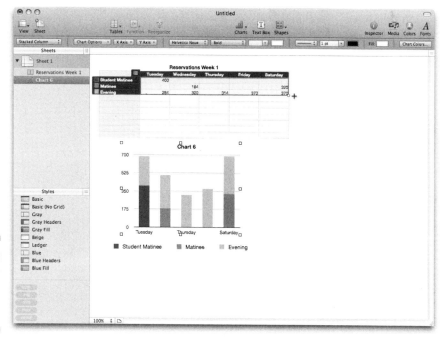

Figure 15-9: Change the data included in the chart.

Moving charts and tables

Whether you start from a chart or start from a table, you'll wind up with the chart and table next to one another on a single sheet. Once both are created and Numbers has created the link between them, you can move either one or both to other sheets — the connections remain. Just copy and paste the tables or charts to the sheets where you want them to be.

Evaluating your charts

You'll probably go through a process like the steps in this section as you develop your charts. Sometimes you know exactly what the data series orientation should be, but other times you'll experiment with the orientation and different types of charts. For example, compare the charts in Figures 15-7 and 15-8. What do they tell you?

In Figure 15-7, it's clear that each bar shows the total attendance for each day. That's a simple idea, and it's probably what you want to see. The stacked bars show how that attendance is divided between types of performances. In Figure 15-8, you can clearly see the total attendance by performance type; different colors distinguish between the days of the week. Both charts show the same data, but if you're a theater manager, you probably want the chart in Figure 15-7.

The fact that Numbers makes it easy to experiment helps to make your chart-making work faster and more productive.

Using Chart Inspector

You can change the chart type and many other attributes of a chart using Chart inspector in the Inspector window. Select Chart inspector by clicking the Chart button at the top of an Inspector window. Click to select the chart to inspect and adjust.

You can customize a chart just as you want with the Chart inspector, but for many people and many charts, you don't need to ever use Chart inspector. The default settings are often just fine. (Numbers even matches the colors to your template's colors.) You may find that just experimenting with switching the data series orientation is sufficient customization.

Changing chart types

To change a chart's type, you can always delete the chart and create a new one. But it's much easier to use Chart inspector. Select the chart you want to change and use the menu at the upper left of Chart inspector to open the same menu of chart types you see in Charts on the toolbar or choose Insert⇨Charts. Figure 15-10 shows Chart inspector with the chart types menu.

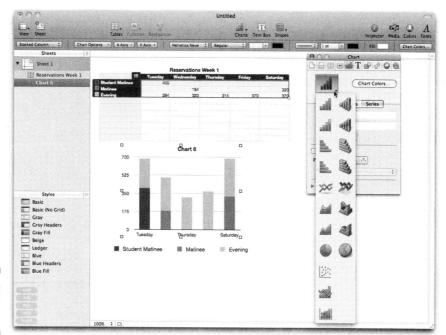

Figure 15-10:
Change the chart type.

Together with changing the data series orientation, changing the chart type gives you the widest range of major changes. As you change the chart type, notice that the size and shape of the chart can change so you may have to rearrange on your sheet objects such as graphics, titles, tables, and even other charts.

Changing chart colors

The Chart Colors button at the top of Chart inspector opens the window shown in Figure 15-11.

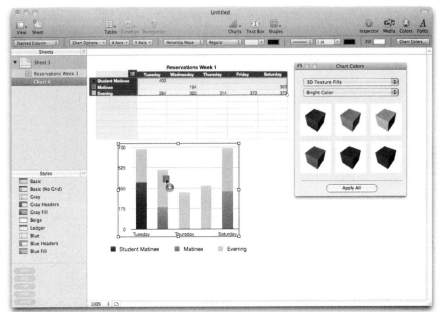

Figure 15-11:
Change
chart colors.

Select the set of colors you want to use for your chart. Drag each color to the color on the chart you're replacing. You see a small color swatch and a plus sign on the pointer as you move the new color into place. That color will replace the previous color everywhere it's used on the chart.

Formatting chart titles, legends, and bar formats

The Chart tab in Chart inspector lets you show or hide legends, titles, and hidden data. The legend, which identifies categories by name and color, is shown at the bottom of the chart.

The chart title, if it is shown, appears above the chart. To change it, simply double-click and type a new name.

If your table has hidden data, you can control whether or not it is shown in the chart. You probably will choose not to show it; if it's hidden in the table, it usually should be hidden in the chart. Be careful about hiding data. If you're hiding it for reasons of confidentiality, it may make sense to hide identifiable data in the table and chart. If you're hiding data because it's distracting and the chart is clearer without it, make certain that you're not misleading the viewer.

Finally, in bar charts you can adjust the width of individual bars as well as the space between sets of bars, as shown in Figure 15-12. A stacked bar chart stacks all the bars for a given category on top of one another, with no space between sets of bars.

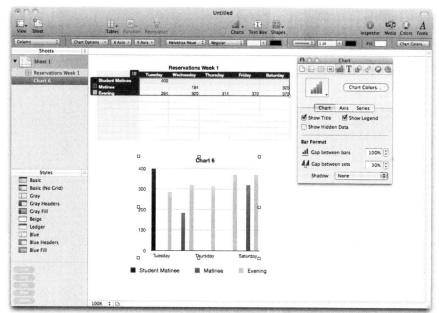

Figure 15-12:
Format titles, legends, and bars.

The category legend names and color codes are in their own section. You can move it and adjust its width (and therefore its height) as shown in Figure 15-13.

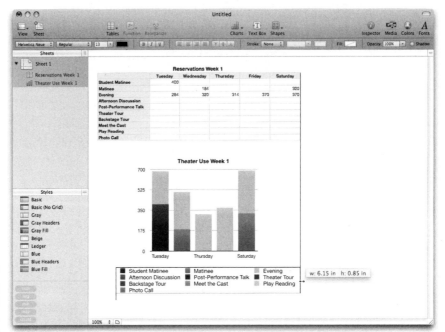

Figure 15-13:
Format
legends.

Setting axes, labels, ticks, and grids

You use the Axis tab in Chart inspector to control axes, labels, ticks, and grids. There are separate settings for the x- and y-axes, and they can depend on the chart type.

In Figure 15-14, you can see the settings for the y-axis. These are the default settings for a stacked bar chart. Notice that the axis pop-up menu is where you set ticks and grids — the marks on the axes that provide a scaled reference for numbers and categories of an axis.

You can choose the maximum and minimum values for the y-axis, as shown in Figure 15-15. If you don't choose your own values, Numbers will choose appropriate settings.

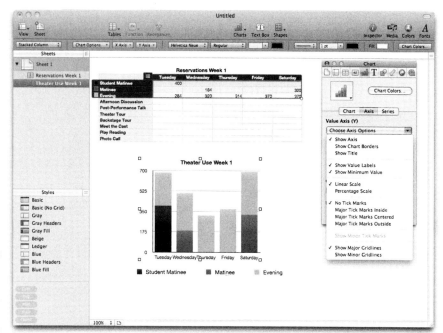

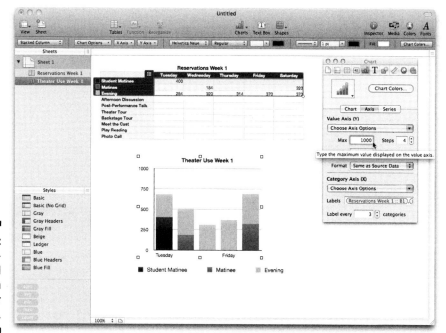

If you're preparing charts that will be compared to one another, you usually want to set the same minimum and maximum values for the y-axis for like data. In other words, if you have several charts that are plotting grades, they might all be scaled from 0 to 100. A separate set of charts plotting audience attendance in the 400-seat theater might all be scaled 0 to 410 (to allow for standing room). If you present like information with different scales, the result is misleading. This is a common mistake in preparing charts. Unfortunately, it is also a deliberate step that some unscrupulous chart designers take.

At the bottom of the Axis tab of Chart inspector, you can set the intervals between category names. In Figure 15-14, labels are shown for every category. In Figure 15-15, labels are shown for every third category, and the bottom of the chart is much cleaner. This works very well when the categories have some obvious sequence. Most people can guess that the two categories between Tuesday and Friday are Wednesday and Thursday. On the other hand, if your categories are Plumbing, Haberdashery, Gifts, and Accounting, showing the labels for only Plumbing and Accounting won't give people a clue as to what those other two categories are.

Adjusting series in Chart inspector

The Series tab in Chart inspector lets you adjust and inspect the data series in your chart. Select a series in the chart (not the chart itself). You do that by clicking any of the bars or data points in the series. In Figure 15-16, you can see that the Matinee series is selected: Round dots appear at the top and bottom of each bar that applies to that series. In addition, the corresponding row in the table is highlighted.

You can also see that a data series is a formula. You can edit it just as you would any other formula. In addition to the data series data, the labels are also taken from a range in the table; you can change this range as well so that the labels will change.

Perhaps most important, you can change the order of each data series. You don't have to rearrange the data in your tables to put one series on top of another in your stacked bar chart. Just as with the minimum and maximum values on the y-axis, keeping your data series in the same order across several charts can make it easier for people to compare one chart with another.

You can turn value labels on and off as well as change their location and formatting, as shown in Figure 15-17.

The chart in Figure 15-17 is a stacked bar chart, so the final label position option (placing it above the bar) is not available. If you choose to place the value labels in a specific position, remember that the chart will usually look best if you use the same position for all data series.

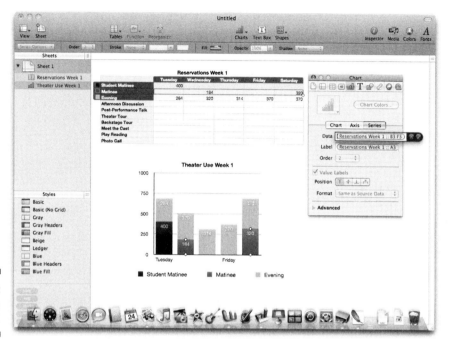

Figure 15-16:
Select a
data series.

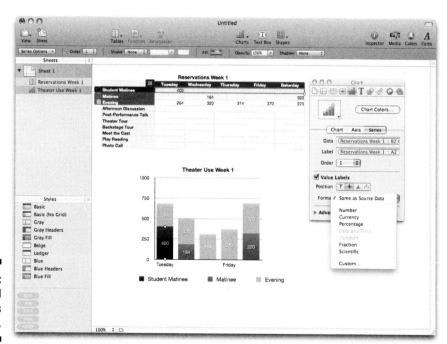

Figure 15-17:
Set label
positions
and formats.

Chapter 16

Formatting and Printing Numbers Documents

In This Chapter

▶ Displaying charts and tables effectively on paper

▶ Reorganizing, sorting, and categorizing data

▶ Searching for data values

*E*ach iWork app has its own settings for its documents and their major subdivisions (sections for Pages documents, slides for Keynote documents, and sheets for Numbers documents). For Keynote presentations and Pages documents, the size of the canvas you're working with is set for the document. In the case of Numbers documents, each sheet can have a different size; it's only when it comes time to print a sheet that you need to worry about its actual size. That's one of the reasons why the procedures for formatting and printing Numbers documents are somewhat different from the procedures for formatting and printing other iWork documents.

Formatting Multiple Charts on a Single Sheet

Creating multiple tables and charts on multiple sheets in Nunbers so that you can track data is simple. Figure 16-1 shows a multiple-sheet solution (it's one used previously in Chapter 15).

Keeping each sheet focused on one set of data (a single week in this case), makes it easy to manage just the information you care about.

But you can also create a new sheet to provide a summary so that you can see all the data together. This section shows you how to combine the tables and charts and how to reorganize and reformat them so that they look their best.

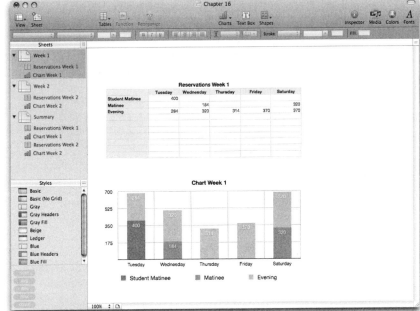

Figure 16-1:
Create
multiple
sheets,
each with
its own
tables and
charts.

The sequence of steps depends on your charts and tables as well as your preferences. As you are rearranging and reformatting your own tables and charts, you may notice something that appears wrong to you. Feel free to jump ahead (or back) in this chapter to fix that issue.

Formatting charts on a single sheet

Here's how you make charts placed together on a single sheet look as good as possible:

1. **Create a new sheet and name it Summary.**

   Click Sheet on the toolbar and double-click to rename it in the Sheets pane.

2. **Copy and paste each chart from its own sheet into the Summary sheet.**

   Don't worry what the sheet looks like as you proceed — you'll clean it up in this section.

   Be careful that you copy only the charts (not the accompanying tables). Do this by clicking once in the center of each chart so that the chart's eight handles are visible. Then copy and paste each chart to the Summary sheet. In this way, the chart on the Summary page and the chart on the original sheet page will both reference the same table.

3. **Rearrange the charts so that they look the way you want them to look.**

   As you move the charts, guide lines appear, as shown in Figure 16-2. In this case, the charts are aligned on their horizontal centers. Experiment with different types of alignment; this will help you uncover errors. For example, if you place the charts next to one another, you'll see a mistake.

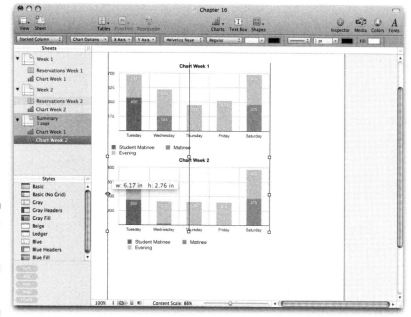

Figure 16-2: Create a single summary sheet with all the charts.

4. **Check the axes to make certain they are consistent.**

   In Figure 16-2, the y-axis goes from 0 to 700 in the Week 1 chart; in the Week 2 chart it goes from 0 to 800. Two charts displaying the same type of data that are placed next to one another should have the same values on their axes. If you take out a ruler and measure the height of bars with similar values, you'll see that they are different heights. This becomes increasingly apparent if you place them next to one another.

5. **Change the axis minimum or maximum value to make them consistent.**

   Usually, you want the values from the larger range of values. Use Chart inspector to change the values of the y-axis, as shown in Figure 16-3.

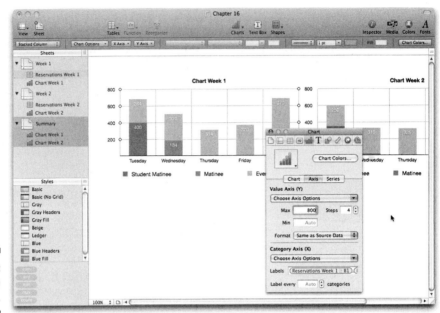

Figure 16-3:
Adjust the
axes scales.

Print charts on a single sheet

Now that you have your charts looking good on the screen, it's time to make them look good when they're printed. Here's how:

1. **Switch to Print view to see how your sheet will look when it's printed.**

   Use any of these commands:

   • Choose View⇨Show Print View.

   • Click View on the toolbar and choose Show Print View.

   • At the bottom of the window, choose Show Print View (see Figure 16-4).

   When Print view is displayed, the Sheets pane shows the number of pages it will take to print that sheet, as shown in Figure 16-4.

2. **Scroll to make certain that the page breaks are appropriate.**

   In this case, a page break toward the right side of the Week 2 chart looks terrible.

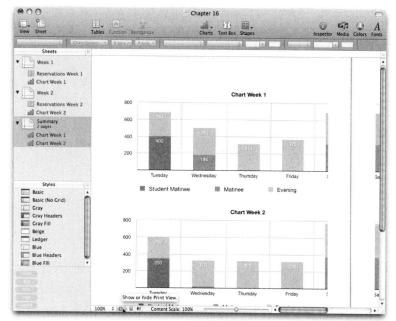

Figure 16-4:
Show Print
view.

3. **If necessary, fix the page breaks.**

   Here's where judgment comes in. You have a variety of options:

   - Rearrange the sheet so that one table or chart appears on each page. This approach, however, is usually overkill.

   - Use the Content Scale slider in the center of the bottom of the window to change the size of the sheet's content. If almost everything fits on a single page, this may work for you. If you reduce the content size, though, print it to check it for readability before distributing the chart.

   - Use the controls in the bottom of the window to switch between portrait (vertical) and landscape (horizontal) orientations.

   - Manually adjust the content. Instead of scaling all the content, make informed judgments about specific rescaling choices. For instance, in this case, you might want to reduce the size of the charts while leaving the legends the same size.

Sorting and Reorganizing Data

Like other spreadsheets, Numbers can sort and reorganize data quickly. As you think about how to print data, you may want to consider not just the layout but also the way in which the data is organized and selected. This section provides an example of how to do that. Both sorting and reorganizing data help people focus on the points you're trying to make.

Many of the examples in this book and the Numbers documentation focus on small problems because it is usually easier to see the basic principles. But the example in this section is chosen to show you the power of Numbers. The data used here is from the United Status 2000 census. The complete data file is a quarter of a million records; several thousand are enough to demonstrate Numbers in action. You'll see how to display the data, format it, and create subtotals by category.

Sorting data with the Reorganize dialog

First I describe how to sort data using iWork's Reorganize dialog:

1. **Download the `censususa` data file as described in the Introduction.**

   Open the file in Numbers.

2. **Use Table inspector to set headers for each column.**

   Type names for each header (Age, Count, Sex, and State). The spreadsheet should appear as shown in Figure 16-5.

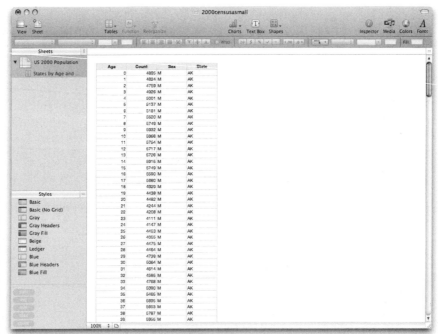

Figure 16-5:
Open the census file in Numbers and set headers for the columns.

3. Select the entire table and click Reorganize on the toolbar to open the Reorganize dialog, as shown in Figure 16-6.

Sort the table based on ascending age as shown in Figure 16-6. Note how quickly the sort is performed: Numbers is fast. Also note that by supplying header values for the columns, you've made it easier to use the Reorganize dialog. There's no question that you're sorting by age because that's the name of that column.

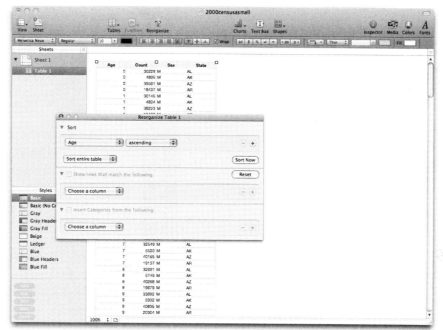

Figure 16-6:
Sort the
table
by age.

Using data categories

Numbers makes it easy to categorize data. Just follow these steps to categorize the census data by state and age:

1. Download the censususa data file as described in the Introduction.

2. Use Table inspector to set headers for each column.

You also may want to use Cell inspector to format the data values as numbers with thousands delimiters.

3. **Select the entire table and click Reorganize on the toolbar to open the Reorganize dialog. Select the State category, as shown in Figure 16-7.**

   (Use the Insert Categories From the Following check box to turn categories on and off.) You can collapse or expand any category by using its disclosure triangle.

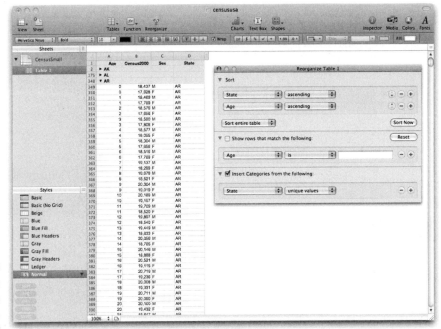

Figure 16-7:
Use
categories.

4. **Use the plus sign at the right to add a category to the Reorganize dialog.**

   Add the Age category below the State category. The display changes as shown in Figure 16-8.

5. **Clean up the display.**

   You can hide the columns for State and Age — they are shown as categories. The table that results is shown in Figure 16-9.

6. **Add a summary function for the categories.**

   Click any summary cell (such as a state) and use the disclosure triangle that appears at the right to open the menu shown in Figure 16-10. Choose a summary function for that category and the column you've clicked in. For example, if you click in the Age column and the State category, you can create subtotals for all ages and all states as shown in Figure 16-11. There's nothing more to click: Numbers just goes to work.

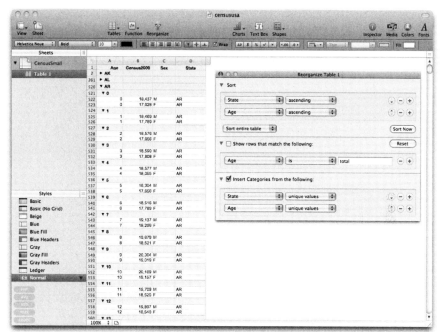

Figure 16-8:
Use sub-
categories.

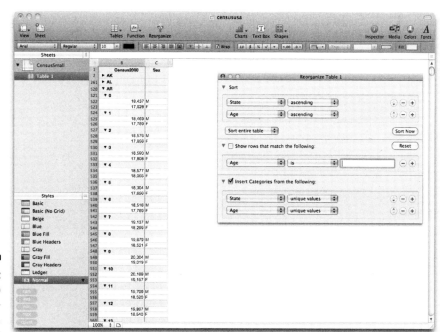

Figure 16-9:
Clean up
the spread-
sheet.

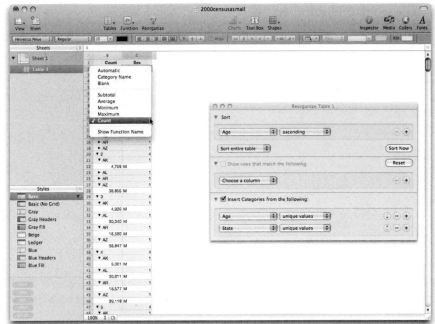

Figure 16-10:
Add
summary
functions for
categories.

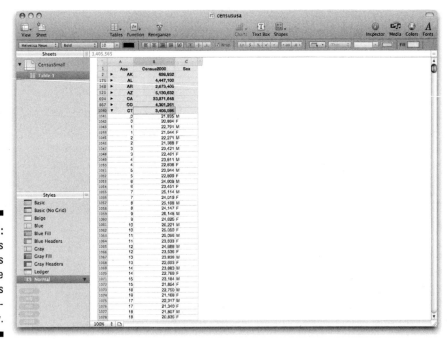

Figure 16-11:
Numbers
performs
the
summaries
auto-
matically.

TIP

Subtotals in large tables can take a while to calculate. Some people are tempted to go wild with summaries. Consider what it is you're trying to communicate. It may be that separate smaller tables with fewer summary fields (or a chart!) can make your point more simply.

Finding data

When you have a small table, you can look at it and understand the data at a glance (particularly if you've used charts). But when you have a large table with hundreds or thousands of cells, you need help to find the data you're looking for.

Here's how to search a table for data:

1. **Select the table or part of a table you want to search.**

2. **Select the column you want to search, as shown in Figure 16-12.**

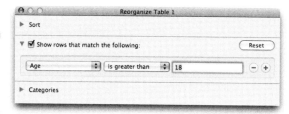

Figure 16-12:
Select the column to search.

3. **Provide the condition you are looking for, as shown in Figure 16-13.**

   These are the values in the pop-up menu shown in the center of Figure 16-12.

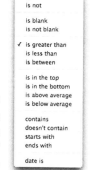

Figure 16-13:
Select the operator for the search.

4. Enter the value to search for.

You can click the + sign to add another condition to the search, as shown in Figure 16-14.

5. Show the data.

When you select the Show Rows That Match the Following check box, Numbers performs the search. The search is very fast because Numbers has been working on it while you've been specifying the search terms.

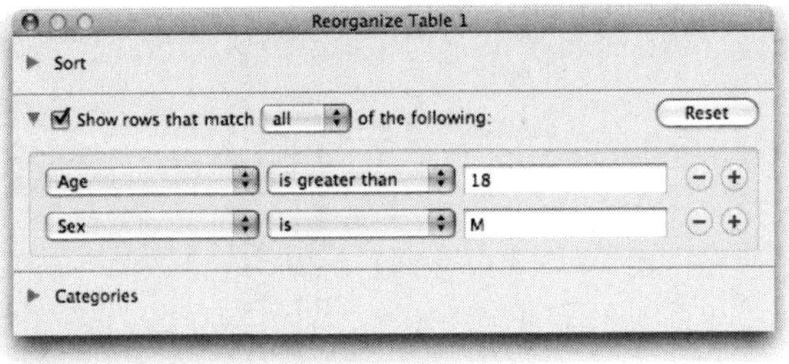

Figure 16-14:
Use multiple
search
conditions.

Part IV

Presenting Keynote

In this part . . .

Keynote started as a project for Steve Jobs, for his presentations at MacWorld and Apple's World Wide Developer Conference. Well-known for his attention to detail, he didn't like the existing presentation software. When you're the head of a company like Apple, you can address the issue by having software written to your specifications.

Over time, Keynote was refined and became the first component of iWork. It's possible to create ugly and boring presentations with Keynote, but it's a lot harder to do so than with some other software.

Although Keynote has great graphics and terrific transitions, its strength is that its features are all focused on the main purpose of the presentation: presenting and clarifying information rather than drawing attention to gee-whiz effects.

Chapter 17

Getting to Know Keynote

In This Chapter

▶ Getting started with a presentation

▶ Using slide masters

▶ Creating handouts, notes, and outlines

Keynote was the first component of iWork. It was originally written for Steve Jobs to use when he gave presentations at conferences and trade shows, including Apple's World Wide Developers Conference and the Macworld conferences. After these "trials by fire," Keynote and Pages became the first two components of iWork.

Word processing programs and page layout programs such as Microsoft Word and Pages focus on preparing paper-based documents. They often are viewed on a computer display, but generally they are tied to paper. When it comes to spreadsheets such as Microsoft Excel and Numbers, there's a different pattern. Spreadsheets are sometimes printed; other times they are designed for interactivity and what-if analyses in which a person uses the spreadsheet's ability to rapidly calculate and recalculate data.

Presentation software is a different type of product. It's really not paper-based like word processing or page layout software, and it's not designed for the kind of interactivity provided by a spreadsheet. Presentation software uses the capabilities of a graphics-based personal computer to let people create effective presentations.

This chapter gets you started with Keynote and its reinvention of presentations for the Mac. It's a reinvention that takes advantage of the built-in features of Mac OS X as well as what people have learned over more than 20 years of using less powerful tools.

Creating Effective Presentations

A lot of confusion and misinformation about presentations exists, creating a bad reputation for presentations and presentation software. By looking at these issues, however, you can find out how to avoid problems and how to make your own Keynote presentations more effective and productive.

Making your presentations effective

Presentations differ from other types of documents in that they are not designed for a person to use on their own. A presenter (usually you) controls the pace of the presentation. And, what's more, because presentations are usually given in a darkened room, you can't always tell if you're losing your audience. Here are some tips for avoiding problems in this area:

- ✔ **Avoid the dark:** Use the least amount of room-darkening you can for your presentation. Make certain you can see your audience.

- ✔ **Use Q&A sections:** Use more (and shorter) Q&A sections in your presentations to involve your audience as much as possible.

- ✔ **Use a roadmap:** Let people know where you're going in your presentation and where they are at any moment. When you're reading a book, the heft of the unread pages gives you an idea of how far you've come. With a presentation, one slide after another can come out of the dark without any clue as to how it fits into the presentation.

- ✔ **Time and rehearse your presentation:** Fortunately, Keynote has excellent presentation tools so that you can make your presentation as efficient as possible. Depending on your topic, your experience with presentations, and who you are, you may find it more important to work on timing or to rehearse your presentation. Some presenters need no more than a few minutes' rehearsal, but many others need hours to come up with a 15-minute presentation.

Using documents that move

What you use for a presentation is a sequence of slides displayed on a large projection screen or sometimes directly on a computer display if the audience is small. You have options for movement that you don't have with a printed document. You can add effects to the transition from one slide to another along with moving elements including QuickTime movies.

These tools, however, are among the most misused of presentation features. In fact, some time ago, one presentation application (not Keynote) even had a feature that allowed you to select a different random animated transition from one slide to the next. The audience had no idea why one transition was used rather than another.

Experiment with the Keynote transitions and use them to help people understand where in the presentation you are. For example, you can use a certain type of transition to go from one slide to another slide that provides details on the first slide. Yet another transition can be used to introduce a new topic.

Your audience is sitting there in the dark trying to figure out what all this means: Give them a helping hand.

Working on a small scale

The last point to remember when working on a presentation is that you're using a very small canvas. Although your slides may be blown up to large sizes on a screen, that's so a roomful of people can see them. Each slide has much less space for information than a piece of paper (or a spreadsheet page).

Given the relatively small size of your slides, you may decide to break up text into multiple slides, such as Strategies (1), Strategies (2), and Strategies (3). This is a time-tested way to antagonize your audience. You're asking them to remember too much. For each slide, make its title clear and its subject understandable. Instead of Strategies (1), try New Customer Strategies. Instead of Strategies (2), try Returning Customer Strategies.

You may think that you have to do more organization for a large document than for a 20-slide presentation, but the opposite may be true. In part, that's because with a large printed document, your readers can always flip a few pages back or forward if they lose the sequence of what you've been writing about. With a slide presentation, they have to remember where they are in the presentation.

Think about these issues as you explore Keynote. Fortunately, with the built-in themes, you'll find plenty of tools. The folks at Apple have used presentations for years, and they're very good at them. Keynote isn't just presentation software; like Pages and Numbers, it's a hands-on training seminar in the nuts and bolts of communicating.

Come back to these issues as you work with Keynote. For now, it's time to explore what you have in that little iWork box.

Introducing the Keynote Themes

When you launch Keynote or create a new document, you are prompted to choose a theme, as shown in Figure 17-1.

Theme Chooser, shown in Figure 17-1, looks very much like Template Chooser you've used with Pages and Numbers. One immediate difference is the pop-up menu in the lower right: You can select the size of your presentation slides when you select a theme.

Another difference between Theme Chooser and Template Choosers you've used before is that the themes are not divided into categories such as Education or Business.

But the biggest difference between themes and templates is that themes are interchangeable. With a template, you normally create a document from the template and go on to customize it. You can modify colors and patterns in the template, but your document has its own logic and structure. If you want to switch to a new template, you can do so by starting a new document, or you can modify the existing document.

With a theme (rather than a template), you can switch back and forth from one theme to another. You can do this because the structure of the underlying document is independent of the theme, so the theme can always be replaced.

Just as a Numbers document can contain a number of sheets, each with its own tables and charts, and a Pages document can contain a number of pages or sections, each with its own formatted elements, a Keynote document consists of a number of slides, each of which has its own formatted elements. Unlike Pages and Numbers, the structure of those slides is specific, and you'll see that the slide structures — called *slide masters* — allow you to switch from one theme to another. In addition, these structures help you implement the type of roadmaps and structures cited previously as ways to improve your presentations.

Slide Masters Provide Consistency and Save Time

Each theme has its own slide masters. Having chosen a theme, you can build a presentation by adding slide masters in whatever sequence you want. Because the slide masters are structured and replaceable, you can always switch themes as you go along.

Not every theme supports every slide master structure, but by and large you'll find that most slide master structures are available. For example, Figure 17-2 shows the slide masters in the Industrial theme.

Title & Subtitle

Title & Bullets

Title & Bullets – 2 Column

Bullets

Blank

Title – Top

Title – Center

Photo – Horizontal

Photo – Vertical

Title, Bullets & Photo

Title & Bullets – Left

Title & Bullets – Right

Figure 17-2:
Slide
masters
for the
Industrial
theme.

Figure 17-3 shows the slide masters for the Typeset theme.

If you enter text or photos on slide masters, you can change the theme of your presentation. Do not do so without checking: Sometimes there are slight differences in fonts and spacing, so you'll need to make manual adjustments to text on the slide master. In general, if you've left a little bit of space around a slide master's text or title, you'll be safer than if you've used every pixel.

The standard suite of slide masters provides the basics for an excellent presentation. You can create your own slides from blank slide masters, but if you use the built-in slide masters, you'll give your presentation not only a consistent look but also a logical structure.

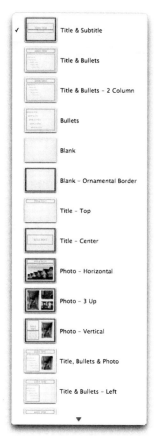

Figure 17-3:
Slide
masters for
the Typeset
theme.

This section provides a preview of the slide masters and how you can use them most effectively. The slide masters in this section are drawn primarily from the Sedona theme, which has several alternate versions of slide masters, providing you with extra choices within the basic presentation structure.

As you start to lay out your presentation, there are several logical parts to consider: the headline and overview, the section headlines and overviews, and the content slides.

Creating your presentation title

Your first slide is usually the Title & Subtitle slide master. For the Sedona theme, that slide master is shown in Figure 17-4.

As you can see in Figure 17-4, you are prompted to enter the title. Some themes use all caps for the title, so if you type lowercase letters, they are converted to uppercase automatically. The best idea is to type uppercase and lowercase letters as appropriate whether or not they appear that way on the slide, because if you change themes later, the capitalization may matter. Figure 17-5 shows the completed title slide. For the subtitle, you can use a true subtitle or the presenter's name. You might want to use a course or conference description as well.

Figure 17-6 shows what can happen when you switch themes.

Here are two common complications:

- **Capitalization can matter.** Although capitalization didn't matter in the slide shown in Figure 17-4, it does now that the theme is changed to Imagine.

- **Spacing can change.** Also, the spacing of the title changes with the new theme. As shown in Figure 17-6, you can double-click and automatically resize the title text to the space available. Figure 17-7 shows the modified title slide.

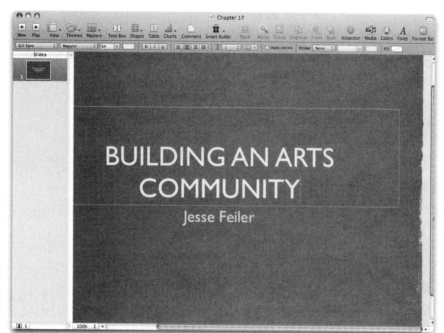

Figure 17-5:
Type the
description.

Figure 17-6:
Switching
themes
can pose
spacing
problems.

Figure 17-7:
Modify the
title slide if
necessary.

When you change themes, you'll probably have the types of issues described
here and will need to check spacing for titles and slide text. You'll quickly
learn that you can minimize these changes by leaving a bit of extra space.

Structuring your presentation

Providing a roadmap to your presentation is critical. Without it, your audience won't know where you are and where you're going; a lack of a roadmap
is what gives rise to the common impression of many presentations as just a
speaker droning on and on. Set up your roadmap and point out its signposts
as you go along. You don't have to be fussy about this; just let people know
what's coming next.

Keynote sets this structure up for you. Look at the slide masters shown in
Figures 17-2 and 17-3. Almost every slide master on every theme has space
for a title. Even a slide that features a photo has space for a title. Your titles
are the signposts to your roadmap.

A presentation is not a vacation slideshow. That's a misunderstanding that ruins many a presentation. When you're showing your vacation slides, it's fine to show a photo and say, "Here we are on the Matterhorn." You can even vary your slideshow with questions, "Can you tell where we are in this photo?" Most of the time, that doesn't work for a presentation for work or a similar environment. There's no question that you can create presentations of vacation images, but Keynote and its tools aren't the best choice for that. Rather, use iPhoto or iMovie to construct a photo album, a slideshow, or a movie. A Keynote presentation with its speaker's notes, the ability to print handouts, and other such features provides much more power and sophistication than iPhoto or iMovie when it comes to presentations.

Providing bulleted content

Most of your slides will consist of some variation on a title and bullets, perhaps with an image as shown in Figure 17-8.

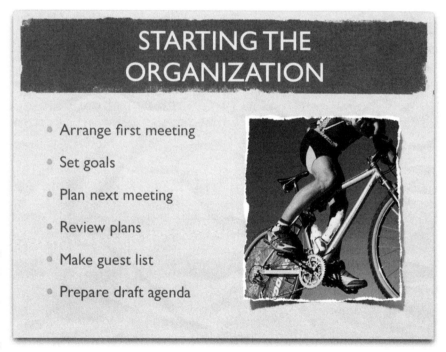

Figure 17-8: Use a title and bullets with an image.

This is the Title Bullets & Photo slide master from the Sedona theme. Most themes have a similar slide master. Bullets are an effective way of structuring your presentation. You can create a hierarchical bullet structure that provides a sturdy roadmap to your presentation. On the initial bullet list, provide an outline of your presentation. Each bullet on that slide then becomes the title for a new slide with its own bullets.

If you use this strategy, repeat the overview slide so that you can provide a summary of what you've talked about. When you use a Keynote bullet slide master, look carefully at what Keynote has given you. As shown in Figure 17-8, a half dozen bullets fill a slide when there's an image next to them. If you don't have an image, you're still usually limited to a half dozen bullets; each one can be longer, but using the extra space for more bullets is an invitation to clutter and confusion.

Using a Q&A slide

All themes have a blank slide master. You can put anything on these slides. A great use of them is to create a discussion or Q&A slide. You can use a bulleted slide to launch a discussion, with the bullets as discussion topics. But for many purposes, nothing beats a blank side with a simple headline such as Q&A or Feedback. Turning the presentation over to your audience involves them and gets things moving.

In general, anything you can do to break the formal pattern of a presentation will involve your audience more and make the presentation go better.

Creating Handouts, Outlines, and Notes

Take a few moments to explore the Keynote Print dialog. Choose Keynote from the pop-up menu in the center of the dialog, and you'll find a wide range of options. You can prepare handouts with up to six slides per page. You can add presenter notes to the handouts if you want. You can also print an outline that Keynote constructs automatically from slide titles and bullets.

Many people prepare two sets of handouts: one set to be distributed and a second set for the speaker (and possibly as a leave-behind for a teacher or administrator).

Chapter 18

Creating a Keynote Presentation

In This Chapter

▶ Using the Keynote window

▶ Creating a simple Keynote presentation

*L*ike all iWork apps, Keynote has its own window features. The basics of the window are the same as for the other apps: a toolbar, a format bar, and an Inspector window. But, as in the other apps, each of those components has customized features for Keynote.

When you compare Keynote to the other apps, you may be able to see that it is the original iWork app: Its interface is the most complex. Partly this is because it has evolved over the longest time, but it's also because presentations can be much more complex than Pages documents or Numbers spreadsheets. When you prepare a presentation well, you bring together the information to be presented along with visuals and slides of text. The presentation can involve notes for yourself as well as a structured sequence of slides. By organizing the presentation in this way, you provide the most interesting and useful presentation.

Perhaps you've had the experience of sitting through a presentation in which the speaker reads every word on every slide: It quickly becomes tedious. Organizing your presentation into separate components of visuals, speaker's notes, planned discussion topics, and time for questions can provide a useful and interesting presentation for your audience — and for yourself.

This chapter is the overview of the basic Keynote tools that help you create and present your Keynote presentations.

Exploring the Keynote Window

Everyone prepares a Keynote presentation differently. There is no one right way — not for a specific topic, not for a specific audience, and not for a specific speaker. The Keynote window is flexible enough to let you work in the way that's easiest for you.

The Keynote window has six major areas that you can show or hide. If you hide an area, however, the information in that area remains in the presentation. If you hide the presenter notes, for example, that's all you've done: hidden them. Want to see them again (perhaps during your presentation)? Just display them. You don't lose anything.

The Keynote window lets you work on a presentation. When it comes time to present the presentation, you can use the techniques in Chapter 19.

As with other iWork apps, an area to the left of the window provides quick access to the structure of your document. This area, called the Navigator, is shown in Figure 18-1.

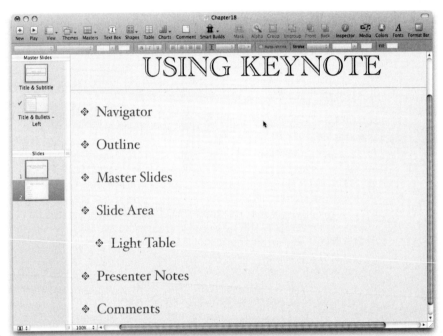

Figure 18-1:
Use the
Keynote
window.

The Navigator

The Navigator has two components: master slides and slides. Slides are always displayed, but the display of master slides is optional.

You create the slides for your presentation using the New button on the toolbar or by choosing Slide⇨New Slide. As you add information to the slides, you can rearrange them by dragging them up or down in the Navigator.

Remember that the structure of a slide is part of Keynote; this means you can select a slide and switch its slide master to another format. You may have to do some reformatting, but you won't lose any data.

You can show slide masters using the View menu on the toolbar (or the View menu in the menu bar). If you've shown them, the appropriate slide master appears with a check mark next to it when you select a slide that uses that slide master.

Slide outlines

If you choose to show slide outlines, the Keynote view changes as shown in Figure 18-2. You can show slides and slide masters together, but neither of them can be shown with slide outlines. Compare the slide in the main section of the window in Figure 18-2 with the outline shown at the left. The outline is generated automatically from the slide's total text, including bullets.

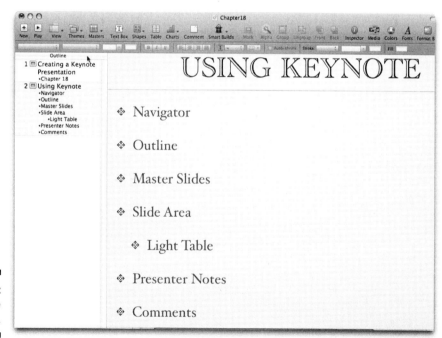

Figure 18-2:
View slide outlines.

This automatic synchronization between slides and outlines works in both directions. For example, in Figure 18-3 a new inner bullet is being typed (*Basic Sli* is all that has been typed so far). As you type in the slide outline area, the appropriate text and bullet appear in the main slide.

Bullets in Keynote presentations, like outlines and bullets in Pages documents, rely on the tab key. To indent some text for an outline or bullet, just tab to the indented position. To outdent (that is, move a bullet up), use Shift-tab. With bulleted or outlined text selected, use the Bullets tab of Text inspector to choose the image for the bullet and to verify the indent level.

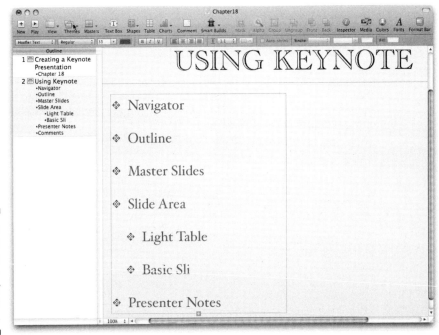

Figure 18-3:
Type the slide outline and automatically update the slide.

When you're creating slides, sometimes it makes sense to bounce between typing in a slide and typing in a slide outline. The outline helps to show you the structure of the slide, and that outline sometimes makes gaps and omissions easier to see and quickly repair.

Master slides

Each Keynote theme has its own master slides, and many themes have variations on some of the master slides (usually marked with *Alt* for *alternate*). To make your Keynote presentation consistent, display the slide masters, and then scroll through them, deleting the ones you won't be using. That way you'll limit your slide masters to a smaller and consistent set.

The light table

If you're used to arranging slides, you may have used a light table — either an actual light table lit from below or one generated by software. In Keynote, you can move slides around as shown in Figure 18-4. This is also another way of doing a consistency check. As you organize your slides into a logical sequence, you'll quickly be able to see if something about the sequence is distracting (perhaps a repeated graphic or too many bulleted slides in a row).

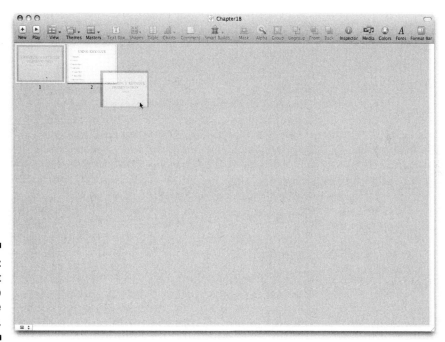

Figure 18-4:
Use a light table to organize your slides.

Presenter notes

One of the techniques that skilled presenters use is presenter notes, as shown in Figure 18-5. Presenter notes can provide you with reminders of questions to ask as well as issues to raise. Don't bother providing a preview of the next slide. In most cases, you can use Keynote's presenter's display (discussed in the next chapter) so that you can see where you're going next.

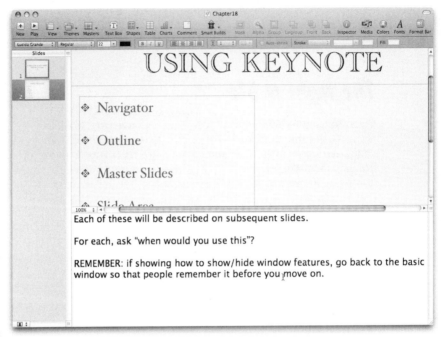

Figure 18-5:
Use
presenter
notes.

If you have good speaker's notes, your presentation is a combination of the slides and your talk. If you rely on your memory, you may find that you're putting everything onto a slide so you don't forget it; that means you will have little to add and will soon bore your audience.

Your speaker's notes shouldn't be too long; otherwise you'll spend too much time reading them and not talking to your audience. You can enlarge the speaker's notes pane at the bottom of the window so that there's more room. This is useful as you're preparing your presentation. When you're actually presenting it, if you use the speaker's display as described in the next chapter, there's plenty of room for speaker's notes alongside the full image of each slide.

Comments

Each iWork application allows you to add comments; those for Keynote appear much like sticky notes, as shown in Figure 18-6.

Comments are free-format; you can place them anywhere on a slide. The best use for them in a Keynote presentation is as a reminder of something still to be done to prepare the presentation. Don't use comments for speaker's notes; they won't show up with other speaker's notes on the speaker's display and can easily be overlooked.

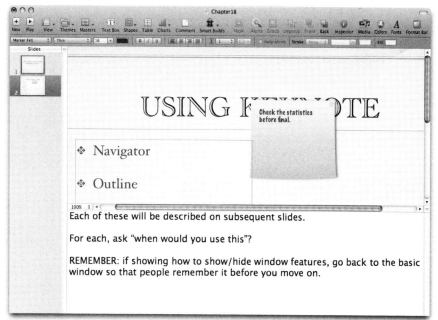

Figure 18-6:
Use
comments.

Creating Your Own Keynote Presentation

You can create a Keynote presentation in many ways, depending on the content, the audience, and yourself. I give various presentations on a number of topics; here's one technique that I use:

1. **Identify your subject and audience, and determine the length of your presentation.**

   This last point is critical whether you're creating a presentation or a document. Most projects have a given length: a 50-page document, for example, or a 30-minute presentation. This is a presentation for public library trustees that I've given as a volunteer on a number of occasions for the Clinton-Essex-Franklin Library System in upstate New York (CEFLS).

2. **Choose File⇨New from Theme Chooser to display Theme Chooser, as shown in Figure 18-7.**

Figure 18-7:
Choose a
theme.

3. **Choose a Keynote theme.**

   You don't have to worry much about the theme you choose; unlike templates for Numbers or Pages, you can always switch to another theme as you work.

4. **Use the View menu on the toolbar to show outlines at the left of the window, as shown in Figure 18-8.**

Figure 18-8:
Show
outlines.

5. Start to type the outline, as shown in Figure 18-9.

At this point, you may just want to type your main points. You can rear-range and reword them as you proceed.

6. Review each slide by selecting it. Change the slide master if desired.

To change the slide master, select a slide and use the Masters menu on the toolbar. Figure 18-10 shows the third slide; it has been properly for-matted with bullets from the outline, so you don't need to do anything else.

7. Check for and correct overflowing text.

The second slide has more content than fits on the slide (see the + box in the center of the bottom in Figure 18-11).

8. Check the revised slide.

As shown in Figure 18-13, the two-column layout works well to solve the spacing issue. In addition, by sheer luck, the two columns have a logic to them (libraries on the left, the system on the right). You may have to perform manual adjustments with return characters to provide a logical two-column structure.

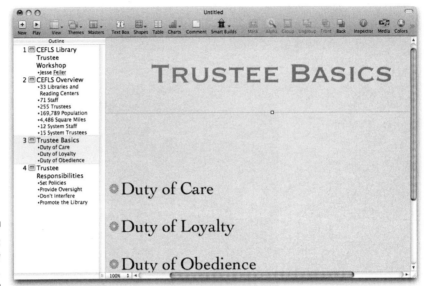

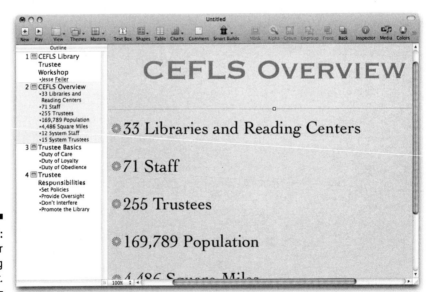

You can fix the overflow text by splitting the slide into two.
Alternatively, choose a new slide master, as shown in Figure 18-12.

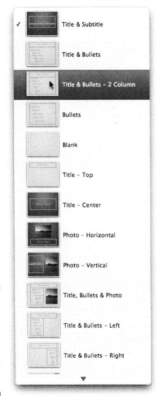

Figure 18-12:
Choose a slide master with multiple columns.

Don't think that this is a text-first process. It starts with the outline but then bounces back to the layout of slides. As you check the formatting, you'll need to reformat some slides and split some into two (or more). Remember that you're dealing with a limited amount of space. A book's section can vary from a few pages to 20 or more, but a slide is a slide is a slide.

Many things follow from the standard size of slides. Not the least is the fact that you can keep track of your presentation's length. For a given speaker and a given presentation, you can probably use a standard amount of time for each slide. Too much time and people get antsy; too little time means those slides come quickly one after the other. Everyone uses their own techniques. (I plan on five minutes per slide.)

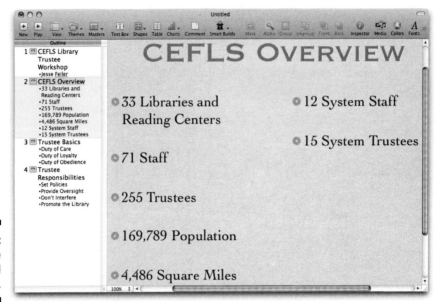

Figure 18-13:
Review the
reformatted
slide.

Like any presentation software, Keynote allows you to specify transitions for slides. The basic process outlined here uses default transitions. It's one of the fastest ways to get your presentation on its feet so you can try it out for a test audience.

In the next chapter you see how to present your work. Then, in Chapter 20, you find out about some advanced techniques for slide transitions.

Chapter 19

Presenting a Keynote Presentation

In This Chapter

▶ Using the Presenter Display

▶ Controlling your presentation with your iPhone

*U*nlike Numbers spreadsheets and Pages documents, Keynote presentations aren't designed to be given to someone to read or study: You're a key component of your Keynote presentation. Sometimes you prepare a presentation for someone else to use or vice versa. But most of the time, you run the show, stage center. Fortunately, Keynote has a host of tools that make it easy for you to fulfill the dual roles of presentation author and presenter. This chapter gives you an overview of those tools.

Choosing Your Presentation Options

The earliest presentation software tools used the computer monitor to display slides. Often, a second monitor, frequently a projection TV, was connected. Keynote lets you select your primary display (usually the projection TV) and configure the other one with timers and presenter's notes.

With the advent of iWork '09, you have another way of working with Keynote — at least if you have an iPhone. You can download Keynote Remote, an app for iPhone and iPod Touch. It's available from the App Store in iTunes and currently costs $0.99. You can use the iPhone or iPod Touch, both of which communicate wirelessly with the computer running Keynote, to control the slides. Another wrinkle in this scenario is that speaker's notes can be visible along with the slide on your iPhone or iPod Touch. This means you have two displays for presenter's notes and other non-slide information: the presenter's display on a computer as well as your iPhone or iPod Touch. You see how to use all these features.

iPhone/iPod Touch

Most apps that run on iPhone also run on iPod Touch provided they don't use the telephony features of iPhone. Rather than using the phrase "iPhone or iPod Touch," from this point on, I simply refer to iPhone. A great deal of complicated forestry analysis has determined that this shortening of the phrase will save 43.25 trees. Again, unless used in the context of telephony, *iPhone* includes *iPod Touch.*

Setting Presentation Preferences

You can set preferences for how Keynote handles multiple displays, for how the slideshow will be managed, for the presenter's display (if you have multiple displays), and for using a remote (if you have one). In most cases, the default preferences for iWork apps are fine. However, when it comes to customizing your environment — particularly if you're using multiple displays — you need to pay attention to these settings.

Setting preferences for two displays

Laptops and iMacs have built-in displays; desktop Macs do not. All Macs have a plug for another display in addition to the built-in display or the main display for a desktop Mac. You use System Preferences⇨Displays to manage the displays on your computer. Three basic display configurations are available:

✔ **Single display:** You have a single display, built-in or not. All windows you open with any program on your Mac are shown on this display. You can move them around, but you can't totally move a window off a single display. (You can minimize it in the dock, but it remains part of the main window.)

✔ **Mirrored display:** This configuration allows you to have two displays connected to your computer. In the Displays section of System Preferences, use the Mirror Displays check box to ensure that the same image appears on both displays. When it comes to presentations, many times the second display for a computer is a projection TV. By mirroring the displays, you can work with the computer's display as you normally would, and the mirrored display (the projection TV) displays that image in an enlarged version.

✔ **Separate displays:** The Displays section of System Preferences shows all screens attached to your computer (some people have more than two!). Only one of them shows a menu bar at the top of the screen. Drag that menu bar to the primary screen. Often the primary screen will be your desktop or laptop screen; the secondary screen (without the menu bar) can be used for other windows that you can use for your work.

If you're going to be giving a Keynote presentation that uses two screens, try to use Displays in System Preferences before you're ready to begin. If you can get to the presentation area ten minutes before the audience arrives, you can arrange screens so that they see what's important. If you can't do this, temporarily create a new user account on your computer, and copy your presentation and any other needed files to that user's Public folder. Do this without connecting to any publicly visible screen. Then, log on as the new user. The desktop will be empty and the only visible files will be your presentation. If you need to move files around and adjust the screen layout, you can do this without everyone looking at the files you have on your computer. Still, the better choice is to use your actual account and set things up before the audience arrives.

Regardless of how you arrange the screens, use Energy Saver to prevent the screen from dimming. If you're using a laptop, plug it in. You'll use a bit more power, but you won't have to jiggle the mouse button to prevent the computer from going to sleep.

Like all iWork applications, you can set preferences for Keynote. Begin by choosing Keynote⇨Preferences to open the Preferences window shown in Figure 19-1.

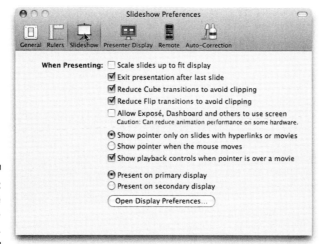

Figure 19-1:
Set Keynote preferences.

The General, Rulers, and Auto-Correction preferences are standard for all iWork apps. The ones that matter for your presentations are Slideshow, Presenter Display, and Remote. I go over each in this section.

Slideshow preferences

The Slideshow preferences are shown in Figure 19-1. Here are the choices for you to consider about those preferences:

- ✔ **Scale slides up:** This option scales (that is, enlarges) the slides to fill the display. Particularly on a projection TV, you have plenty of space to play with, so you might as well use it. However, if your presentation will be made at different times on different size displays, you may want to reset this preference for the display just before you give your presentation.

- ✔ **Exit presentation after last slide:** Consider what will happen at the end of your presentation. If you exit the presentation, there you'll be (along with your audience), looking at your desktop and the files on it. Consider placing a special slide at the end of the presentation. It can be a simple "The End" slide, but you can also make it more useful. "For more info, contact XXX" provides a neutral final slide that can remain visible until the last person has left the room.

- ✔ **Minimize distractions from transitions and other applications:** That's the idea behind reducing Cube transitions, reducing Flip transitions, and not allowing Exposé, Dashboard, and other apps to intrude on your Keynote presentation.

- ✔ **Set pointer preferences:** You have three pointer preferences. If you're used to pointing with the pointer, use the option to show the pointer when the mouse moves. (The alternative is to have a separate pointer for your presentation, which seems like overkill.)

- ✔ **Choose the display for slides:** If you have more than one display, choose the one for slides to appear on. If you have a single display or a mirrored display, you don't have a choice. Otherwise, choose the display that is connected to a projection TV. It doesn't matter if it's a primary or secondary display: Keynote will do the right thing.

Also consider a special introductory slide that can play as a movie before your presentation begins. Create a movie or an iPhoto slideshow from relevant photos and images. You can add music. If you watch various presentations, you'll see that such introductory movies or slideshows can consist of excerpts from previous presentations, promotional materials, or even advertisements. Your goal is to provide a lead-in to your presentation.

Presenter Display preferences

Figure 19-2 shows the Presenter Display preferences. The Presenter Display is available only if you have two displays connected to your computer or if you're using Keynote Remote on an iPhone, but the Presenter Display preferences are available even if you only have one display at the time you're setting the preferences. This means you can configure your Presenter Display preferences before you get to the auditorium with the big projection display.

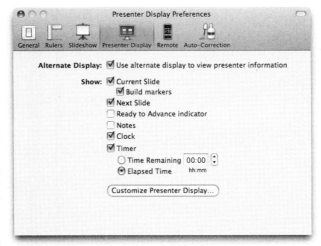

Figure 19-2:
Set
Presenter
Display
prefer-
ences.

In addition to customizing the Presenter Display preferences, you can format the presenter's display by using the Customize Presenter Display button at the bottom of the Presenter Display Preferences screen. Click that button to open the window shown in Figure 19-3; drag items to rearrange them on the presenter's display.

If you're accustomed to giving presentations, two features are absolute gifts. The first is the time. Elapsed time for a slide is useful, but if your presentation is scheduled from, say, 2:00 to 2:45, knowing the exact time can help you speed up as needed or stop for a Q&A period if you see that there's time to spare. Of course, you don't need Keynote to do this: You can step up to the podium and take your watch off so you can keep track of time. There is a technical word for this frequently repeated gesture: tacky. It's almost as bad as a speaker rifling through the remaining pages of a speech to see how much material is left. Keynote hides what should be hidden and shows it to you if and when you need it.

Equally valuable is the ability to see the next slide. Transitions from one slide to another are often left to the speaker, as in "But how does that work in practice?" or "What's a good example of this?" If you see the next slide cued up, you can make the appropriate transition.

Another feature of the Presenter Display is shown in Figure 19-4: You can add presenter's notes to the display. By being able to see the current slide and the next slide along with notes you have prepared, everything you need for your presentation is in front of you without distracting the audience.

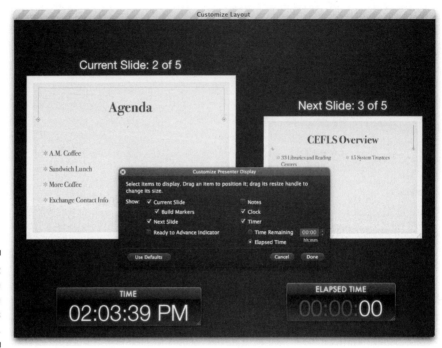

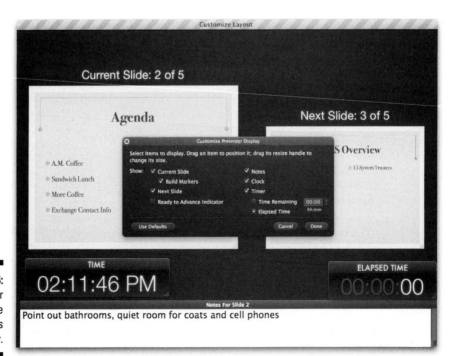

You enter presenter's notes for a slide by choosing View➪Show Presenter Notes or clicking View on the toolbar. This preference controls where and if the presenter's notes you've entered for slides are shown on the presenter's display.

Remote preferences

As mentioned, with iWork '09 you can control presentations and view presenter's notes by downloading the Keynote Remote application from iTunes and installing it on your iPhone or iPod Touch.

Launch a Keynote presentation on your computer, and then launch Keynote Remote on your iPhone. You'll be asked to make a connection to your computer. The iPhone will locate a nearby computer running Keynote, and Keynote will ask you to confirm the connection, as shown in Figure 19-5. If you want to connect to that iPhone, click the Link button at the right.

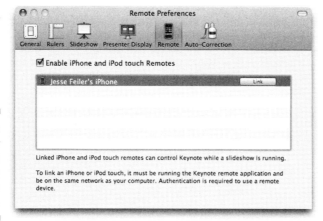

Figure 19-5:
Accept (or decline) the invitation to link to an iPhone.

When you click Link, a code is displayed on Keynote Remote on your iPhone. Type that code as shown in Figure 19-6.

The connection between iPhone and Keynote is now complete. You'll see the first slide of the current presentation on your iPhone. Buttons on the screen let you skip to the beginning or end of the presentation. For standard movement, just use your finger to drag the current slide aside on your iPhone. You don't need to touch your computer.

Add Remote for iPhone and iPod touch

Please enter the passcode displayed on your Keynote Remote to
allow it to control Keynote.

6 9 2 ☐

Cancel

Figure 19-6:
Accept the
pairing.

An option on Keynote Remote shows presenter notes below the slides on
your iPhone. This means you now have two places for presenter's notes: on
the computer or on an iPhone.

Using your iPhone means that you can wander around more: The computer
with its projection TV output doesn't need hands-on attention from you
because you're driving the slides from your iPhone. However, now that
you're untethered from the computer, you can no longer use the mouse to
point to parts of a slide. (You could use a laser pointer or a wooden pointer.)

Another mixed blessing is the absence of a presenter's display. You can have
speaker's notes on Keynote Remote, but if you like being able to see the next
slide, that feature is available only from an alternate display on your computer. The feature that shows you the current time is available on Keynote
Remote, in the top center of the iPhone screen as always.

Chapter 20

Improving Your Keynote Presentation

In This Chapter

▶ Adding motion

▶ Adding sound and packaging your presentation

*W*hen it comes to Numbers and Pages, you have a variety of choices for sharing your documents. But those choices are insignificant next to the choices for sharing and automating Keynote presentations. This chapter shows you some of the features you can add to your presentations. Because presentations involve text, images, and a variety of media components, you can export them to any of the movie and DVD formats available on your Mac. You can also share them through the Web — using the various iLife apps as well as Web-sharing sites such as YouTube.

In general, the features you can add using Keynote transfer without effort to these other formats and platforms. The first part of this chapter shows you how to add Keynote features for motion, sound, and automation to your presentation.

Creating Different Types of Presentations

The Keynote themes are interchangeable, and each has certain basic slides that suggest the types of presentations you can create. It's easy to fall into a trap of thinking that these are the only types of presentations you can create with Keynote. This section will give you some additional ideas.

Reviewing the slide masters

First of all, Figure 20-1 shows the basic slide masters available in Keynote, although remember that some themes have alternate versions.

Figure 20-1:
Explore
Keynote's
slide
masters.

You don't have to use all the slide masters in a given theme. Here are some of the types of presentations you can create with the various themes and slide masters:

✔ **Basic structured presentations:** These are presentations that emphasize content and organization. They typically use bulleted lists of information. Keynote's organizing tools help people follow your presentation without getting lost.

✔ **Catalogs, albums, and event presentations:** These tend to use slide masters with space for photos. Whereas basic structured presentations tend to use bulleted lists to create a hierarchical structure, these presentations have a less hierarchical structure. Their organizing structure can be chronological (a wedding day, for example) or informational (a product catalog is a good example).

✔ **Creative presentations:** Keynote is part of iWork, but that doesn't mean you can't use it to explore your creative side. You can merge the structure of bulleted slides with images for an art appreciation presentation. You can also use a Keynote presentation to tell a story or create a scrapbook. Depending on your resources and your audience, it may be easier to construct your story as a Keynote presentation than as an iPhoto slideshow. One deciding factor may be whether you have photos and video that you can use in telling your story. If you don't, Keynote, with its excellent handling of text, can be more effective than iPhoto.

Planning your presentation

Different types of presentations lend themselves to different types of interactions with their audiences. Keynote lets you package and automate your presentation. Most people find that self-running presentations work well for catalogs and albums; they can stand on their own, like advertisements or magazine articles.

Complex structured presentations such as those used at trade shows or in classrooms often don't work well as self-running presentations. Instead, having someone (probably you) control the presentation and stop for questions and discussions can help get the message across.

The choices are built into Keynote, mostly through its themes, so it's just a matter of experimenting with your options to find the most effective method for your own presentation.

One way to improve your Keynote presentations is to watch other presentations. What interests you? What do you like? If there's a live audience, watch them and see what they like. There are no hard-and-fast rules. A presentation designed for a college class is different from one designed for a Bridal Faire (and not just in spelling of the title). Some presentations benefit from a serious approach, while others work well with humor and added features.

Adding Motion to Your Presentation

Your Keynote slideshows can use motion in three ways. This can make the slideshow more interesting and keep people's attention. (Or it can be distracting: Use your judgment.)

Here are the three basic ways to add motion to your Keynote presentation:

- ✔ Insert a QuickTime movie onto a slide.
- ✔ Add transitions between slides.
- ✔ Add builds within slides.

Adding a movie to a slide

The most basic way of adding movement to your presentation is to add a QuickTime movie to a slide. Here's how you do it:

1. **Click Media on the toolbar to open Media Browser, from which you can choose movies, photos, and audio, as shown in Figure 20-2.**

Figure 20-2: Add a movie to your presentation.

2. **Drag the movie into the slide where you want it.**

   Remember that in Media Browser, the movie is shown as a single-frame thumbnail image. When you drag it into a slide, it appears either as a shape with the typical eight handles or as the movie itself (not the thumbnail). That's why you see the FlorenceMovie.mov thumbnail in Figure 20-2, and part of the movie itself in Figure 20-3.

Figure 20-3:
Position the movie on the slide.

3. **Select the QuickTime movie on the slide and use QuickTime inspector, as shown in Figure 20-4, to set up the movie.**

   Depending on the movie, you may want to vary the settings shown in Figure 20-4. If the movie is to start with a click, most likely you'll want to set a poster frame so that a still image is visible on your slide before the movie starts playing. If you're using the movie for an introductory or final slide, you may want to set the Repeat options so that the movie loops over and over or loops back and forth. If you're using the movie as part of your presentation (that is, as a movie to be played from start to finish with the click of a mouse), you probably don't want any looping.

Figure 20-4:
Use
QuickTime
inspector to
set up the
movie.

Adding a transition between slides

Another way to add motion to your presentation is to use one of the transition effects between two adjacent slides. Here's how to do that:

1. **Select the slide for the transition.**

   The transition will come into play when you move from this slide to the next one.

2. **Click the Slide button in Slide inspector and then click the Transition tab, as shown in Figure 20-5.**

Figure 20-5:
Use Slide
inspector
and the
Transition
tab to set up
a transition.

3. **Select the transition you want from the list of effects shown in Figure 20-6.**

   Not all effects are available on all computers (some require advanced video cards). Try to avoid turning your presentation into a presentation about transitions. If you limit your transitions to a few, and if you choose consistent directions, you'll find that your transitions serve your presentation rather than the other way around.

Figure 20-6:
Select the transition and its direction.

One technique many presenters use is to home in on two or three transitions, each of which plays a distinct role. For example, if your presentation is highly structured, you might want to use a dramatic transition such as a 3-D effect to introduce each major section of the presentation. Then, within each major section, use simpler 2-D effects for minor transitions. If you're consistent with the use of transitions, they add to your presentation.

As you can see from Figure 20-6, transitions are available that use text and graphics so that you can move from one slide to another without causing distraction. One interesting transition is Magic Move, which you use when you have the same object, such as a text box, on both slides that are part of the transition. If the same object appears on both slides in different locations,

Keynote performs a transition that appears to move the object from its location on the first slide to its location on the second slide. This transition is powerful when you're discussing the object and its text or graphics.

Adding builds within slides

Builds work within a single slide; they let you bring slide items such as bullets onto the slide with animation effects.

Builds have three aspects: Build In (for items appearing on the slide), Build Out (for items disappearing from the slide), and Action.

You set the builds as follows:

1. **Begin with the complete slide.**

   Make certain that all bullets, titles, and graphics are visible.

2. **Open Build inspector, as shown in Figure 20-7.**

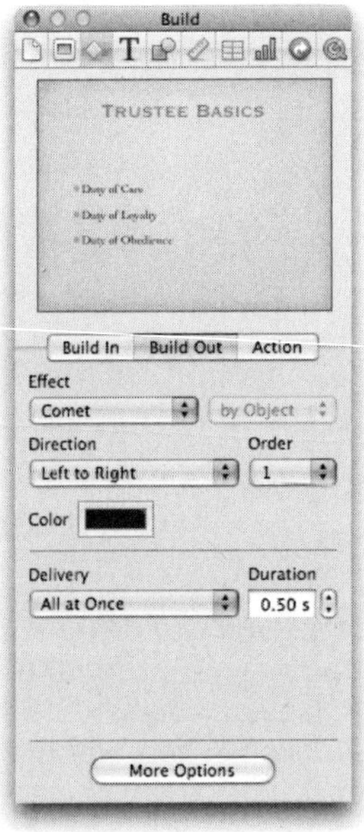

Figure 20-7:
Build
inspector.

3. **On the slide itself, select the first item to build (it doesn't matter if it's built in or out).**

   With the item (such as a bullet) selected, choose Build In or Build Out, and then choose an effect, a direction, an order, and a color. The order determines the sequence in which builds are performed.

   The Delivery option lets you set items within a group: all at once, by bullet, by bullet group (such as a subgroup), and by highlighted bullet. Watch out, because this is an area where you can obscure the content of your presentation with too many and too varied builds.

4. **Using the same process, select all the build ins and build outs you want.**

   You don't need to have both build ins and build outs. In many cases, a single style of build is more than enough.

5. **Use effects for movement that may be less structured than the sliding in and out of a build.**

   Figure 20-8 shows the available effects. Letters and images will appear from all directions in many of these effects.

Figure 20-8:
Select an
effect.

Adding Sound to Your Presentation

You can add sound to your presentation in three ways:

- ✔ **QuickTime movies:** If you're adding a movie to your presentation, that movie can have a soundtrack and you can play it with the movie.

- ✔ **Voice-over slideshow recording:** You can prerecord your narration of a presentation. This prerecording adds a soundtrack; it also automatically saves the timing of slides so that they are synchronized with your soundtrack. By adding a soundtrack like this, your presentation is playable automatically.

- ✔ **iTunes music for a soundtrack:** You can add iTunes music to your presentation.

Recording a slideshow

To add a voice-over soundtrack, begin with the Audio tab of Document inspector, as shown in Figure 20-9.

Figure 20-9:
Use
Keynote's
Document
inspector.

Click the Record button in the Slideshow Recording section at the bottom of the window. You walk through the presentation; in the upper left, a sound level appears as you speak, as shown in Figure 20-10. Keynote keeps track of when you have advanced to the next slide so that the presentation and the soundtrack are both recorded.

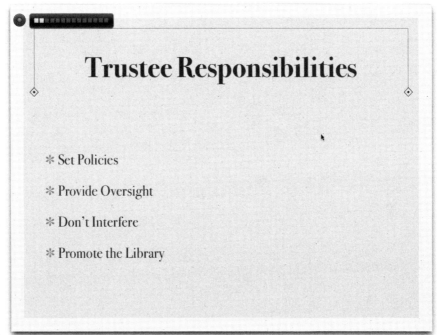

Using the recorded slideshow

Figure 20-11 shows how you can use Document inspector with a recorded presentation. The Presentation pop-up menu includes a Recorded option and a Self-Playing option after you have recorded the presentation. Together with the option to automatically play when the Keynote document is opened, you have a powerful self-running presentation.

Adding an iTunes song

You can add an iTunes track to your presentation (refer to Figure 20-9). You can use the looping feature to repeat it behind all the slides. Note that adding an iTunes song is in addition to the ability to use Media Browser's Audio tab (click Media on the toolbar and then click the Audio tab) to add an iTunes track to an individual slide.

Part V
The Part of Tens

The 5th Wave   By Rich Tennant

"He seemed nice, but I could never connect with someone who didn't have iWork on his Macbook."

In this part . . .

The chapters in this part are top ten lists. They provide you with ways to share content (a much-enhanced feature of iWork '09) and ways to let iWork do the work for you with Automator and AppleScript.

The features described in this part of the book apply to all iWork applications. It makes for a full circle with Part I, which also applies to all iWork applications.

If you come away with the impression that iWork has a powerful set of commands and features available in any of its applications, that's good. The differences between Numbers, Pages, and Keynote reflect their specific objectives, but what you have in iWork is perhaps the most robust and full-featured user interface for productivity tools that has yet been created.

Chapter 21

Ten Ways to Share Content

*Y*ou don't have to start from scratch every time you create an iWork document. You can build on other documents you've created, and you can build on the templates that are part of iWork. You can also include content that has been created with other applications. iWork and Mac OS X make it easy to reuse your work. This chapter provides you with ten ways to accomplish that goal.

There are two basic ways to share content:

✔ **Copying content:** You can copy content to a flash drive or other place from which you and others can retrieve it.

✔ **Accessing content:** You can provide a mechanism that lets people access the data. You don't copy the data: There is one file, and everyone accesses it. This eliminates problems with data synchronization because there are no copies.

Sharing Content with MobileMe

MobileMe is Apple's subscription-based service that provides email addresses (yourname@me.com) along with disk storage on Apple's servers. MobileMe is integrated with many features of Mac OS X. For example, your calendars and Address Book entries can be automatically synchronized between your Mac and your iPhone. Your iDisk, which is part of MobileMe, appears as just another folder in your Finder window. With the sophisticated synchronization features of the second version of the iPhone, more and more iPhone users are using MobileMe.

MobileMe lets you use a Web browser to access your calendars, Address Book, and me.com email. You also can access disk storage that comes with MobileMe. You can use this disk storage for backups; you can also use it to share files with other people.

If you have a MobileMe account, your Web storage (called iDisk) can be accessed in a browser window (see in Figure 21-1).

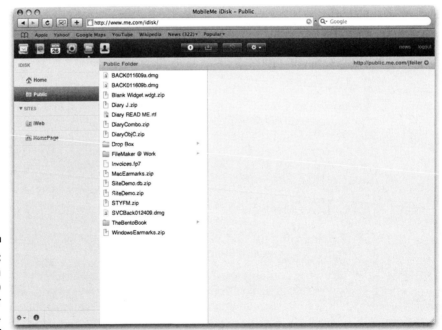

Figure 21-1:
Use a browser to access your iDisk.

You can also access your iDisk using the Finder on a Mac, as shown in Figure 21-2.

Figure 21-2:
Use a Finder window to access iDisk.

If you don't see your iDisk in the Finder window, choose Finder⇨Preferences to open the dialog shown in Figure 21-3. Make certain that iDisk is checked.

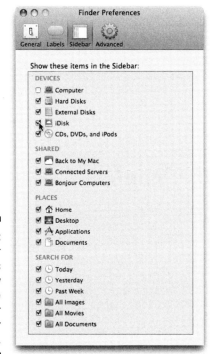

Figure 21-3:
Use Finder Preferences to show iDisk in the sidebar of Finder windows.

You can drag files or folders to your Public folder on your iDisk so that other people can share them. In the MobileMe section of System Preferences, shown in Figure 21-4, you can determine how people can access your Public folder on your iDisk (read only or read and write, as well as whether or not they need a password to log on).

Figure 21-4:
People can log on to your MobileMe Public folder.

People can access your Public folder on your iDisk by choosing Go⇨iDisk⇨ Other User's Public Folder. If necessary, they will be prompted for the Public folder password you set. They can also choose Go⇨iDisk⇨Other User's iDisk, which does use this special Public folder password. Instead, they need your full iDisk account name password, which you should always be hesitant to give out.

Sharing Content with People on Your Network

If you are working on a local network, letting people access your Public folder is handled differently than when you're using MobileMe on the Web.

If you want to allow other people on your network to access your Public folder, choose System Preferences⇨Sharing to open the pane shown in Figure 21-5.

Figure 21-5:
Set sharing
privileges
for public
folders
on your
computer.

The settings in Figure 21-5 determine what other people can see when they navigate to your public folder. Figure 21-6 shows the view of your home directory that you can see yourself.

Figure 21-6:
Set privileges for
folders.

With the default settings for your folders in place, other users would see the folders but not be able to see inside them. The Public folder's sharing preferences are set as shown in Figure 21-5. The result is shown in Figure 21-7. Users can see only a drop box folder inside the Public folder. A special icon next to Jesse Feiler's Public Folder indicates that it's a drop box. Anyone can drop files and folders into the drop box, but they cannot see the contents — even if the contents consist of files and folders that they have dropped into the drop box. For a drop box, no users (except the owner) can see inside the folder. That includes all information, including the modification date, which is not shown in Figure 21-7.

Figure 21-7: View access to a drop box folder inside someone's Public folder; there's nothing to see if you're not the owner.

Sometimes you need to log on to another user's folder on your network with a different user ID than the one you are currently logged in with. (This could happen if you have saved settings in KeyChain and now want to log on with a different ID.) Here's how you do it:

1. **Log out from the remote server.**

   In the Finder, drag the remote server to the trash. Or select it, ⌘-click to open the contextual menu, and choose Eject. A third method is to click the eject button next to the remote server's name in the Finder sidebar.

2. **Log on again with the new ID you want to use.**

   Click the Network icon, as shown in Figure 21-8.

Figure 21-8: Connect again.

3. **Make certain you log on as a registered user, as shown in Figure 21-9.**

Figure 21-9:
Log on with
the correct
password
and user ID.

Sharing Content on iWeb

If you have a MobileMe account, you can share content through iWeb. You can post files automatically to your iWeb blogs from any of the iWork apps, as shown in Figure 21-10. Choose Share⇨Send to iWeb to begin the process. The process continues by letting you select the file type for the file you will be sending to iWeb. After you've uploaded the files, people can download them.

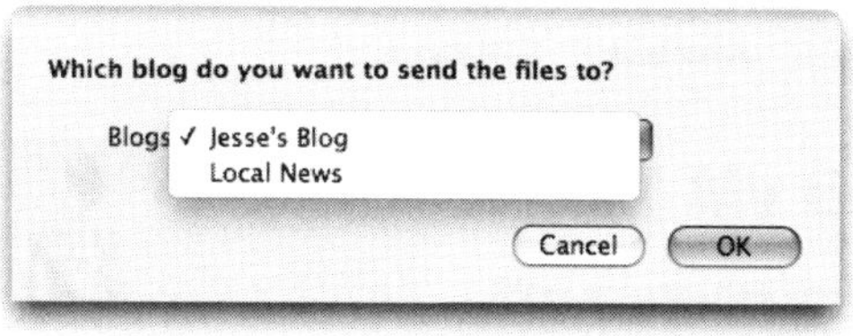

Figure 21-10:
Post files on
your iWeb
blogs.

You can always save an iWork document as a PDF file or its own file type (Numbers, Keynote, or Pages). In addition, Keynote documents can be saved as podcasts.

Sharing Content Using Send To

Share⇨Send via Mail lets you send documents via email. The Send To command lets you send a PDF file or a native iWork file; in addition, you can send the corresponding Microsoft Office file type (Word, Excel, or PowerPoint).

Using Media from iPhoto, iTunes, and iMovie

All of the iWork applications let you insert media from iPhoto, iTunes, or iMovie. Begin by clicking Media on the toolbar to open Media Browser, shown in Figure 21-11.

Figure 21-11:
Use Media
Browser
to insert
media.

The iWork apps have tools to adjust inserted media. These adjustments don't affect the basic media file itself, so you don't have to worry about accidentally making changes to your valued photos, music, and movies.

Using PDF Files as Images

PDF files can serve as images for your iWork documents. Remember that you can save almost any type of document as a PDF file. After the document has been saved as a PDF file, you can insert it in an iWork app. This is a backup strategy for sharing files; iWork apps can open many types of files directly.

For example, the standard File➪Open command in Pages lets you open a Microsoft Word document; Pages takes care of the conversion for you. The PDF strategy works well for any type of document that you can print as a PDF file and that you are not able to open directly in an iWork app.

Adding Hyperlinks to iWork Documents

You can add hyperlinks to iWork documents so that you can click the hyperlink and see the hyperlink's data on the screen. Here's how to add a hyperlink to an iWork document:

1. **In an iWork document, select the text that will become the hyperlink.**

2. **Open Link inspector, as shown in Figure 21-12.**

3. **Select the type of link and then type the link's URL in the inspector.**

Figure 21-12: Use Link inspector to create a hyperlink in an iWork document.

Moving Data from Other Applications into iWork

The all-purpose method for moving data from other applications into iWork is Insert➪Choose. This opens the standard file dialog shown in Figure 21-13. Among the types of files you can open are standard GIF and JPEG files, Photoshop files (.psd), HTML files, and PDF files.

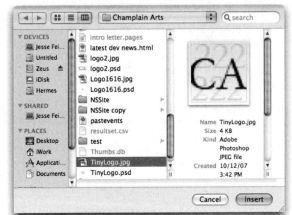

Figure 21-13:
Import a
variety of
file types.

Chapter 22

Ten Ways to Let iWork Do the Work for You

*A*re you pointing and clicking your way through the tasks at hand? With the Mac OS X automation tools, you can specify what you want to do and then have Mac OS X and apps such as the iWork apps carry out your wishes.

A wide variety of automation tools are available. Some construct scripts using scripting languages found not only in Mac OS X but also in other operating systems. Two of the most important Mac OS X–only tools are AppleScript and Automator. They're the jumping-off point for this chapter. After you see the basics of AppleScript and Automator, you find specific ways to use them to automate your iWork projects.

AppleScript's syntax is built into Mac OS X and many applications, including the iWork applications. There are two major components to AppleScript:

Letting iWork do your work

A host of timesaving features are built into the iWork apps. The most obvious are the built-in themes and templates. Instead of starting from a blank document, you can start from a document with built-in pages, sheets, and sections. You don't have to worry about laying out your documents. You can perform the much simpler task of modifying existing documents.

There's a second way to save time with the iWork apps. Rather than retype content, you can copy and paste it from other documents (not just from iWork documents) or drag it over to your new document. This reuse of material

helps you get the most out of your previous analysis and keystrokes (not to mention movies and graphics you've already stored in your media libraries on Mac OS X).

With AppleScript, you have yet another way of saving time. You can construct scripts that create and format sections of iWork applications. These can work together with the built-in themes and templates. To get the most out of iWork (and the most out of your time!), you'll probably want to explore all these ways of working. Use whatever feels most convenient at any given time.

✔ **Script Editor:** This is the primary application that you use to create scripts for AppleScript. It is within the AppleScript folder, which is inside the Applications folder on your hard disk. You don't have to do anything to turn on Script Editor; it's part of the normal Mac OS X installation.

✔ **AppleScript dictionaries:** Every AppleScript-aware application has its own AppleScript dictionary. The AppleScript dictionary for an application is built automatically from the AppleScript commands that the developer supports in the application; no external documentation is required. If AppleScript is supported by the app, the AppleScript dictionary is visible.

Finding and Browsing the Pages AppleScript Dictionary

The first step in using AppleScript is to browse the dictionary for the appropriate application. Here's how to browse the Pages dictionary. As you'll see, it's the first step to scripting the creation of a Pages document.

1. **Launch Script Editor.**

   Choose Applications⇨AppleScript⇨Script Editor. By default, you see the basic window shown in Figure 22-1.

2. **Open the script dictionary by choosing File⇨Open Dictionary.**

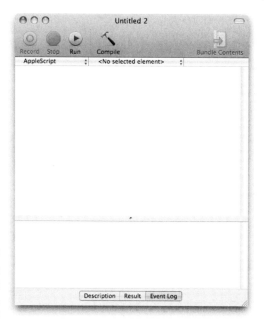

Figure 22-1:
Open Script
Editor.

Locate the application you're looking for, as shown in Figure 22-2. Note that each application has its own version number. In the case of iWork '09 Pages, it's version 4.0. You'll probably find a number of previous versions of your various software products.

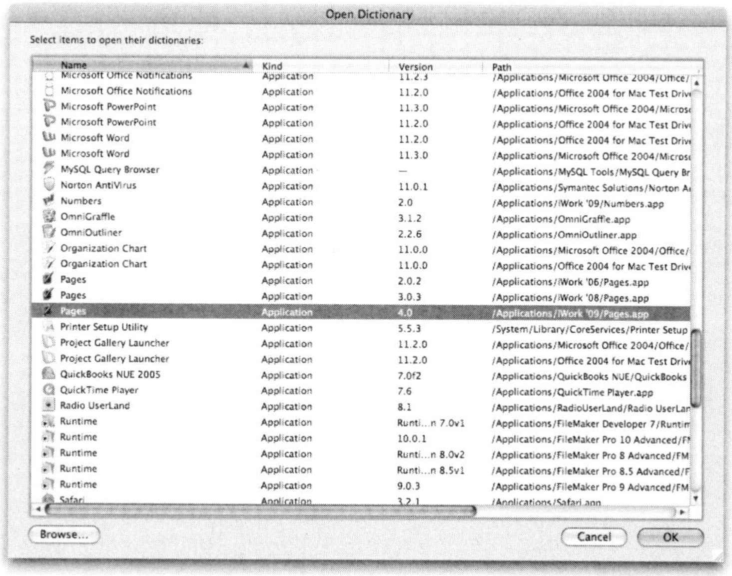

Figure 22-2:
Open the
appropriate
dictionary.

3. **View the suites.**

AppleScript dictionaries are divided into suites, as shown in Figure 22-3. Each suite can have commands (a C in a circle) as well as components (a C in a square). Each has a syntax description.

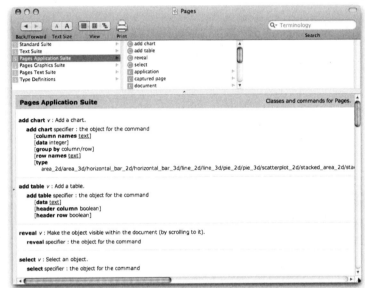

Figure 22-3:
Look at the
suites.

Now that you've briefly looked at the dictionary, you can begin to explore commands to automate your work.

Creating a Script

If you've used any programming languages, you'll find using the syntax for a script even simpler because Script Editor has the full syntax and examples in its Help menu.

Scripts are usually addressed to specific AppleScript objects: These can be applications or objects within applications. (The dictionary tells you what objects are addressable.) Figure 22-4 provides a basic script for use with Pages.

Counting tables on a Pages page

Commands are addressed to scriptable items. Spacing is generated automatically in Script Editor when you click either Run or Compile. If there are syntax errors, the text coloring or spacing (or both) clearly indicates that there's a problem.

The script shown in Figure 22-4 is simple. Here's what's happening:

- ✔ **`tell application "Pages"`:** All commands within this section (called a `tell` *block*), are sent to Pages.

- ✔ **`tell document 1`:** Within Pages, each opened document is given a number automatically when it is opened. 1 is the frontmost document, and Pages makes certain that it receives the next line of code.

- ✔ **`count tables`:** Document 1 is asked to count the number of tables it has.

The dictionary for Pages includes the `count` command in the Standard Suite, as shown in Figure 22-5. As soon as you've spent some time with AppleScript, you'll become familiar with the basic suites such as the Standard Suite. Developers are encouraged to implement the basic parts of AppleScript in the same way for each application. This is made easier because the Mac OS X development framework (Cocoa) handles a lot of this implementation so neither user nor developer needs to worry much about the implementation of the `count` command.

Adding a table to a Pages document

The script shown in Figure 22-6 is a variation on the previous script. It tells the current page to add a table and then to count the resulting number of tables. The code to add the table was shown in Figure 22-3. It's part of the Pages application suite.

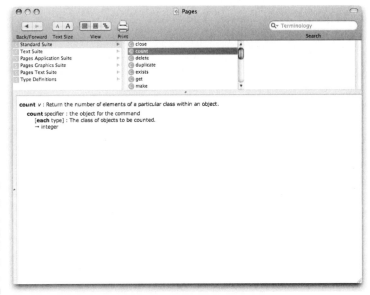

Figure 22-5:
The count
command is
described
in the
dictionary.

This is a fairly typical structure of suites for an AppleScript-enabled application. Suites such as the Standard Suite are implemented by almost all AppleScript-enabled applications. Then a specific application such as Pages is likely to have its own application suite that can act on objects within the application, such as Pages. Further focused suites such as the Pages Graphics Suite and Pages Text Suite handle specific types of operations.

Figure 22-6 shows the script that adds the table.

Figure 22-6:
Tell a docu-
ment to add
a table and
count its
tables.

Retrieving properties about a table in Pages

You can always get properties for objects that are addressable in AppleScript. Figure 22-7 shows you how you can get the properties for the table you just created.

Figure 22-7:
Tell a document to get the properties for a table.

Compare the properties of a table as retrieved through AppleScript with the properties for the same table as shown in Table inspector in Pages. If you really want to get into the nuts-and-bolts of an application like Pages (or any other iWork app), you can get used to this cross-referencing of settings. Often a slightly different terminology is used for an Inspector window than for AppleScript properties. Sometimes the difference in terminology reflects different audiences for interactive users of the software and people who are writing scripts.

Setting properties for a table in Pages (version 1)

As you saw in Figure 22-7, you can get the properties for a table (or any other Pages object). You can set those properties interactively using the Inspector window or using Apple Script. This section shows you one way of setting preferences (you'll find another method in the next section).

In previous scripts, you've seen how you can get or set information through AppleScript. In general, you create a *tell block* to send information to Pages (or whatever app you're dealing with). Within that `tell` block, you send one or more commands to a specific document, and that document is then charged with referencing the table or other object you need to handle. In the previous examples, you've been asking Document 1 to get information about Table 1.

To set properties, you can use the structure shown in Figure 22-8. Here, the same `tell` block sends commands to Pages; within that `tell` block, messages are sent not to Document 1 but instead to Table 1 of Document 1.

Figure 22-8:
Set preferences
(version 1).

A final `tell` block is addressed to Document 1, not to Table 1 of Document 1, because the document needs to retrieve the properties for the table it contains.

The section that sets properties is based on the output shown previously in Figure 22-7. Although you can look up properties in the AppleScript dictionary, the fastest way to find the correct names and spelling of properties is to get the properties for a similar object (such as a table), and use the names and spellings such as those shown in Figure 22-7 as the basis for setting properties as shown in Figure 22-8.

Setting properties for a table in Pages (version 2)

This version of setting properties uses a `tell` block that goes directly to the appropriate document. Instead of dispatching commands to Table 1 of Document 1, the commands are dispatched to Document 1, and those commands reference Table 1, as shown in Figure 22-9.

Neither of these two versions is better than the other; you can use whichever one seems easiest to you at the time.

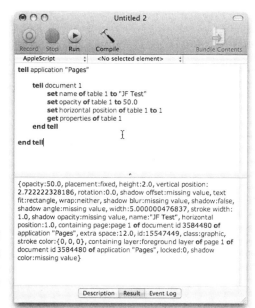

Figure 22-9:
Set pref-
erences
(version 2).

Using Automator with Keynote

One of the other major components of Mac OS X automation is Automator. Like AppleScript, it's installed automatically as part of your operating system. You can find Automator in your Applications folder.

Figure 22-10 shows you the basics of Automator. With Script Editor, you can create scripted code for operations you want to perform. With Automator, you're developing a workflow that brings together sequences of events.

Figure 22-10:
Use
Automator
to import
images to
Keynote
slides.

At the left side of the Automator window are various actions that you can use to build a workflow at the right. When you select an action at the left, its description is shown at the bottom of the window. As you drag it into the workflow area, the actions are added, one to the other. The arrows between the actions indicate that output from one action can flow into the next action as input.

The sample Automator workflow shown in Figure 22-10 lets you select Finder items. It then automatically creates new Keynote slides from each image you've selected.

Using Automator with Images

Automator comes with a number of actions that you can assemble into workflows to handle images. Figure 22-11 shows how you can use three actions in a workflow to prepare images for use in any application (including the iWork applications).

Simply drag these three actions into the workflow. As you drag the scaling and rotating actions, you'll be warned that these actions will permanently affect the files you've selected. Automator not only warns you but also offers to add actions to the workflow to copy the files before they're adjusted. Those steps have been omitted from Figure 22-11 for simplicity.

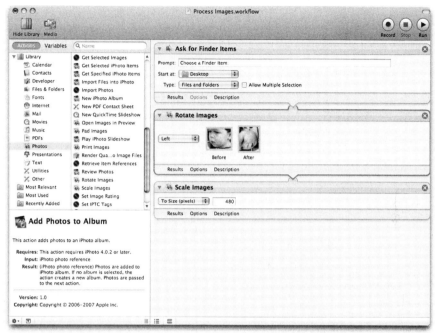

Figure 22-11:
Rotate
and scale
images with
Automator.

This type of workflow can make your use of images more consistent so that they are scaled appropriately.

Using Automator with Multiple Files

Many of your Automator workflows start with the Ask for Finder Items action. You set up the workflow you want to perform, and everything is automatic once you start it running and select the files.

Instead of selecting an individual file, create a folder into which you put a number of files that you want to process. You can put those files into the folder whenever you feel like it — possibly over a period of days. Then, when it comes time to carry out the workflow, start with the Ask for Finder Items action as usual to select the folder, but then insert one of the two actions that can automatically select the individual files:

- ✔ Get Folder Contents. This action starts from the folder you select in Ask for Finder Items, and then takes each file within it and sends the whole set of files into the next action. An option lets you repeat this for subfolders (*recursively*, as programmers would say).

- ✔ Filter Finder Items. Selects all the files within a folder based on criteria you specify, such as the file name (or part of a name) or the type of file.

You can combine both actions so that you get the contents of a folder (and possibly its subfolders), then filter only the JPEG files, and pass them on to image manipulation or to another action, such as Create Image Slide.

Remember that the Finder handles alias files just as it does actual files. This means you can create a folder into which you place aliases of files you want to process in Automator. (To create an alias, select the file and choose File⇨Make Alias or ⌘-L.) You can keep the actual files wherever you would normally store them on your computer. When you've finished with the Automator action, you can trash the folder with the aliases.

Looping Around Automator

Automator excels at combining actions and sending the output from one action into the next one as input. It easily picks up all the items in a folder, possibly filtering them. "All" is an important part of Automator. It means you don't have to write code that is repeated for each folder or other object.

But sometimes that's important. A recent addition to Automator is the Loop action. Along with the Run Workflow action, you can create powerful workflows that can help you with iWork and other applications.

The Loop action lets you run the following action a certain number of times. You can take any action you have already created and run it with Run Workflow. This means that you could modify the workflows suggested previously so that you can make slides from the first 10 JPEG images in a folder. That's a handy workflow to use to test if your slide layout is going to work with those images. When you're satisfied, take out the loop and let the workflow run overnight with 3,000 images.

You can use Loop and Run Workflow to create handouts for a meeting. Create a workflow that prints several documents. You can use Ask for Finder Items, but you have to interact with it (so it can't run unattended). Use Get Specified Finder Items so that you can specify the items you want in advance and the workflow can then run unattended.

For each document that you want to print for the handout, use Get Specified Finder Items to select that one document. In the workflow, place Print Finder Items below it so that document will be printed. Then repeat the process with each document you want for the handout. The workflow will then print them in the order you have specified. Add the Loop action to run that workflow, and you'll have an automated way to print and collate 100 copies of your handouts (provided you don't run out of paper).

Appendix A

Using iWork.com

*i*Work '09 comes with a new feature: a public beta version of iWork.com. This is a new way of sharing your iWork documents as you work on them.

Want to work with two colleagues on a presentation? No big deal: Start by uploading your Keynote document. Then a friend can download it and make changes in the document as a Microsoft PowerPoint document. Back it goes to the Internet, and someone else can download it in yet another format. This is an example of a new trend called *cloud computing.* It's also an example of people being able to work together on their own terms. You don't have to get together and decide which presentation (or spreadsheet or word processing) application you'll all use.

The Share menu (new in iWork '09) lets you send documents from Keynote, Numbers, and Pages via email; it also lets you send an iWork document to GarageBand, iDVD, iTunes, iPhoto, iWeb, and YouTube.

iWork.com adds another way of collaborating on a document. You can post an iWork document to your iWork.com area, where it is visible to you and to people you invite to view it. Those people can then add notes and comments to the documents on the Web.

You can download documents from iWork.com in a variety of formats. This makes two types of interactions possible:

✔ **Comments and notes on iWork documents:** You can add comments to specific parts of iWork documents (a section of text, for example); you can also add notes to the document as a whole (rather than to a specific part of it). As a result, a number of people can work together on a document.

✔ **Multiple revisions to iWork documents:** You can download the documents to your own computer in a variety of formats. Many of these formats include the comments that you and others have added. Once a document is downloaded, it can be modified and more comments can be added describing the modifications.

As the iWork.com public beta proceeds, the software will change. There are indications that Apple may charge for the use of the service at some point, but no formal announcement has been made.

Logging On to iWork.com

When you are using an iWork app, the Share menu allows you to log on to iWork.com as shown in Figure A-1. You need an Apple Account to log on to iWork. If you have a MobileMe subscription account with an email address, your AppleID is your email address, for example, jfeiler@me.com. If you've used the Apple Store or iTunes, you most likely have an Apple account; it may be the same format as a me.com email address, but it could be something different (such as an old-style mac.com email address).

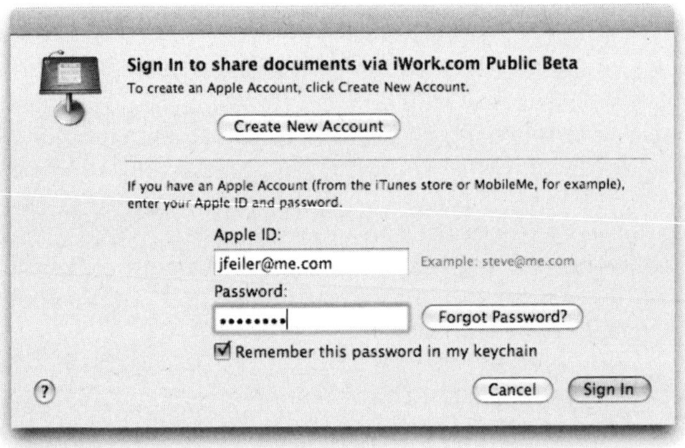

Sign In to share documents via iWork.com Public Beta
To create an Apple Account, click Create New Account.

    Create New Account

If you have an Apple Account (from the iTunes store or MobileMe, for example),
enter your Apple ID and password.

Apple ID:

    jfeiler@me.com   Example: steve@me.com

Password:

    ••••••••   Forgot Password?

☑ Remember this password in my keychain

                              Cancel   Sign In

Figure A-1:
Sign in to
iWork.com.

As you can see in Figure A-1, you can create a new Apple account if you need to. Before you go through that process, check to see whether you have an existing account by logging on to iTunes or the Apple Store. If you don't have an existing account, go ahead and create a new one.

Depending on whether or not you already have an AppleID, the Share menu can take various formats. For example, the Sign In command allows you to log on as shown in Figure A-2.

Figure A-2:
Sign in
with your
AppleID.

If you're already signed in, you can sign out from the Share menu as shown in Figure A-3.

Figure A-3:
Sign out
from the
Share menu.

If you're using a computer in a public area (such as a public library), it makes sense to log out from any private areas that you're using so that the next person using the computer doesn't have access to your data.

Sharing Documents with iWork.com

Choose Share⇨Share via iWork.com to share an open iWork document. You're prompted to specify the ways in which the document can be downloaded, and you're also prompted to supply an email address for your colleague (see Figure A-4).

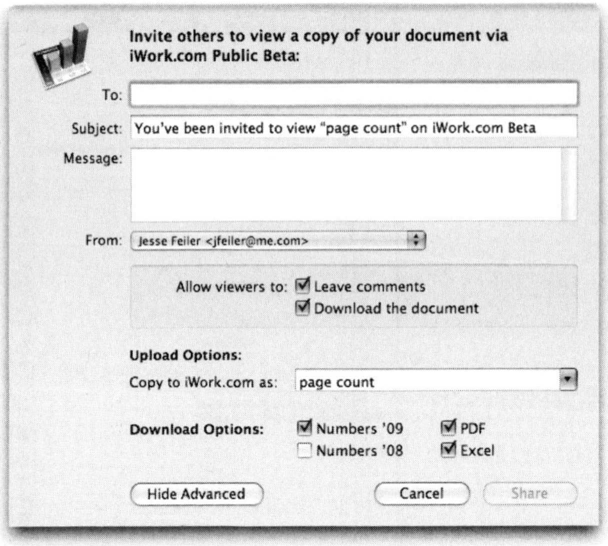

Figure A-4: Prepare documents for sharing on iWork.com.

Viewing Your Shared Documents

After you've logged on, you can choose Share➪Show Shared Documents to open the browser window shown in Figure A-5. (iWork uses the default browser for your computer, and you must have an Internet connection to view your shared documents.)

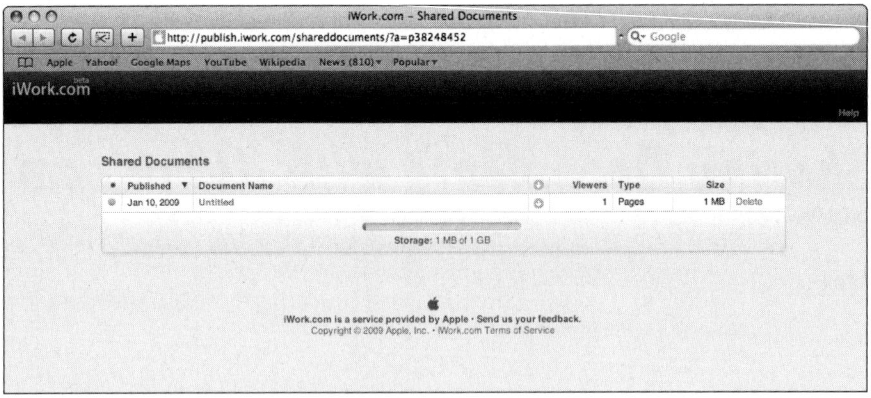

Figure A-5: View shared documents in a browser.

In constructing the Share menu, the iWork application you're using will take note of whether or not you're logged on. In addition, it may post information about notes or changes that have been made, as shown in Figure A-6.

Figure A-6:
The Share
menu
provides
summary
informa-
tion about
changes
to shared
documents
on iWork.
com.

You can download your shared iWork documents from iWork.com. Use
the Download menu at the right to choose a download format as shown in
Figure A-7. You'll find the appropriate iWork format, but you usually also find
cross-platform formats such as PDF as well as Microsoft Office formats such
as PowerPoint, Excel, and Word.

Figure A-7:
Download
your shared
iWork docu-
ment in the
format you
want to use.

In general, changes and comments appear in all formats; document notes on the iWork document itself generally appear only if you download the document as an iWork document.

In the case of complex documents, you may want to save copies of the downloaded files before you make changes to them.

Inviting People to View Shared Documents

You can add individuals to the list of people who can share a document. Click Add at the right of the window shown in Figure A-8. Enter the name and email address for the new person.

Figure A-8: Invite new people to share your documents.

As you can see in Figure A-9, you are given a link that you can send to that person; the link lets the person view the document.

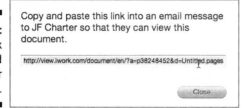

Figure A-9:
Get the link
to send
to your
colleague.

If you ever want to see the link again, select the triangle next to the person's name and email address, as shown in Figure A-10. You can then send it to a colleague who has lost his or her link.

Figure A-10:
You can
always
retrieve the
link.

Adding Document Notes

Someone who is invited to view your document and make changes can add document notes to it. When logged on to iWork.com, he or she simply needs to click Add at the right of the window to add a document note. It will be appropriately identified and time-stamped, as shown in Figure A-11.

Figure A-11:
Add docu-
ment notes.

Document notes are downloaded when you download a document as an iWork document, but they are not always downloaded when you download the document in another format. You don't have to worry about document notes being visible on iWork.com; as you can see in Figure A-12, they are added to a chronological list.

Adding comments to document objects

You can select an element of an iWork document and add a comment to it. Follow these simple steps:

1. **Select the object to annotate.**

   You can select text, a text box, or anything else that's selectable in your iWork document. Figure A-13 shows part of the For Sale banner selected for annotation.

2. **Click Add Comment at the top of the window, as shown in Figure A-14.**

Figure A-12:
View document notes on iWork.com.

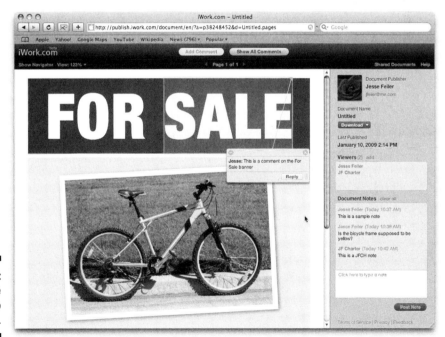

Figure A-13:
Select the object to annotate.

Figure A-14:
Click Add
Comment.

3. Type the comment.

The comment is identified with your name and time-stamped automatically. As shown in Figure A-14, you can reply to a comment from someone else and they can reply to a comment from you (it's called working together).

Appendix B

Chapter Guide to iWork Techniques

*H*ere's a big non-surprise: Similar tasks are done the same way in most iWork applications. In some cases, though, the techniques are located in a chapter designed for one of the applications because that helps the flow of the narrative. For example, despite the fact that a chart or a table can be equally at home in a spreadsheet, a word processing document, or a presentation, most people will look up charts and tables in a spreadsheet chapter, so that's where you'll find details of charting (Chapter 15).

Table B-1 shows a variety of tasks you can do with the iWork applications and the chapter in which that task is discussed. (If you see *n/a,* the task is not available for that particular app. For example, you can add a slide transition only to a Keynote presentation document.)

Table B-1	iWork Techniques by Chapter			
Category	*Task*	*Pages*	*Numbers*	*Keynote*
Charts	Creating a chart	Chapter 15	Chapter 15	Chapter 15
Charts	Using Chart inspector	Chapter 15	Chapter 15	Chapter 15
Charts	Formatting and printing numbers	n/a	Chapter 16	n/a
Do it for me	Using AppleScript	Chapter 22	Chapter 22	Chapter 22
Do it for me	Using Automator to scale and rotate images	Chapter 22	Chapter 22	Chapter 22
Document layout	Modifying links and autodetected email addresses and URLs	Chapter 4	Chapter 4	Chapter 4

(continued)

Table B-1 *(continued)*

Category	Task	Pages	Numbers	Keynote
Document layout	Setting pagination	Chapter 6	Chapter 6	Chapter 6
Document layout	Moving headers and footers	Chapter 6	n/a	n/a
Document layout	Using section headers and footers	Chapter 6	n/a	n/a
Document layout	Adding a section to a document	Chapter 11	n/a	n/a
Document layout	Creating and updating tables of contents	Chapter 11	n/a	n/a
Document layout	Formatting headers and creating a new style	Chapter 13	Chapter 13	Chapter 13
Document layout	Adding hyperlinks to iWork documents	Chapter 21	Chapter 21	Chapter 21
Graphics	Formatting Graphics with Graphic inspector	Chapter 4	Chapter 4	Chapter 4
Graphics	Masking images with shapes	Chapter 3	Chapter 3	Chapter 3
Graphics	Adjusting images	Chapter 3	Chapter 3	Chapter 3
Keynote	Creating a Keynote presentation	n/a	n/a	Chapter 18
Keynote	Setting Keynote remote preferences	n/a	n/a	Chapter 19
Keynote	Adding a movie to a slide	n/a	n/a	Chapter 20
Keynote	Adding a transition between slides	n/a	n/a	Chapter 20
Keynote	Adding builds within slides	n/a	n/a	Chapter 20
Media	Using Media Browser	Chapter 4	Chapter 4	Chapter 4

Category	Task	Pages	Numbers	Keynote
Numbers	Creating sheets	n/a	Chapter 13	n/a
Numbers	Creating tables	n/a	Chapter 13	n/a
Numbers	Creating a multi-sheet and multi-table summary	Chapter 14	Chapter 14	Chapter 14
Objects	Checking and setting positions with Metrics inspector	Chapter 4	Chapter 4	Chapter 4
Preferences	Setting Pages Preferences	Chapter 5	n/a	n/a
Shapes	Creating a predrawn shape from the toolbar	Chapter 3	Chapter 3	Chapter 3
Shapes	Drawing a predrawn shape from the toolbar	Chapter 3	Chapter 3	Chapter 3
Shapes	Editing a shape's geometry	Chapter 3	Chapter 3	Chapter 3
Sharing	Sharing content with Mobile Me	Chapter 21	Chapter 21	Chapter 21
Sharing	Sharing content with iWeb	Chapter 21	Chapter 21	Chapter 21
Sharing	Sharing content by using Sent To	Chapter 21	Chapter 21	Chapter 21
Sharing	Using photos from iPhone	Chapter 21	Chapter 21	Chapter 21
Sharing	Using music from iTunes	Chapter 21	Chapter 21	Chapter 21
Sharing	Using movies from iMovie	Chapter 21	Chapter 21	Chapter 21
Sharing	Using PDF files as images	Chapter 21	Chapter 21	Chapter 21
Sharing	Moving data from other applications into iWork	Chapter 21	Chapter 21	Chapter 21
Tables	Adjusting headers in a table	Chapter 13	Chapter 13	Chapter 13

(continued)

Table B-1 *(continued)*

Category	Task	Pages	Numbers	Keynote
Tables	Creating formulas using the SUM function and a range of cells	n/a	Chapter 14	n/a
Tables	Creating formulas by selecting individual cells	Chapter 14	Chapter 14	Chapter 14
Tables	Working with functions	Chapter 14	Chapter 14	Chapter 14
Tables	Sorting and reorganizing data	Chapter 16	Chapter 16	Chapter 16
Tables	Finding data	Chapter 16	Chapter 16	Chapter 16
Templates	Creating a Pages document from a template	Chapter 5	Chapter 5	Chapter 5
Text	Formatting Text with Text inspector	Chapter 4	Chapter 4	Chapter 4
Text	Setting vertical spacing	Chapter 6	Chapter 6	Chapter 6
Text	Setting indents with the Inspector window	Chapter 6	Chapter 6	Chapter 6
Text	Setting indents with the ruler	Chapter 6	Chapter 6	Chapter 6
Text	Setting tabs	Chapter 6	Chapter 6	Chapter 6
Text boxes	Creating a text flow link	Chapter 7	Chapter 7	Chapter 7
Text boxes	Adding objects to text boxes	Chapter 7	Chapter 7	Chapter 7
Toolbar	Customizing the toolbar	Chapter 3	Chapter 3	Chapter 3

Index

E

F

BUSINESS, CAREERS & PERSONAL FINANCE

Accounting For Dummies, 4th Edition*
978-0-470-24600-9

Bookkeeping Workbook For Dummies†
978-0-470-16983-4

Commodities For Dummies
978-0-470-04928-0

Doing Business in China For Dummies
978-0-470-04929-7

E-Mail Marketing For Dummies
978-0-470-19087-6

Job Interviews For Dummies, 3rd Edition*†
978-0-470-17748-8

Personal Finance Workbook For Dummies*†
978-0-470-09933-9

Real Estate License Exams For Dummies
978-0-7645-7623-2

Six Sigma For Dummies
978-0-7645-6798-8

Small Business Kit For Dummies, 2nd Edition*†
978-0-7645-5984-6

Telephone Sales For Dummies
978-0-470-16836-3

BUSINESS PRODUCTIVITY & MICROSOFT OFFICE

Access 2007 For Dummies
978-0-470-03649-5

Excel 2007 For Dummies
978-0-470-03737-9

Office 2007 For Dummies
978-0-470-00923-9

Outlook 2007 For Dummies
978-0-470-03830-7

PowerPoint 2007 For Dummies
978-0-470-04059-1

Project 2007 For Dummies
978-0-470-03651-8

QuickBooks 2008 For Dummies
978-0-470-18470-7

Quicken 2008 For Dummies
978-0-470-17473-9

Salesforce.com For Dummies, 2nd Edition
978-0-470-04893-1

Word 2007 For Dummies
978-0-470-03658-7

EDUCATION, HISTORY, REFERENCE & TEST PREPARATION

African American History For Dummies
978-0-7645-5469-8

Algebra For Dummies
978-0-7645-5325-7

Algebra Workbook For Dummies
978-0-7645-8467-1

Art History For Dummies
978-0-470-09910-0

ASVAB For Dummies, 2nd Edition
978-0-470-10671-6

British Military History For Dummies
978-0-470-03213-8

Calculus For Dummies
978-0-7645-2498-1

Canadian History For Dummies, 2nd Edition
978-0-470-83656-9

Geometry Workbook For Dummies
978-0-471-79940-5

The SAT I For Dummies, 6th Edition
978-0-7645-7193-0

Series 7 Exam For Dummies
978-0-470-09932-2

World History For Dummies
978-0-7645-5242-7

FOOD, GARDEN, HOBBIES & HOME

Bridge For Dummies, 2nd Edition
978-0-471-92426-5

Coin Collecting For Dummies, 2nd Edition
978-0-470-22275-1

Cooking Basics For Dummies, 3rd Edition
978-0-7645-7206-7

Drawing For Dummies
978-0-7645-5476-6

Etiquette For Dummies, 2nd Edition
978-0-470-10672-3

Gardening Basics For Dummies*†
978-0-470-03749-2

Knitting Patterns For Dummies
978-0-470-04556-5

Living Gluten-Free For Dummies†
978-0-471-77383-2

Painting Do-It-Yourself For Dummies
978-0-470-17533-0

HEALTH, SELF HELP, PARENTING & PETS

Anger Management For Dummies
978-0-470-03715-7

Anxiety & Depression Workbook For Dummies
978-0-7645-9793-0

Dieting For Dummies, 2nd Edition
978-0-7645-4149-0

Dog Training For Dummies, 2nd Edition
978-0-7645-8418-3

Horseback Riding For Dummies
978-0-470-09719-9

Infertility For Dummies†
978-0-470-11518-3

Meditation For Dummies with CD-ROM, 2nd Edition
978-0-471-77774-8

Post-Traumatic Stress Disorder For Dummies
978-0-470-04922-8

Puppies For Dummies, 2nd Edition
978-0-470-03717-1

Thyroid For Dummies, 2nd Edition†
978-0-471-78755-6

Type 1 Diabetes For Dummies*†
978-0-470-17811-9

* Separate Canadian edition also available
† Separate U.K. edition also available

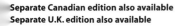

Available wherever books are sold. For more information or to order direct: U.S. customers visit www.dummies.com or call 1-877-762-2974.
U.K. customers visit www.wileyeurope.com or call (0)1243 843291. Canadian customers visit www.wiley.ca or call 1-800-567-4797.

INTERNET & DIGITAL MEDIA

AdWords For Dummies
978-0-470-15252-2

Blogging For Dummies, 2nd Edition
978-0-470-23017-6

Digital Photography All-in-One Desk Reference For Dummies, 3rd Edition
978-0-470-03743-0

Digital Photography For Dummies, 5th Edition
978-0-7645-9802-9

Digital SLR Cameras & Photography For Dummies, 2nd Edition
978-0-470-14927-0

eBay Business All-in-One Desk Reference For Dummies
978-0-7645-8438-1

eBay For Dummies, 5th Edition*
978-0-470-04529-9

eBay Listings That Sell For Dummies
978-0-471-78912-3

Facebook For Dummies
978-0-470-26273-3

The Internet For Dummies, 11th Edition
978-0-470-12174-0

Investing Online For Dummies, 5th Edition
978-0-7645-8456-5

iPod & iTunes For Dummies, 5th Edition
978-0-470-17474-6

MySpace For Dummies
978-0-470-09529-4

Podcasting For Dummies
978-0-471-74898-4

Search Engine Optimization For Dummies, 2nd Edition
978-0-471-97998-2

Second Life For Dummies
978-0-470-18025-9

Starting an eBay Business For Dummies, 3rd Edition†
978-0-470-14924-9

GRAPHICS, DESIGN & WEB DEVELOPMENT

Adobe Creative Suite 3 Design Premium All-in-One Desk Reference For Dummies
978-0-470-11724-8

Adobe Web Suite CS3 All-in-One Desk Reference For Dummies
978-0-470-12099-6

AutoCAD 2008 For Dummies
978-0-470-11650-0

Building a Web Site For Dummies, 3rd Edition
978-0-470-14928-7

Creating Web Pages All-in-One Desk Reference For Dummies, 3rd Edition
978-0-470-09629-1

Creating Web Pages For Dummies, 8th Edition
978-0-470-08030-6

Dreamweaver CS3 For Dummies
978-0-470-11490-2

Flash CS3 For Dummies
978-0-470-12100-9

Google SketchUp For Dummies
978-0-470-13744-4

InDesign CS3 For Dummies
978-0-470-11865-8

Photoshop CS3 All-in-One Desk Reference For Dummies
978-0-470-11195-6

Photoshop CS3 For Dummies
978-0-470-11193-2

Photoshop Elements 5 For Dummies
978-0-470-09810-3

SolidWorks For Dummies
978-0-7645-9555-4

Visio 2007 For Dummies
978-0-470-08983-5

Web Design For Dummies, 2nd Edition
978-0-471-78117-2

Web Sites Do-It-Yourself For Dummies
978-0-470-16903-2

Web Stores Do-It-Yourself For Dummies
978-0-470-17443-2

LANGUAGES, RELIGION & SPIRITUALITY

Arabic For Dummies
978-0-471-77270-5

Chinese For Dummies, Audio Set
978-0-470-12766-7

French For Dummies
978-0-7645-5193-2

German For Dummies
978-0-7645-5195-6

Hebrew For Dummies
978-0-7645-5489-6

Ingles Para Dummies
978-0-7645-5427-8

Italian For Dummies, Audio Set
978-0-470-09586-7

Italian Verbs For Dummies
978-0-471-77389-4

Japanese For Dummies
978-0-7645-5429-2

Latin For Dummies
978-0-7645-5431-5

Portuguese For Dummies
978-0-471-78738-9

Russian For Dummies
978-0-471-78001-4

Spanish Phrases For Dummies
978-0-7645-7204-3

Spanish For Dummies
978-0-7645-5194-9

Spanish For Dummies, Audio Set
978-0-470-09585-0

The Bible For Dummies
978-0-7645-5296-0

Catholicism For Dummies
978-0-7645-5391-2

The Historical Jesus For Dummies
978-0-470-16785-4

Islam For Dummies
978-0-7645-5503-9

Spirituality For Dummies, 2nd Edition
978-0-470-19142-2

NETWORKING AND PROGRAMMING

ASP.NET 3.5 For Dummies
978-0-470-19592-5

C# 2008 For Dummies
978-0-470-19109-5

Hacking For Dummies, 2nd Edition
978-0-470-05235-8

Home Networking For Dummies, 4th Edition
978-0-470-11806-1

Java For Dummies, 4th Edition
978-0-470-08716-9

Microsoft® SQL Server™ 2008 All-in-One Desk Reference For Dummies
978-0-470-17954-3

Networking All-in-One Desk Reference For Dummies, 2nd Edition
978-0-7645-9939-2

Networking For Dummies, 8th Edition
978-0-470-05620-2

SharePoint 2007 For Dummies
978-0-470-09941-4

Wireless Home Networking For Dummies, 2nd Edition
978-0-471-74940-0

OPERATING SYSTEMS & COMPUTER BASICS

iMac For Dummies, 5th Edition
978-0-7645-8458-9

Laptops For Dummies, 2nd Edition
978-0-470-05432-1

Linux For Dummies, 8th Edition
978-0-470-11649-4

MacBook For Dummies
978-0-470-04859-7

**Mac OS X Leopard All-in-One
Desk Reference For Dummies**
978-0-470-05434-5

Mac OS X Leopard For Dummies
978-0-470-05433-8

Macs For Dummies, 9th Edition
978-0-470-04849-8

PCs For Dummies, 11th Edition
978-0-470-13728-4

Windows® Home Server For Dummies
978-0-470-18592-6

Windows Server 2008 For Dummies
978-0-470-18043-3

**Windows Vista All-in-One
Desk Reference For Dummies**
978-0-471-74941-7

Windows Vista For Dummies
978-0-471-75421-3

Windows Vista Security For Dummies
978-0-470-11805-4

SPORTS, FITNESS & MUSIC

Coaching Hockey For Dummies
978-0-470-83685-9

Coaching Soccer For Dummies
978-0-471-77381-8

Fitness For Dummies, 3rd Edition
978-0-7645-7851-9

Football For Dummies, 3rd Edition
978-0-470-12536-6

GarageBand For Dummies
978-0-7645-7323-1

Golf For Dummies, 3rd Edition
978-0-471-76871-5

Guitar For Dummies, 2nd Edition
978-0-7645-9904-0

**Home Recording For Musicians
For Dummies, 2nd Edition**
978-0-7645-8884-6

**iPod & iTunes For Dummies,
5th Edition**
978-0-470-17474-6

Music Theory For Dummies
978-0-7645-7838-0

Stretching For Dummies
978-0-470-06741-3

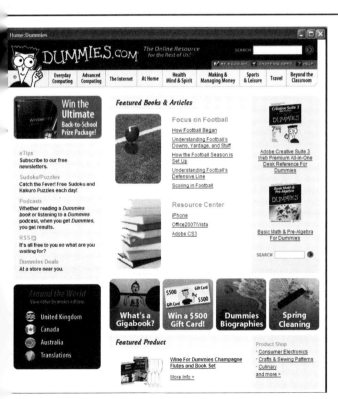

Get smart @ dummies.com®

- **Find a full list of Dummies titles**
- **Look into loads of FREE on-site articles**
- **Sign up for FREE eTips e-mailed to you weekly**
- **See what other products carry the Dummies name**
- **Shop directly from the Dummies bookstore**
- **Enter to win new prizes every month!**

Separate Canadian edition also available
Separate U.K. edition also available

Available wherever books are sold. For more information or to order direct: U.S. customers visit www.dummies.com or call 1-877-762-2974.
U.K. customers visit www.wileyeurope.com or call (0) 1243 843291. Canadian customers visit www.wiley.ca or call 1-800-567-4797.

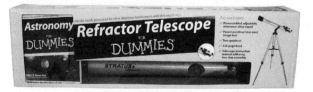